Recent Studies in School Psychology

Recent Studies in School Psychology

Edited by

Panch. Ramalingam

AUTHORSPRESS
PUBLISHERS OF SCHOLARLY BOOKS

Worldwide Circulation through Authorspress Global Network
First Published 2010
by
Authorspress
E-35/103, Jawahar Park
Laxmi Nagar, Delhi-110 092
e-mail: authorspress@yahoo.com

Recent Studies in School Psychology
ISBN 978-81-7273-536-4

Printed in India at Tarun Offset, Delhi.

Foreword

Prof. William (Bill) Pfohl, *Psy.D.*
International School Psychology Association, USA.

Across the world, school psychology as a profession continues to grow and flourish. Countries that had been unaware of school psychology as a profession are now faced with the task of training school psychologists and governing their practice. From well established practice in parts of Europe and the United States of America to an emerging profession in other countries such as India, it is exciting to see this book addressing a wide range of topics. It illustrates that issues of training and practice are very similar across the world; however, there are some unique issues in a country as diverse and vast as India. This book also illustrates the wide range of theory and practice practised in India. The variety of topics in *Recent Studies in School Psychology* confirms the universality of school psychology training issues and practices. This is an excellent resource showing the breadth and depth of the knowledge base in both research and practice of school psychology in India.

The various chapters speak of the wide ranging topics that school psychologists must be familiar with in their training and practice. From understanding change in system theory to the practice of Rational Emotive Behaviour Therapy (REBT), this book provides valuable knowledge to both the university educator and school-based practitioner to enhance their practices. The topics are current, well thought out, and relevant to the field of school psychology. School psychologists and university trainers are committed to high quality education and practice. Serving the children, families, and school-based educators of a country/

community is a high calling. The information contained in these chapters will provide the necessary information base to better serve these diverse populations.

School psychologists have a unique perspective in viewing the development of a children's educational achievement and their mental health growth. If this developmental process is possibly faced with barriers, the school psychologist must be able to intervene early (prevention) before problems become too large or complex. By working closely with teachers, administrators, parents and communities, the school psychologist can facilitate students' progress both academically and emotionally. This unique occupation carries high expectations. Internationally, school psychologists have delivered an "evidence-based" solution to many problems found with today's students and schools. By working with those who have lives steeped in poverty, to those from whom much is expected because of their gifts, school psychologists are ready to assist. This book and its range of topical information bodes well for India and the profession of school psychology to be able to provide the necessary research-based information and skills to benefit India's children, educators and school communities. All children of the world deserve an education that allows them to be successful in their lives.

It is a pleasure to see a book such as this which will join a strong library of titles that school psychologists can draw on internationally. India shares common issues with many other countries and their school communities draws us together even more to share our research and skills. These are exciting times for India and the rest of the world as school psychologists help schools and their communities face complex and difficult problems. School psychologists typically appear at the cutting edge of change, pushing for better schools, better education and achievement, improving mental health in the children, families and school communities they serve. School psychologists readily accept this position of leadership, training, and practice. Through its affiliation with the International School Psychology Association, India is able to draw upon a broad base of research and practice to build education programmes for training practitioners to deliver a high quality service. Meeting the challenges of today's children across the world is daunting. Together we can *make a difference* in children's lives. We can impact educational policy and laws to better the learning environment. We can set standards for both training and practice. ISPA stand ready to assist any country in its establishment of "best practices" in training or practice. This book helps push that agenda forward by raising important issues and discussing their solution.

My hope is that we all can come together internationally to share research, knowledge, and practices. This book is a stepping stone for this to happen.

Best Wishes,

Professor ***William (Bill) Pfohl,*** Psy.D.

Professor of Psychology,
Western Kentucky University
Bowling Green, Kentucky,
USA and President,
International School Psychology Association

Preface

I received an email on 22 March 2009 from Dr. Janet Muscutt, U.K., Chair of the Cal Catterall Fund Committee (CCF) of the International School Psychology Association (ISPA), USA, notifying me that I had been awarded Cal Catterall Funds to attend the 31st ISPA International Conference in Malta from 7 to 11 July, 2009. It was an exciting moment for me to share this with Prof. B. Mukhopadhyay, Secretary of the Indian Academy of Applied Psychology (IAAP), who was instrumental in helping me apply for the grant.

From day one I started preparing for the conference in Malta, getting permission to attend the International conference and preparing for my presentation. I would like to express my sincere gratitude to Professor J.A.K. Tareen, the Vice-Chancellor of Pondicherry University, for his encouragement and support for all academic endeavours in Pondicherry University and for permitting me to attend this International Conference.

On 6 July 2009, I landed in Malta. This journey was not only to represent the IAAP and the Pondicherry Psychology Association (PPA), but also to enhance my knowledge of diversity in international school psychology. The conference began on 7 July with several concurrent workshops including the Leadership workshop given by ISPA central office, in which I participated. The workshop was an eye-opener for me to understand the effective functioning of ISPA and its keen interest in uplifting school psychology at the international level. I attended all the five days and enjoyed the interaction with fellow colleagues in Malta. I visited other European countries and reflected on the academic experience that I had in Malta. The ISPA Conference was excellent and I learned a lot during my visit to Malta.

This experience induced me to search studies related to school psychology in India. Being the Editor of the *Journal of the Indian Academy of Applied Psychology,* I am able to get the studies related to school psychology from various authors. Most of the papers included in this book were published in the *Journal of the Indian Academy of Applied Psychology* between 2006 and 2009.

I wish to record my sincere gratitude to Professor J.A.K. Tareen, Vice-Chancellor, Pondicherry University, Puducherry, and Member, University Grants commission, New Delhi, for his continuous support and guidance. He is the man of excellence in planning and execution of academic and administrative changes in the higher education sytem in the country in general, and Pondicherry University in particular, to reach the heights of world class standard in higher education. He has already proved his eminance in the all-round development of Kashmir University as Vice-Chancellor.

I thank Professor A. Balasubramanian, Director of Culture and Cultural Relations of Pondicherry University, Puducherry, who is a renowned personality to shape and guide the future teacher generation of the country. He inspired me to achieve many things in my academic career and guiding me for professional development.

I thank Professor S. Hariharan, Director, UGC-Academic Staff College, Pondicherry University, Puducherry for his encouragement in completing this work. I wish to record my sincere thanks to Dr. P. Bhaskaran Nair, Department of English, Pondicherry University, and Ms. Razia, Department of English, Bharathidasan Govt College for Women, Puducherry for their valuable suggestions and guidance in completing this work.

My sincere thanks are due to Prof. R. Karpagakumaravel, Vice-Chancellor, Madurai Kamaraj University, Madurai, Prof. N. Balasubramanian, Director, School of Distance Education Bharathiar University, Coimbatore for their help whenever sought; to Prof. K.K. Tiwari, Former Director, UGC-ASC, RD University Jabalpur, Prof. R. Seshadri Naidu, Director, UGC-ASC, Sri Venkateswara University, Tirupati, and Prof. G. Venkatesh Kumar, Director, UGC-ASC, Mysore University, Mysore.

During this project, I frequently approached Prof. B. Mukhopadhyay, Prof and Head, Department of Educational Management and Applied Psychology, NITTTR, Chennai, Prof. G.P. Thakur, President, Indian School Psychology Association, New Delhi, Prof. Habib Ahmad, President, Indian Academy of Applied Psychology, New Delhi, Prof. K.V. Kaliappan, President of Madras Psychology Society, Chennai, and Dr. S. Renuka Devi, Asst. Professor, Department of Education, Natioanl Institute of Technical Teachers' Training and Research, Chennai. They were very cordial while helping me to complete the task by way of providing useful resources. I am indebted to them for their kind advice and continuous guidance in my academic endeavours.

My sincere thanks are always due to Sudarshan Kcherry, Authorpress, New Delhi for his active involvement in the process of publishing this book.

And last but not least, I thank all the authors from various parts of the country for having given their contributions to complete the work. Their kindness and cooperation helped me a lot to remember them for ever. This is being a new practical approach in the field of school psychology to encourage the teachers for their professional development by applying one or more ways and means possible to experiment and practice.

I personally request psychologists, educational administrtators, educational consultants to offer thier views and comments to further improve the quality of the publication.

Dr. Panch. Ramalingam

List of Contributors

Abid Husain, Ph.D. Research Scholar and Counsellor (VCTC), Department of Psychology, Jamia Millia Islamia, New Delhi -110 025.

Akbar Hussain, Ph.D., Sr. Lecturer, Department of Psychology, Jamia Millia Islamia, New Delhi -110 025.

Alireza Beygi, Department of Psychology, University of Mysore, Manasagangotri, Mysore - 570 006.

Anindita Chaudhuri, Department of Applied Psychology, Calcutta University, Kolkata - 700 009.

Anjana Mukhopadhyay, Professor, Mahila Mahavidyalaya, Banaras Hindu University, Varanasi-221 005.

Annalakshmi Narayanan, Bharathiar University, Coimbatore.

Anupama Shrivastava, Research Scholar, Department of Psychology, Banaras Hindu University, Varanasi-221 005.

Ashutosh Kumar, Sr. Lecturer, Patna Training College, Patna University, Patna-800 004.

Ayatollah Karimi, Research Scholar, All India Institute of Speech and Hearing, Mysore - 570 006.

Debdulal Dutta Roy, Ph.D., Psychology Research Unit, Indian Statistical Institute, 203, B.T. Road, Kolkata – 700 108.

Erika E. Voigt, Ph.D., School Psychologist, Nikolausberger Weg 76 A D-37073, Gottingen, Germany.

Gowramma I. P., Department of Special Education, All India Institute of Speech and Hearing, Mysore, 570 006.

Gururaj, B. Urs, Asst. Professor & Program Coordinator, Institute of Health Management Research, Hosur Road, Bangalore. Bangalore 560 058.

Hardeo Ojha, Ph.D., Former Professor and Head, Department of Psychology, T.M. Bhagalpur University, Bhikhanpur (Siyaram Nagar), Bhagalpur- 812 001.

Jayanti Basu, Ph.D., Department of Applied Psychology, Calcutta University, Kolkata - 700 009.

Jayaraju, R., Department of Psychology, Karnataka State Open University, Manasagangotri, Mysore –570 005.

Kalpana Vengopal Mridula K., Regional Institute of Education (NCERT), Mysore.

Kannappan, R., Ph.D., Associate Professor in Clinical Psychology, Vinayaka Mission Medical College, Salem.

Khaja Rahamtulla, T., Andhra University, Visakhapatnam.

Lancy D'Souza, Department of Psychology, Maharaja's College, University of Mysore –575 005, India.

Madhavi Latha, M., Faculty, ICFAI Business School, Hyderabad.

Majda Tarannum, Research Scholar, Department of Psychology, Aligarh Muslim University, Aligarh.

Manju Mehta, Ph.D., Professor and Head, Department of Psychology, University of Rajasthan, Jaipur, Rajasthan.

Mridula K, Regional Institute of Education (NCERT), Mysore

Naima Khatoon, Ph.D., Reader, Department of Psychology, Aligarh Muslim University, Aligarh, U.P.

Naved Iqbal, Jamia Millia Islamia, New Delhi.

Neerpal Rathi, Indian Institute of Technology, Roorkee.

Partha Malakar, Research Scholar, Department of Applied Psychology, Calcutta University, Kolkata - 700 009.

Pooja Yadav, Jamia Millia Islamia, New Delhi.

Prachi Maheshwari, Research Scholar, Department of Psychology, University of Rajasthan, Jaipur, Rajasthan.

Prakash Padakannaya, PhD, Department of Psychology, University of Mysore, Manasagangotri, Mysore 570 006, e-mail: prakashp99@yahoo.com

Raju, M.V.R., Andhra University, Visakhapatnam.

Ramalingam, Panch, Reader; UGC-Academic Staff College, Pondicherry University, Puducherry – 605 014.

Renu Rastogi, Indian Institute of Technology, Roorkee.

Roshan Lal Zinta, Lecturer Department of Psychology, Himachal Pradesh University, Summer Hill, Shimla - 171 005.

Rumki Gupta, Indian Statistical Institute, Kolkata.

Sandhya Gupta, Dayalbagh Educational Institute, Agra.

Sinha, S.P., Dayalbagh Educational Institute, Agra.

Suneetha Hangal, Karnatak University, Dharwad.

Venkatesan, S., PhD, Professor in Clinical Psychology, All India Institute of Speech and Hearing, Mysore - 570 006.

Venkatesh Kumar, G., Ph.D, Professor of Psychology, Director, UGC-Academic Staff College, Mysore University, Mysore-570 006.

Vijayalaxmi A., Aminabhavi Karnatak University, Dharwad.

Vineeth Kumar, V., Research Scholar, Department of Psychology, University of Rajasthan, Jaipur, Rajasthan.

Indian School Psychology Association (InSPA)

(Regd No.583/2009)

No.12, Qutab View Apartments, Shaheed Jeet Singh Marg, New Delhi-110 016

www.ispaindia.org Email: indianpsychology@gmail.com

PROFILE

India is a multi cultural and multilingual developing country in the Asian subcontinent. It has multifaceted schooling systems which cater to the needs of the children. In India, the schools run by the state governments, both in urban and rural areas differ in many respects from the private English-medium schools that draw children by and large from economically prosperous families. Thus, the Indian setting today is characterised by the existence of schools of various standards, which may be distinguished on the basis of a number of indicators, including teaching methods, physical infrastructural facilities, and policies of administration. The children of these schools need proper psychological guidance to learn and acquire skills and abilities. We strongly believe that School Psychologists alone can provide the necessary professional guidance to the children in schools. At present Indian schools are badly in need of such professional school psychologists to create an ambiance to teach and learn so as to provide desired high quality school education in the country.

In India, academic psychology is predominantly dominated by the Western concepts and principles. The psychology graduates mostly get training on educational and clinical psychology. School Psychology is a new area to study and research based on International models. The competency requires both knowledge and skills in a particular domain. To provide a platform to get these inputs in School Psychology, a six member team of psychologists met under the guidance of the renowned psychologist Prof B. Mukhopadhyay and evolved the Indian School Psychology Association.

The national level association is expected to take an initiative at the policy making levels of the State and Central governments to introduce School Psychology as a subject in the curriculum and to appoint at least one trained school psychologist in each school by creating the post of school psychologists all over the country to develop school education more effective.

There is a pertinent need for school psychologists to propagate the basic concepts of School Psychology and to impart proper training on the basis of the guidelines issued by the International School Psychology Association, and the National Association of School Psychologists, USA.

The Indian School Psychology Association is the need of the hour to help young and energetic psychologists to promote school psychology. To initiate the process the association has been started in Puducherry on 15th August, 2009.

Registered Office: No.17, 14th Street, Krishna Nagar, Puducherry - 605 008, India.

Base of Operation: Its base of operation shall be India.

Character

The Indian School Psychology Association shall be a voluntary non-profit educational service society. All its income shall be applied solely for the promotion of its aim and objectives and no part of it shall be distributed to any of its members.

Aim and Objectives

The primary aim of the association is to develop and promote School Psychology, Human Values-based education and training to meet the needs of society and particularly to elevate the poor from poverty through school education. To realise the aim, the following are the objectives:

i. To promote the use of sound psychological principles within the context of education, internationally.

ii. To promote communication among professionals who are committed to the improvement of the mental health of children in schools.

iii. To encourage the training and employment of school psychologists in India.

iv. To promote the psychological rights of all children throughout the country.

v. To initiate and promote cooperation with other organisations working for causes similar to those of ISPA in order to help children.

vi. To condemn any discrimination of a racial, religious or sexual nature and recommend its members conduct their professional life consistent with this principle.

vii. To mobilise human resources and other resources to utilise them effectively to realise the aim.

viii. To establish education, training and counselling centres/ units to promote social and economic development of the community through education.

ix. To establish and promote high quality School Psychology Programmes and Centres to meet the needs of specific groups, particularly the children and teachers.

x. To establish education, training and counselling centres at schools, colleges and universities to promote School Psychology.

xi. To organise local, regional, national, and international seminars, conferences, exhibitions, lecture meetings, workshops and training programmes.

xii. To propagate the aim and objectives, the association shall publish a quarterly Newsletter.

xiii. To function as an academic- cum- research organisation to undertake relevant research related activities to promote education and human development.

The InSPA is an affiliating association of the International School Psychology Association, and Indian Academy of Applied Psychology, India.

Governing Council

The management of the affairs of the InSPA is entrusted in accordance with the Rules and Regulations of the association to the Governing Council of the association:

Sl. No	*Name*	*Designation*
1	Dr. G.P. Thakur	President
2.	Dr. B. Mukhopadhyay	Vice-President
3	Dr. V. Muthu	Vice-President
4.	Dr. Panch. Ramalingam	Secretary
5	Dr. S. Renukadevi	Joint Secretary
6.	Mr. V. Sendhil	Joint Secretary
7	Dr. B. Rangaiah	Treasurer

Membership, Admission and Fees

There shall be two classes of membership, namely

a) *Life Member:* All those who are qualified Graduates with psychology, known to be of good character in the community, may become Members of the Association and shall be members by remitting Rs. 2000/- and will be called Life Members.

b) *Institutional Member:* Institutions with interests related to the Association may become Institutional Members by remitting Rs. 10,000/- on one time basis.

Special Features

- First 100 members will get the title of "Founder Member".
- Quarterly update of activities will be given in the InSPA website.
- Members will get quarterly InSPA Newsletter free of cost. First issue appears in January, 2010.
- Members are entitled for concession in the Registration fee at the annual conferences.
- The ISPA-India has initiated National Journal for School Psychology in India. The Journal publishes a wide range

of original empirical research related to School Psychology, cross-cultural replications of promising procedures and descriptions of technology transfer.

- Members will be united with the help of State level conveners. The list of conveners is available in the InSPA website.
- Members will be given preferences to undergo International training in School Psychology
- Members will be recommended for participation in the International conferences on request.
- ISPA-India Best School Psychologist Award has been instituted to encourage Indian School Psychologists. Members may recommend/apply/nominate suitable persons every year.
- Members may suggest best practices for School Psychology Programmes.

Contents

1

Recent Studies in School Psychology— An Introduction

—Panch. Ramalingam

In recent years various dimensions of school education are examined from the perspective of equity, access and relevance, keeping in view the requirements of education for all. The impact of industrialisation, globalisation, privatisation and urbanisation has created tremendous opportunities and challenges to educational institutions of learning. The newly emerging scenario will bring about socio-political and economic changes on a grand scale. The imperatives of national development are such that competent teachers must produce quality students to contribute to all-round development. Given these national priorities, the school psychology is an essential discipline to promote in India. Hopefully, the present work is a serious academic attempt towards recent studies in school psychology. The editor has made an indepth study of the recent research trends, methodology and operational dynamics of the school psychology in the country.

This book is the need of the hour to India to train our teachers in school psychology. It has undergone tremendous growth in the Western countries for the last 25 years. Current and future perspectives of school psychology meet the challenges and needs of children in schools. The goals of this book are as follows: (i) explore the possibilities of current and future demands for school psychology and how the psychologists can meet those demands in India; (ii) conceptualise the theory and practice of school psychology in the face of children, and (iii) develop a base to use school psychology resources to maximise the benefits to children, families, and schools.

The Republic Union of India comprises twenty-eight states and seven union territories. The Constitution of India provides directives regarding the development of education throughout the country. Indian education is multifaceted in all respects. Education is the subject of concern for central and state governments. It has been identified in the Constitution as the *central* list, *state* list and *concurrent* list. Until the late 1970s, school education had been on the *state* list, which meant that states had the final say in the management of their respective school systems.

In 1976, education was transferred to the *concurrent* list through a constitutional amendment, the objective being to promote meaningful educational partnerships between the central and state governments. The present central government establishes broad education policies so as to improve the school system and management practices. It has also been decided to have common curricula so that the standard of education should be maintained throughout the country.

School psychology is an unheard of discipline in India. But, Educational psychology is the study of how humans learn in educational settings, the effectiveness of educational interventions, the psychology of teaching, and the social psychology of schools as organisations. Although the terms "educational psychology" and "school psychology" are often used interchangeably, researchers and theorists are likely to be identified as educational psychologists, whereas practitioners in schools or school-related settings are identified as school psychologists. Educational psychology is concerned with the processes of educational attainment among the general population and sub-populations, such as gifted children and those subject to specific disabilities.

Educational psychology both draws from and contributes to cognitive science and the learning sciences. In universities, departments of educational psychology are usually housed within faculties of education, possibly accounting for the lack of representation of educational psychology content in introductory psychology textbooks.

Lightner Witmer is called the 'father of school psychology' (Fagan, 1996). He opened the first psychology clinic in the U.S. in 1896 at the University of Pennsylvania. Witmer's clinic provided services that combined educational and clinical interventions related to school psychology. Clinic staff treated children with psycho-educational difficulties by working directly with the children at the clinic, and also by consulting with educators at the local school (Fagan, 1996). However, the first person to hold the title "School Psychologist" was Arnold Gesell (Fagan, 2000).

It has been stated that the profession of school psychology in the U.S. grew tremendously following the passing of laws mandating compulsory schooling for children in the early twentieth century. These laws led to a spurt in the number of children with physical and mental problems in schools who previously would have not attended school, and educators struggled to serve them. These are all challenges to the school psychologists in USA.

The strength of school psychology as a profession is closely associated with a country's economic wealth and its commitment to use this wealth to promote the education of all children. Hence, typically, school psychology services are more successfully established and embedded in countries characterised by highly developed and legally mandated education systems that provide universal education for all children, including special education services for students with chronic, severe and complex learning and behavioural disorders. These conditions are present in Australia, Canada, Israel, New Zealand, the United States and in most Western European countries. In contrast, the governments of India, Pakistan and Zimbabwe lack sufficient economic resources to adequately fund general education. Thus, governmental resources that are needed to support special education and school psychology are meagre. School psychologists (SP) working in countries that provide little to no financial support for public school services may find employment in private schools that obtain financial support from middle class families or from Non-Governmental Organisations (NGOs).

Given the diversity in the economic wealth of the countries in which SPs work and the impact that this can have on the development of SP services, it is perhaps surprising that the roles and functions of SPs around the world are so similar. In all countries core SP work includes the following:

- the psychological assessment of individual children with learning and/or behaviour problems.
- advice to teachers and parents on the planning and implementation of learning and behavioural programmes for individual children.
- direct support and counselling of individual children.
- consultation with, and advice to, schools and other organisations on the development of whole school intervention programmes and policies.
- In-service training of teachers and other professionals.

In countries where the ratio of SPs to children is extremely favourable (e.g. one SP to 500 pupils, as in Turkey) they tend to be more involved in offering therapy/counselling to individual children. However, this is rare in other so-called developed countries, e.g., in the UK.

Although the tasks listed above are almost universal across all countries, there are increasing examples of SPs offering additional services although this is by no means apparent in all countries. This includes work with preschool children in nurseries, homes and health service settings, with children who are in the care of the social services and with students in further and higher education. Increasingly, in many countries, SPs work in multi-agency teams alongside teachers, therapists and heath service staff. In the UK SPs are also being asked to act as expert witnesses by the legal profession and to appear in court.

School psychology, the professional application of psychology to education environments and programmes, has evolved during the last hundred years to become a critically valuable source of support for the learning and development of children and youth throughout the world. This review of *The Handbook of International School Psychology* found it to be the best available source for understanding the profession's history of development, nature, present status characteristics and the challenges and potentials for its future internationally and for the diverse sample of 43 countries included for specific attention (Hart, 2007).

In this book the following 24 papers have been included to establish studies related to school psychology in India. These studies prove that the authors are regularly contributing to the field of school psychology so as to meet the challenges and opportunities.

Erika E. Voigt has discussed how school psychology can help the school-system and thus societal transformation. She also quoted the recently published handbooks of German and International School Psychology, over viewing more than 50 years development of our profession, which allow to make some conclusions on basic principles, influential structural conditions, directions and examples of good practice. From this perspective some fundamental challenges for the contribution of our profession to societal change are discussed.

Panch. Ramalingam, in his paper, highlights some of the activities for school teachers, how they can learn school psychology so as to suit to the Indian traditional school system. It is an encouraging trend in the field of education in India to promote school psychology as a separate discipline by following the guidelines of International School Psychology Association (ISPA).

Alireza Beygi, Prakash Padakannaya, and Gowramma, I. P., investigated the impact of remedial intervention on students' performance with dyscalculia in teaching addition and subtraction. Forty male students with dyscalculia (20 in experimental, and 20 in control groups) from fourth and fifth grades in Arak, Iran were the participants. The experimental group received a remedial program in addition to their regular classroom teaching (every other day). Data analysis indicated a significant increase in the subtraction and addition performance after remedial intervention. The article discusses implications for teachers, administers, researchers, teacher training institutions, and students with learning disabilities.

G. Venkatesh Kumar has examined the impact of Rational-Emotive Behaviour Therapy on adolescent students with conduct disorder. It was hypothesized that the REBT psychotherapy would have a positive impact on adolescents' conduct disorder symptoms. The results revealed that the treatment decreased the symptoms of conduct disorder. The results showed that REBT has a positive impact on conduct disorder, and other emotional and behavioural disorders co-morbid with conduct disorder experienced by adolescents.

M.V.R. Raju and T. Khaja Rahamtulla have examined the adjustment problems of school students from urban and rural schools of Visakhapatnam district. Adjustment is a process by which a living organism maintains a balance between the needs and the circumstances. The variables included for the study apart from adjustment (family, social, academic, financial and emotional) are age, gender, class, type of school, etc. The major findings of the study have shown that adjustment of school children is primarily dependent on the school variables like the class in which they are studying, the medium of instruction present in the school, and the type of management of the school. Parental education and occupation of the school children also significantly influenced adjustment.

Kalpana Vengopal and Mridula K. have aimed at examining the hemispheric preferences for information processing and styles of learning and thinking in children. Results revealed that there was significant difference in the right and left (brain) hemisphere preference for information processing among children and that boys were more right-hemispheric-oriented and girls were more left-hemispheric-oriented in information processing. Significant difference in the styles of learning and thinking and concept preference among right-hemisphere and left-hemisphere dominant children was also observed with respect to both genders.

Pooja Yadav and Naved Iqbal have studied the impact of life skill training on self-esteem, adjustment and empathy among adolescents. The result showed that subjects improved significantly in post-condition on self-esteem, emotional adjustment, educational adjustment, total adjustment and empathy. However, no significant difference was found on social adjustment in pre- and post-condition. Overall training was very effective as subjects improved in the post condition on all measures except one, thus showing that life skill training do show positive results in bringing change in adolescent's attitude, thought and behaviour by providing supportive environment to them.

Annalakshmi Narayanan has investigated the relationship between resilience and certain cognitive variables. The findings showed that among the aspects of attributional schemata investigated in this study, complex explanation and metacognition had significant effect on resilience. The highly resilient had higher preference for complex rather than simple explanations for explaining human behaviour and used metacognition concerning explanations more than those who had low resilience.

Partha Malakar, Jayanti Basu and Anindita Chaudhuri have conducted a study to explore whether there is any difference in intelligence-achievement relationship between low and high obsessional thought groups among late adolescent students. The aims of the study were to determine (i) whether there is any sex difference in obsessional thoughts (ii) whether there is any sex difference in achievement scores and (iii) whether there exist any difference in intelligence-achievement relationship between low and high obsessional thought groups. The analyses revealed significant differences between high and low obsessional thought groups indicating substantial loss in intelligence-achievement relationship attributable to obsessional thought. The results have been discussed in terms of future research directions and therapeutic implications.

Majda Tarannum and Naima Khatoon have attempted to study certain demographic variables as determinants of self-esteem and emotional stability of visually challenged students. The results reveal that demographic variables of gender, age, class, family system and area of living, only gender emerged as the significant predictor of emotional stability of visually challenged students, and none of the demographic variables emerged as predictors of self-esteem of these students.

Ayatollah Karimi and Venkatesan investigated whether the CBGT has any impact on mathematics anxiety of high school students. Analyses of data of pre- and post-test by repeated measures ANOVA have shown that CBGT was highly effective in reducing mathematics anxiety and two subscales of this scale (test anxiety and numerical anxiety). Moreover, with respect to gender, there is a significant difference between boys and girls in mathematics anxiety in post-test of experimental group.

R. Kannappan studied 60 female children who had the symptoms of depression, such as tension, irritability, social withdrawal, weeping spells, sleep disturbance, loss of appetite, forgetting, fear of examination, low activity level, palpitation, and diminished ability to concentrate, and they, came for treatment. Children's Depression Rating Scale (CDRS) was used at the assessments of before, after, and follow-ups of the therapeutic intervention. Results indicate a significant reduction of depressive symptoms in female children and better maintained at follow-ups in Pharmacotherapy (PT) and combination of Pharmaco and Psychological Therapies.

Anupama Shrivastava and Anjana Mukhopadhyay have assessed the levels of alienation and emotional intelligence of adolescents with internalising symptoms. The result obtained from ANOVA revealed that the affected group is significantly alienated and emotionally immature in awareness and management compared to their comparative normal group.

Akbar Hussain, Ashutosh Kumar and Abid Husain examined the level of academic stress and overall adjustment among public and government high school students and also to see relationships between the two variables (academic stress and adjustment). Results indicated that the magnitude of academic stress was significantly higher among the public school students whereas government school students were significantly better in terms of their level of adjustment. However, inverse but significant relationships between academic stress and adjustment were found for both the group of students and for each type of school.

Manju Mehta, Prachi Maheshwari and V. Vineeth Kumar have made a comparative study of the personality patterns of SC, ST and non–backward higher secondary boys. The prolonged social discrimination has produced an adverse impact on the development of the personality of these downtrodden, which is a severe stumbling block in providing 'social justice' and 'social equality' to the masses. Results revealed significant differences in personality patterns among SC, ST and non-backward boys. These differences were more prominent in rural areas in comparison to urban areas.

Lancy D'Souza, Gururaj B Urs and Jayaraju R. have made an attempt to find out the extent of shyness and related guidance needs, if any, among adolescent students. Results revealed that shyness had a direct relationship with two areas of guidance needs—social and educational—and total guidance needs, and as the shyness levels increased, guidance needs also increased. Shyness did not influence the guidance needs in the areas—physical, psychological, and in vocational areas. Male and female adolescents also did not differ significantly in their guidance needs. Treatment aspects of shyness have been delineated.

Madhavi Latha M. has studied the emphasis on improving problem-solving skills in children with developmental delays by designing a model called as Problem-solving Interactive model. The pre- and post-test differences on all the intervention outcome indicators were highly significant in experimental group MA (t=5.70), MDI (t=4.099), DMeQ (t=2.64) and Battery of Problem Solving Tasks (t=27.93), indicating the efficacy of the Problem-Solving Interactive Model. The variations in intervention outcomes with respect to chronological age of infants and toddlers with developmental delays showed that children in the age group of 24-33 months showed the highest rate of gain of 0.99 in experimental group and 0.76 in control group. The lowest rate of gain of 0.77 and 0.24 in experimental and control group was seen in children from 4 to 13 months chronological age. These variations in intervention outcomes indicate the need to plan and implement specialised early interventions targeting specific child characteristics.

Debdulal Dutta Roy has studied the rapid change in web technology, training method gradually shifts from manual to web-based computer adaptive training. Here, each trainee is not exposed to the same stimuli. Stimulus exposure depends upon individual differences in proficiency level accounted by the computer. Therefore, usual validity estimating statistical tools (ANOVA with repeated measurement) are not applicable. The aim of the current research is to examine the criterion related validity of one web-based computer adaptive training programme (Fast ForWord Language Gateway Edition Product). The programme is based on the adaptive training techniques such as frequency, reward, intensity and motivation allowed for more rapid learning. It includes seven modules. Results identified very poor validity in two modules out of seven. Finally, the role of box whisker plot analysis on validity assessment was discussed.

Hardeo Ojha aimed at exploring the relationship between perceived parental behaviours and children's Machiavellian orientation (MO) and also between parents' MO and children's MO. The data analysed by product moment correlation coefficient revealed that loving and permissive behaviours of parents were negatively and significantly related with their sons' MO. It was also found that the MO of parents and their sons was positively and significantly associated, providing support for modelling hypothesis.

Neerpal Rathi and Renu Rastogi have examined meaning in life and psychological well-being in male and female students of pre-adolescence and adolescence periods. It was hypothesized that there will be significant differences in the perception of life as meaningful and psychological well-being of different groups of students; t-test was applied to analyse the data. Besides discussing the results, applied aspects of a meaningful life and psychological well-being are also discussed.

Suneetha Hangal and Vijayalaxmi A. Aminabhavi have assessed the impact of maternal employment on the self-concept, emotional maturity and achievement motivation of adolescents. The results revealed that the adolescent children of homemakers have significantly higher self-concept. It was also noticed that children of employed mothers have high emotional maturity and female children of employed mothers are highly achievement oriented.

S. P. Sinha and Sandhya Gupta have examined self-worth protective subjects who intentionally withdraw efforts from situations reflecting low ability. On occasions, when failure is unavoidable, self-worth protective subjects attribute their failures to internal attributions. This learned helplessness leads to low self-esteem, low self-concept, hopelessness and worthlessness. Results showed a significant increase in self-esteem and external attributions, and a significant decrease in internal attributions of high self-worth protective subjects, following reattribution training.

Roshan Lal Zinta has investigated the impact of rural and urban background on performance among the high and low self-efficacious students studying in various senior secondary schools of Shimla District of Himachal Pradesh in India. The results revealed that there was a non-significant difference ($p>0.05$) in the performance of boys and girls with high and low in self-efficacy within rural and urban settings but highly significant ($p<0.01$) differences in performance were found between rural and urban setting with the males and females high and low in self-efficacy. The urban students high as well as low in self-efficacy significantly ($p<0.01$) outperformed the rural students in problem solving task. Urban high self-efficacious females significantly ($p<0.01$) outperformed both rural males and females with high and low in self-efficacy as well as urban females with high and low in self-efficacy and urban females with low in self-efficacy. Overall the urban self-efficacious students significantly outperformed rural self-efficacious students and the females of rural and urban backgrounds competed equally well with males in problem solving task.

Rumki Gupta has studied how the secondary education serves as a bridge between primary and higher education and also as entry into the higher education. All the students enrolled under the West Bengal Board of Secondary Education (WBBSE) participated in a challenging standard-based curriculum, the first public school leaving examination, i.e., Madhyamik Examination, which is conducted by the WBBSE at the end of class X in West Bengal. The factor analysis of Madhyamik curriculum subjects score of the students for a particular year 2000 was done considering marks of all subjects and separately for the oral part of the respective subjects.

These studies are pioneering research contributions in India and reflect some of the more current schools of thought as well as fairly recent research in specific issues. The widely ranging topics include the impact of cancer prevention education on students, affiliation with universities, academic assistance for youth at risk of failure, classroom token economies used to manage destructive behaviours in preschools, violence and victimization among adolescents at school, the relationship between girls' friendships and their adulthood adjustment, classroom structure and behaviour management practices with at-risk students, childhood resilience in the classroom, effectiveness of school interventions.

References

Fagan, T.K. (1996), Witmer's contributions to school psychological services, *American Psychologist,* 51.

_______________ & Wise, P. S. (2000). *School Psychology: Past, Present, and Future,* (2nd ed.). Bethesda, MD: National Association of School Psychologists.

Stuart N. Hart (2007), *School Psychology International,* 28, (5), 523-539. DOI: 10.1177/0143034307085656

2

How School Psychology can help the School-System and Thus Societal Transformation

—*Erika E. Voigt*

Our task and challenge: "Meeting Individual and Community Needs!" - What can our science and professional experience contribute to education in nowadays rapidly changing society? Here a look from the perspective of a practitioner, over viewing more than 25 years of work in the German School System, also relying on some own experience from research and teaching in less developed countries and enriched by exchange with colleagues from many parts of the world, thanks to our dedicated Professional Association of International School Psychology (ISPA). The recently published handbooks of German and International School Psychology, over viewing more than 50 years development of our profession, allow to make some conclusions on basic principles, influential structural conditions, directions and examples of good practice. From this perspective some fundamental challenges for the contribution of our profession to societal change are discussed.

Keywords: School Psychology, Societal Transformation.

Last summer the International Psychology Association (ISPA)[1], held its annual Colloquium in Finland, the country praised for the excellence of its educational system, its outstanding results in achievement and social behaviour and its well developed school psychology. The theme of our conference was: "Meeting

This paper originally appears in the *Journal of the Indian Academy of Applied Psychology,* April 2008, Vol.34, special issue, pp. 9-15.

individual and community needs" — with this message our Finish colleagues named and explained their success: "care for quality of education" and "let no child behind". The role of school psychologists in the words of the Colloquium Organiser: "help the teacher ... meet all the children's basic needs of safety and belonging ...help headmasters cope with their teachers to create a safe and friendly school for all, where learning and social and emotional needs are fully answered ... enable each child to feel he/she has a place in his/her particular class, school, community and world."

So, "Meeting individual and community needs", the key to success in education! We all know the hydra-headed blessings of modernity, globalisation, consumption, exploitation ... With Jerome Bruner[2] in mind, "Human psychology must be meaning-making", I agree, that this must be *the way to societal transformation*: "Help create a learning environment, where all can participate and needs of all are dealt with in a responsible way."

Fifty Years of Counselling Individuals and Schools in Germany

In Germany, after World War II, parents, social services, teachers were searching for psychological help: the first child guidance centres were established. At the same time training in psychology developed and also became part of teacher training programmes and schools started to demand more support from psychology. School psychologists focused mainly on one of two approaches (1) problems of individuals by applying clinical psychology or (2) problems of teaching, managing classrooms, tackling youth problems by using different specifics of psychology. Organisational psychology was not yet well developed. In 1970 the request for support, the growing group of professionals, their increasing influence on educational politics, finally recommendations from UNESCO resulted in the political decision to establish countrywide, school-psychological services in state responsibility. The declared target was to gradually raise the ratio of school psychologist per student towards 1/10,000 and of counselling teachers to 1/500. Concrete actions followed up to about a half-way realisation, until at least every district had one school psychologist.

Luckily we were two in our large district with nearly 200 schools, 45,000 students and responsibility for a quantity of tasks to be fulfilled on the state level. In my state were about 40 districts with 80 colleagues, who had a diploma in general psychology plus several years of practice. We had specialists with different psychotherapeutic training. Thanks to an excellent promoter on the ministerial level, a psychologist and former head of a special school, we were allowed to build a network and cooperate statewide and bring our experience together. This was an optimal use of resources and an excellent chance for professional development. We developed training programmes for counselling—teachers, tutors, headmasters, administrators, school—teams. We often worked in multi-professional teams. Our themes were: organisation development, motivating women for leadership, mental health, prevention, school climate, etc.

Teaching, training, working with groups became my major activity also on the local level — pure economy in our large area. Besides I was engaged in some long-term research: We had whole-school projects to prevent failure among students at risk; we were running pilot classes on inclusive education and we took part in the development of a four-year-mental health education programme for primary school-children and their parents. But as my knowledge derives mainly from psychological counselling of individuals, my focus is the well-being of the individual child, so I want to bring in some case examples.

Beginnings

When I started with my profession, the predominant expectation of teachers was to send students, to have them cured. The third day in my office: an upset father with his wife dropped in, sent by the teacher, with their seven-year-old boy, blaming his hyperactivity, his inability to concentrate on homework, his disobedience and poor achievement. I didn't use tests, but observed him doing his homework in my office. I saw: he was nervous to not make mistakes and he was afraid that his handwriting would be criticised by the teacher. The writing was fairly good, in spite of a crippled arm.

When he visited me a second time, to show what he liked to do after school, he brought a box, scissors, glue and in half an hour of highest concentration, kneeling, drawing overhead, he built a puppet-theatre into the box. A puppet-performance on this stage at the family's next visit greatly helped me to open parent-child communication towards tolerating his fears and giving a chance to his creativity and to advise a better homework procedure. Two more hours were necessary to observe in class and win the teacher's support, stopping her to create a fear of failure in her class. Two later evaluative contacts showed that the life of this boy had changed completely. Accidentally I met him, 12 years later, climbing a high ladder to repair the electricity in my office. The teacher's pushing competition, caused conflicts with other parents several times later, she still had to work on it. *Fear of failure, fed by the tendency of schools to punish mistakes, is one of the main barriers for teachers to seek support from psychologists.*

Developments

Just as I sit, writing this paper, one of my former teachers is calling me. She reports about a 10-year-old-boy, who blames her for having beaten him. It looks like a show he gave to divert from the fact, that he violated the rule to not use a mobile in class. We discuss probable motives, her feelings, his feelings and ways to deal with the conflict, the role of his mother, classmates, tutor, headmaster, and the actual lesson.

My next thought: Some years ago, we were running a project on social behaviour for all newcomers of this school. Should it be repeated, also to support the new, unassertive headmaster? In this case the teacher is seeking support, it shows how the expectations on school psychology have changed. But also the type of problem changed — in the 70's a 10-year-old wouldn't have behaved like that. Be aware: counselling in school does not necessarily find a change-motivated subject. To get this boy to cooperate is the challenge. *To me the task in school counselling is: Look for the strengths of the person, identify barriers to use them and give support to combine inner resources with reality in cooperative and constructive ways.*

A systemic perspective in counselling students and teachers aims at the improvement of the institution for the benefit of all. Counselling a group or whole school or its environment can be a challenging hard work, more still conflict-management, coaching or organisation development. It is always a highlight, when school teams decide on whole-school training. Whereas formerly schools would have asked for a lecture, e.g., on "students' aggressiveness", today the agreement on a theme or problem of relevance may be the first step into a change process with targets like "ways to improve school" or "strengthen cooperation and respect". Such training may include casework, role-play, and changing inefficient habits, sometimes students and parents participate.

One day the headmaster of a big high school asked me to lead a training with all tutors of the school entrance classes — no lecturing, but looking at everyday realities and problems, students, disappointments, ideals. This later was developed to become a state-wide training programme for tutors, called "communication, interaction, cooperation". It is offered since to 100 teachers yearly. Here a researchsummary[3] showing the importance of our main target school climate: (1) "School climate" has a strong positive influence on achievement, motivation, school contentment, self-concept and the reduction of anxiety, stress and misbehaviour. (2) The major stress for teachers is their relationship with students, which tends to become worse across school life. (3) Many teachers have poor awareness and capability to influence social factors in education. What a misery and what a challenge for teachers and psychologists: the ultimate task is to open ways for creative social development of our educational system.

International School Psychology

ISPA published last year the *Handbook of International School Psychology,*[4] with reports on school psychology from 44 countries. It's a resourceful survey, usable like a strategic cook-book. I'll bring in this knowledge-base, concentrating on five of its topics together with my own experience from International Colloquia and from teaching, visiting and exchanging with colleagues from quite a few other countries—in order to look at our profession, conditions of its development and its contribution to societal transformation.

1. ***Context promoting or hindering the development of our profession:*** Clearly: most favourable is a *highly developed, legally mandated education system,* guaranteeing education for all and caring for special needs, but also the availability of good health services.
   - Decisive are on the *political level* efficient structures like a qualified board or commission of education that responds to needs and cares for improvement of public institutions by allocating finances, supporting research and specialists, who help establish standards for education and prepare legislation and the implementation of support services.
   - Challenging are *demographic characteristics:* size and heterogeneity of country and population – like multicultural, multilingual settings, imbalance in infrastructure, high speed of urbanisation, chaotic political situation.
   - One of the most limiting factors is a weak economy without long-term planning.
2. ***Needs and motives that create impulses for the development of school psychology:*** In early twentieth century psychologists, responding to different needs and demands from the educational field, developed mainly two approaches in offering their services:
   - individual measurement-supported counselling and guidance and
   - system-oriented support for schools and teachers.

   Certainly the system-approach is more economical and change-oriented and a necessity, when resources are poor, but it's also a quality characteristic of a well-developed educational system to combine both approaches. Most developments are connected to one of these two, but some countries started or concentrated on priorities as below:

- measurement for school exams and connected curriculum development.
- diagnosing and dealing with Special Education Needs.
- diagnosis, prevention and intervention in critical phases like school entrance, early childhood, transition—and final examinations.
- vocational guidance and preparation for university.
- solve community problems, run programmes of intercultural learning, crisis intervention.
- prevention and intervention of youth problems like addiction, criminality, suicide, AIDS.
- supervision and coaching for personal, beginning teachers or headmasters.

3. ***Comment on roles and functions involved in delivering these services:*** The needs and possible answers are so many, that specialisation may be advisable. Colleagues are often overburdened, as too many expectations cannot be fulfilled. Creating an infrastructure of teamwork, networking, good resource management integrating lay and other services, use of mass-media, phone and internet-counselling may reduce work load and stress.
   - Psychological work needs support systems like team work and supervision, for in everyday work colleagues are often confronted with heavy emotional load.
4. ***Professional Infrastructure, decisive for development:*** The following three are the stronghold of development, when cooperating by effectively:
   - A *higher education institution* of well-trained, recognised professionals, who can provide relevant theory, research and technology to meet social needs and develop programs to prepare practitioners;
   - Educated *practitioners,* who want to use their knowledge and serve the public;
   - A *strong National Professional Association:* Many members give power, but more important are persons, capable of taking leadership and getting influence on

educational policy. These are important goals: (1) provide exchange on good practice and quality of training; (2) develop concepts and establish standards, which can later be used for legalisation, that will establish the professional structure and allow employment; (3) develop statutes, a code of ethics for their services and build a credentialling and licensing system; (4) support cooperation with other professional groups and institutions, who have related goals, (5) edit journals, books, tests and other materials, (6) support professional and public events like conferences, (7) lobbyism and care for public relations.

– Support from *NGO's and other associations*—professional and welfare, also international ones - can be helpful, but need to be integrated carefully. *ISPA* and some of its members gave decisive help in some countries by organising Colloquia, supporting research, giving advice and promoting exchange.

5. ***Impacts and challenges for school psychological services:*** Instead of giving a list of deficits – it would be long—I'll follow the Handbook authors' creative recommendation: *Let us rely on our "inner resources", our professional knowledge and identity*! Here two of its summarising quotations: (1) "The initial and continued acceptance of psychology and school psychology depends, in part, on practitioners' ability to communicate their relevance in meeting important national needs." (The Editors, p. 506)[5] "As soon as psychologists assume the role of improving social comprehension in schools and communities, school psychologists" will be empowered to take responsibility in ensuring children's rights and to implement preventive models of interventions. Only then will some of the big challenges—consolidating the profession and transforming reality—be met." (Brazilian colleagues, p.34)

The authors' recommendations for the development of school psychology: a broadening of traditional roles towards more consultative and preventive services; activities on all levels — institutional, regional and national; combining Western psychology with concepts and knowledge from local culture; developing of awareness for student differences and taking responsibility for all, thereby responding to societal needs and problems.

Responding to Societal Problems — Prerequisite for Societal Transformation

School psychologists can contribute and take a lead in societal change, if they take an active, conscious part in their reactions to societal needs.

Poverty is creating so much misery and not only to those who are directly affected. I took part in building up an NGO on implementing children's rights in my country, our target is to create public awareness for children's poverty, open debates with politicians, etc. We have a dense public social security net, so children are not hungry or left without medical care or schooling, but it's a scandal that a high percentage of families with only one parent or with many children are underprivileged and excluded from full cultural participation, thereby creating a familial heritage of marginalisation for generations. Poverty does not only mean "deficit on a material level" but in consciousness, it creates helplessness, loss of control and confidence. We have to care for both types of poverty. A child may lack means of learning, have poor education before coming to mainstream class, may be pre-occupied to care for their basic needs. All these disadvantages can be ameliorated. But special attention has to be given to a damaged self-concept and lack of self-acceptance, especially in a group of children with quite different experiences, when, e.g., some are using consumption or luxury articles to symbolise exclusiveness. Schools that have a mixture of this students, need to care for targets that help to create identity apart from goals, that can only be reached by those, who have money or better previous education. May the Voices of Nobel Prize (Amartya Sen, R. Pachauri, M. Yunus,) and Right Livelihood Award winners (P. K. Raveendran, Vandana Shiva) from your continent be heard, their examples spread to motivate colleagues. Let's walk their talk: "Strive together for global responsibility", "no economy without justice", "protection of natural resources", "education for all" – these are goals that help to create meaning and identity and thus societal transformation.

"Training of intercultural competences" means prevention of conflicts and peace education in environments with cultural differences deriving from ethnicity, immigration, settlement, urbanisation and other factors. In some of our classes, we have a majority of children from non-German background. Our government realised only late (1) that these children and also their parents need language training and (2) that multicultural environments need planning for social integration. Psychological theories on communication, counselling, organisation and systems change deliver useful concepts and training programmes. They must be adapted to real situations, start from self-reflection and be embedded in a group or institutional process with the target to make all groups and individuals feel accepted and respected members. Building up a school and class as a participative society, in which each person's voice is heard, and 'nobody left behind', is a helpful frame.

Gender-sensitive education needs awareness all around the world. Germany: in early years girls outscored boys in achievement and adaptability. Adversely, the percentage of boys referred to a psychologist, running into behaviour problems or later becoming criminal is much higher. In spite of their success in education, you find fewer women in well-paid jobs and higher careers. We have a law—like you— guaranteeing gender-equality, demanding representatives in all state institutions to work for it. But differences and discriminations are subtle. Roles and expectations are learned at an early age and have their roots in traditions. The way to restructure them is to become aware of differences, to do away with discriminations and unfair advantages, and make decisions towards more justice. Female discrimination worldwide is a violation of human rights, what a waste of human potential, what a poor concept of manliness! In words from UNESCO: education of females is the most rewarding investment for development.

Responsibility for children that need special education or are at risk. Much of the basic knowledge on special needs and risks has been developed by specialists in our profession, but also by those responsible for special education, for daily care and healing. Two rights of children with educational needs tend to be violated: (1) to get best quality special aid and (2) social inclusion. Our task may be to coordinate, bring need and aid together and keep a close look on reality! For what is thought of as special help is sometimes causing segregation and what is thought of as inclusion may cause damage, especially when in a highly competitive school system, children with learning difficulties are torn to fit to preset norms. I was grateful, that in our pilot classes, we were running in the 90s, the children to be included in mainstream classes were mentally and not mildly learning handicapped—so we had to adapt teaching and not children. In Western countries the risks to fail or not complete their school career are the highest for children from the fringe of society. Today in a high quality school means, teachers are regularly checking the learning and social-emotional situation of each child, devising and planning remedial interventions to prevent failure. School psychology can provide high quality to this educational support.

There are risks in our "modern" consumption and media society. We had to realise that modern life is connected with a loss of basic knowledge on environment and traditional ways of coping and production, and that it creates risks like running away, addiction, excessive media-use. Good schools create environments for active learning like school-farms, forest-learning-paths, historical sites, they plan actions to protect nature, cooperate with museums and cultural institutions, care for social learning, stimulate social responsibility, by partnerships with social institutions or schools abroad. I close by referring to the "Credo" of my highly honoured teacher and supervisor, Dr. Erika Landau, Tel Aviv[6], expert on promoting creativity in children: "prepare for each learner — be it student, teacher, psychologist -- to win an attitude of 'what can I do' and get experience and encouragement to bring in intellect, fantasy and emotion on real life problems and social needs."

REFERENCES

1. www.ispaweb.org
2. Bruner, Jerome (1983).*"In Search of Mind"*. New York: Harper.
3. Grewe, N. (2007). Schul- und Klassenklima aktiv gestalten. In Fleischer T., and Grewe N., Jötten, B. (Hrsg.), Handbuch Schulpsychologie. Stuttgart: Kohlhammer. (2007), 22-238.
4. Jimerson, S.R., Oakland, T. D., Farrell, P.T. (Ed., 2007). *Handbook of International School Psychology*. London: Sage.
5. Grewe, N. In Fleischer, T., Grewe, N., & Jötten, B. (Hrsg.) Handbuch Schulpsychologie. Stuttgart: Kohlhammer.
6. www.erika-landau.net/my-credo-en.htm

3

Promoting School Psychology in India

—Panch. Ramalingam

The present paper is aimed at proposing suitable models for the teachers to promote School Psychology to meet the present day requirements of best school education and technological advancements in the country. In the Indian system, higher education begins after 12 year schooling or higher secondary education. Universities offer the Bachelor, Master, MPhil and Doctoral degrees in various disciplines. At present there exist 468 universities/ university level higher education institutions in India and more than 20,000 colleges. Despite such a large and extensive education system, India is woefully short of adequate higher education institutions in view of its younger generation. The students are seeking admission into professional and non professional courses depend upon their interest and availability of courses. At present, applied psychology has been given a prominent place in the field of sciences. Keeping in view of these emerging trends the psychologists may work out a strategy to train the teachers at school levels for developing themselves to meet requirements of school psychologists. This paper highlights some of the activities for school teachers, how they can learn School Psychology so as to suit to the Indian traditional school system. It is an encouraging trend in the field of education in India to promote School Psychology as a separate discipline by following the guidelines of International School Psychology Association (ISPA).

Keywords: Indian Education, School Psychology, School Psychologist, School teachers.

This paper has been presented in the 12th International Conference on Developing School Psychology in India held at Puducherry on 9-10 January, 2010

India is a multi-cultural and multilingual developing country in the Asian subcontinent. It has a multifaceted schooling system to cater to the needs of children. In India, the schools run by the state governments, both in urban and rural areas, differ in many respects from the private English-medium schools that draw children from economically prosperous families. Thus, the Indian setting today is characterised by the existence of good schools and ordinary schools, which may be distinguished on the basis of a number of indicators, including teaching methods, physical infrastructural facilities, and policies of administration. Good schools impart education through well-trained teachers, using new teaching methods supported by technology; they are equipped with fairly good libraries, reading rooms and adequate reading material; they have enough space for accommodating students and members of the teaching staff; they generally provide children with transport and the facilities for games, sports and other recreational activities. Ordinary or poor schools are generally less or not equipped with these facilities (Mishra & Gupta, 1978; Shukla, 1993; Sinha, 1977).

The Government of India has made a commitment to provide free and compulsory education to all children up to the age of 14 as enshrined in its Constitution. The latest Constitutional (86th Amendment) Act 2002 provides the children of India their Fundamental Right to Education in the age group of 6-14 years. The Early Childhood Care and Education (ECCE) to all children up to the age of six years has been expressed through its insertion in Article 45 of the Directive Principles of the Constitution of India. Earlier, the National Policy of Education 1986 had considered two components of basic education – Elementary Education and Adult Literacy which remain relevant and valid, as on today. The Government of India has launched a nationwide comprehensive and decentralised programme of 'Education For All' named as *Sarva Shiksha Abhiyan* (SSA). It may be considered as a significant step towards achieving the long cherished goal of Universalisation of Elementary Education (UEE) through a timebound integrated approach to be implemented in Mission mode in partnership with the states.

At present, 38 million children of 0-6 years age group are covered through 650,000 Integrated Child Development Scheme (ICDS) centres that cater to the nutritional, health and preschool education needs of the 0-6-year olds. Another 190,000 centres are being opened with the intention of universalising coverage. The overall number of these centres is expected to go up to almost 1 million by 2006. India's commitment to ECCE crystallised in the Constitution (86th Amendment) Act 2002, which enjoins the State 'to provide early childhood care and education to all children until they complete the age of six years' (NCERT, 2006a).

Status of School Education

The Indian union comprises 28 states and 7 union territories. It has a parliamentary system of government both at the centre and in the states. While the legislature and the executive have mutually inclusive jurisdictions, the judiciary functions as a truly independent organ of the government. Decentralised governance supported by a large network of local self-governments, both in rural and urban habitations, enable grassroots democracy and the participation of the people of all affiliations in the political process is the hallmark of its vibrancy.

Establishing a schooling system catering to about 150 million people is in itself a significant achievement. The Indian education system is one of the largest such systems in the world. In order to support the states in their efforts at Education for All (EFA), the central government has opted to be an equal partner, placing Education on the concurrent list. India considers basic education as the key to sustainable socio-economic development and peace and stability within and among countries. From a dismal statistic of 16.67 per cent literacy, and despite the burgeoning population, India has achieved an impressive growth of literacy, which stands at 65.38 per cent (male – 75.85 % and female – 54.16 %), according to the 2001 census data. Literacy rates have shown an impressive growth of 11.72 per cent for males and 14.87 per cent for females, over the last census decade (1991-2001).

Modern schools refer to those schools that are modelled on the British system of education introduced by Lord Macaulay. This system was introduced during the British rule in India, and after 1947 it was made a general policy of education for the masses. The history of these schools is not very old, but the impact on the society is widespread. These schools teach languages, arithmetic, history, geography and science that seem to expand a child's knowledge of the external world and promote abilities of analytical reasoning and logical thinking. Religious topics are taught only as lessons of moral education (Mishra & Dasen, 2002).

Gross enrolment at the primary stage has crossed the 90 per cent mark (92.92% overall) and an impressive 90.93 per cent for girls. The Gross Enrolment Ratio (GER) at the upper primary stage has also improved from 54 per cent in 1993 to about 60 per cent in 2002. Drop outs have shown a steady decline at the primary stage from 59 per cent in 1980-81 to 39 per cent in 2001-02. Even the completion rates for classes I - X have shown improvement, dropping from a 82.5 per cent drop out rate in 1980-81 to 66 per cent in 2001-02 (NCERT, 2006b).

Sarva Shiksha Abhiyan

This is an initiative of the Government of India for Universal Elementary Education and introduced in the year 2001–02. Sarva Shiksha Abhiyan (SSA) has been introduced at all levels including rural areas. The Sarva Shiksha Abhiyan (SSA), which is the cornerstone of the government's intervention in basic education for all children, was allocated Rs. 3,057 crore in the budget estimate for 2004-05 while the 2005-06 budget proposed to increase the allocation to Rs. 7,156 crore; 66,147 elementary schools opened, 17,454 new elementary school buildings, and 33,777 additional classrooms, constructed, 3,10,506 additional teachers appointed, about 6.15 crore girls and children belonging to Scheduled Castes (SCs) and Scheduled Tribes (STs) studying in elementary schools, given free textbooks, in 2004-05.

A periodic assessment after every three years has been encouraged at primary and upper primary stages to assess enhancement in children's learning achievement and progress, using the Baseline Assessment Surveys (BAS) findings as a reference point. Research groups at the state, district and sub-district levels have been constituted to facilitate quality improvement in teaching learning (NCERT, 2003). In view of the recommendations of various commissions and committees collected regarding evaluation in general and evaluation practices in particular, the following major concerns of evaluation practices at different stages of school education have emerged: Leaving apart the teaching of psychology, school psychologists do not exist to whom students affected by psychological problems could be referred for behaviour modification, relieving emotional disturbances, solving the learning difficulties of the learning disabled, or structuring and using special educational techniques for the mentally retarded (Paliwal, 1984).

School Psychologists

As far as the present Indian school education is concerned, from nursery school to senior secondary school, there is no position of school psychologist on the academic staff. Among subject-teachers, the school psychologist is out of place because psychology as a course of study does not exist at the high school level. There are in fact no school psychologists to whom students affected by psychological problems could be referred for behaviour modification, or for addressing emotional or learning difficulties (Paliwal, 1984).

In India, the academic psychology is predominantly dominated by Western concepts and principles. Hence it is quite possible to train the psychology graduates in school psychology so as to lay a strong foundation in the teaching and learning process of the school education. Competency requires both knowledge and skills. School psychology programmes ensure that candidates have a foundation in the knowledge base for psychology and education, including theories, models, empirical findings, and techniques in each domain. School psychology programmes ensure that candidates demonstrate the professional skills necessary to deliver effective services that result in positive outcomes in each domain (National Association of School Psychologists, 2000).

As like that of India, no laws or regulations govern the licensure of psychologists and school psychologists in Albania. There is no job security for school psychologists at this time because employment at schools is made possible only through different organisations that often are in existence for only a few years. School psychologists work in schools because of these organisations and they are paid by these organisations because the Ministry of Education has not compiled a plan to implement school psychologists in school and have no budget for this (Gladiola Bashi, 2003). Research on student's satisfaction with school, including teaching, peer- and student-teachers relationships, also is needed. Professional development and the inclusion of school psychologists within the educational system infrastructure were noted as important areas for future emphasis on the 2003 ISPS (Jimerson et al., 2004).

The history of school psychology in Estonia has gone hand in hand with that of vocational counselling. During the period of Soviet influence, career planning received some emphasis. Through vocational orientation programmes, different occupations were introduced to children beginning in the first grades and later in other grades. The purpose of these programmes was to help children to discover their needs, interests, and abilities, and to acquire career understanding and orientations, especially toward the generally unpopular working class occupations. Today, career counselling is a responsibility of several school psychologists (Eve Kikas, & Hele Kanter, 2006).

Rich Gilman (2004) studied the role and functions of school psychologists, and recommended that school psychology reform efforts should involve stakeholders, including education professionals (i.e., teachers, administrators) in their advocacy efforts. However, very few recent empirical studies have investigated educators' perceptions of the discipline. In this pilot study, over 1,600 teachers and administrators from school districts in four states completed the School Psychology Perceptions Survey. Responses to questions pertained to (a) knowledge of school psychology, (b) satisfaction with school psychological services, (c) helpfulness of school psychology services, and (d) future desired roles and functions of school psychologists. Against this background, an initiative has been taken to promote school psychology in India and thereby motivate the teachers for becoming school psychologists so as to meet the challenges in the school education.

Objectives

The major objectives of the present study are:

1. To find out the ways and means to introduce School Psychology in India by analysing the need for the present school system in India.

2. To explore the possibilities of introducing Indian psychological approaches in education so as to analyse the need of School Psychologists in India.

Analytical Discussion

In India, academic psychology predominantly is dominated by Western concepts and principles. Hence it is quite possible to train school psychology graduates so as to lay a strong foundation in the teaching and learning process of school education. Competency requires both knowledge and skills. School psychology programmes ensure that candidates have a foundation in the knowledge base for psychology and education, including theories, models, empirical findings, and techniques in each domain. According to the National Association of School Psychologists (2000), school psychology training programmes ensure that candidates demonstrate the professional skills necessary to deliver effective services that result in positive outcomes in each domain of practice.

In 2009, Erika E. Voigt stated that the role of the school psychologist, as discussed at the ISPA colloquium 2008, is undergoing changes. These changes are connected with new perspectives and trends in our profession. These are mainly: a stronger priority on prevention; a stronger focus on social-emotional functioning; a higher sensitivity to social and cultural diversity; whole-school and community projects, which demand leadership; and handling of organisational and management processes.

Taking these initiatives into consideration, the group of psychologists in India met and discussed in detail initiating a new venture. Based on the initiative, a professional association was established called the "Indian School Psychology Association" (ISPA-India) that would cater to the needs of school psychologists in India. The ISPA - India is just what the Indian psychologists need to help young and energetic psychologists promote school psychology in India.

Several new initiatives have been proposed to introduce School Psychology programmes to train school psychologists in India. Academically it has been proposed to introduce School

Psychology discipline in higher education so as to train the professional school psychologists.

There is a pertinent need for school psychologists to understand the basic concepts of school psychology and get proper training based on the guidelines issued by the International School Psychology Association and the National Association of school Psychologists, USA. In addition to these guidelines, basic concepts of integral psychology, the Indian psychological aspects of yoga and spiritual education components are also to be included in school psychology so as to train the teachers towards Indian culture and traditions.

Indian classrooms are intertwined with more of culture and traditional aspects. To understand the Indian way of training those needs, school psychologists must know the foundations laid by the educationalists and philosophers of the country. Several Indian models have been practised in Indian education such as the Gandhiji model of basic education, the Sri Aurobindo model of Integral education, and so on and so forth. Indian classroom teaching is more complex than any other system since, multicultural and multilingual and multi religious issues also influence school education. Taking all these issues into consideration, School Psychology programmes have to be evolved so as to meet the challenges and opportunities of the children.

Recommendations

It is realised that as a first step to promote school psychology in India, the awareness programmes and school psychology training programmes based on the ISPA guidelines should be organised in various parts of the country.

It is felt that the Indian Academy of Applied Psychology and other national psychology associations should take an initiative to conduct awareness programmes and training programmes for young and aspiring psychologists.

The national level associations should take an initiative at the policy making levels of the State and Central governments to introduce at least one trained school psychologist in each school and also school psychologist posts are to be created all over the country to develop the school education and to make it more effective.

Conclusion

While it is important and necessary to teach 3Rs (Read, Write and Arithmetic), at the same time it is important to remember that educational institutions do not end up as industries turning out 'consumer products' on 'assembly line'. They have the responsibility of developing personality of children providing a future perspective on life, which is healthy and meaningful. Then only the present education becomes holistic. In India, several steps have been initiated to introduce various ways and means in the education by satisfying the social needs. In this process, introducing the school psychologists in all schools is the pertinent need of the hour to meet the present challenges and opportunities in the school education.

References

Cohen, L., Manion, L.M., and Morrison, K. (2000), *Research methods in education* (5th edition), London: Routledge Falmer.

Erika E. Voigt (2009), School Psychology in a Changing Society, *Indian Psychologist, 7, 6-7.*

Eve Kikas, & Hele Kanter, (2006). *A Description of School Psychology in Estonia,* International School Psychology Association.

Gladiola Bashi (2003), *A Description of School Psychology in Albania,* International School Psychology Association.

Jimerson, S. R., Graydon, K., Farrell, P., Kikas, E., Hatzichristou, C., Boce, E., Bashi, G. & the ISPA Research Committee (2004), The International School Psychology Survey: Development and Data from Albania, Cyprus Estonia, Greece, and Northern England, *School Psychology International, 25 (3).*

Mishra, R.C., & Gupta, V. (1978), Role of schooling and exposure in perceiving pictorial sequence. *Psychologia, 21,* 231-236.

National Association of School Psychologists (2000), Standards for Training and Field Placement Programmes in School Psychology. Retrieved 21.04.2009 at www.naspweb.org

NCERT (2006a), Learning achievement of students at the end of class V., Department of Educational Measurement and Evaluation, National Council of Educational Research and Training, New Delhi. Retrieved 21st March, 2009 http://ssa.nic.in/qualityedu/summ_exec.asp

NCERT (2006b). *Seventh All India Education Survey: 2002-03,* New Delhi.

Paliwal, T.R. (1984), The Prospects for Psychology in Indian Schools, *School Psychology International, 5 (1),* 27-30

Palmer, P. (1998), *The Courage to Teach—Exploring the Inner Landscape of a Teacher's Life*, San Francisco: Jossey Boss.

Raina, M.K., & Srivastava, A.K. (2004), Educational Psychology in India: Its Present Status and Future Concerns, *International Journal Group Tensions, 27 (4),* 309-340.

Ramalingam, P. (2009), *Need Analysis for School Psychologists in India,* A paper presented in the 31st International School Psychology Association Colloquium held on 7–11 July, 2009 in Malta.

Ramesh C., Mishra & Pierre R. Dasen (2002), *The Influence of Schooling on Cognitive Development: A Review of Research in India.*

Rich, Gilman (2004), Perceptions of school psychological services by education professionals: results from a multi-state survey pilot study, *School Psychology Review.*

Shukla, A. (1993), A developmental study of pictorial perception in high and low facility schools. Unpublished doctoral dissertation, Banaras Hindu University.

Sinha, D. (1977), Social disadvantages and development of certain perceptual skills, *Indian Journal of Psychology, 52,* 115-132.

4

A Remedial Intervention for Addition and Subtraction in Children with Dyscalculia

—Alireza Beygi, Prakash Padakannaya, and Gowramma, I. P

This study investigated the impact of remedial intervention on students' performance with dyscalculia in teaching addition and subtraction. Forty male students with dyscalculia (20 in experimental, and 20 in control groups) from fourth and fifth grades in Arak, Iran were the participants. The experimental group received a remedial programme in addition to their regular classroom teaching (every other day). Data analysis indicated a significant increase in the subtraction and addition performance after remedial intervention. The article discusses implications for teachers, administers, researchers, teacher training institutions, and students with learning disabilities.

Keywords: Dyscalculia, Addition, Subtraction, Learning Disability.

According to the DSM-IV (American Psychiatric Association, 1994), developmental dyscalculia is a rare form of learning disability (LD), with a prevalence of about 1 per cent in the school-age population. But researches in the United States (Badian, 1983), Norway (Ostad, 1998), Israel (Gross-Tsur, Manor, & Shalev,1996), and Europe (Kosc,1974) have shown that 5 per cent to 8 per cent of school-age children exhibit some form of mathematical disabilities (MD) and associated long-term problems (Geary, 2004; Griffin & Case,1997). With many of these students, reading

This paper originally appeared in the *Journal of the Indian Academy of Applied Psychology*, January, 2009, Vol.36, No.1, pp. 09-18.

disabilities (RD) and attention-deficit/hyperactivity disorder (ADHD) have been identified as co-morbid disorders (Geary, 2004; Gross-Tsur et al.., 1996). Behrangi (1997 cited in Behrad, 2006) studied the prevalence of learning disabilities in primary schools (grades I, II, III, IV, and V) in Tehran, the capital city of Iran and concluded that 5.2 per cent of the children exhibited symptoms of dyscalculia.

Children with LD often have difficulty with symbolic or abstract concepts and reasoning. These students may need extra assistance through hands-on manipulative and pictorial representations of mathematical concepts. Hands-on experiences allow students to understand numerical symbols and abstract equations at a concrete level, making the information more accessible to all students (Maccini & Gagnon, 2000). Concrete-Representational-Abstract (CRA) is an intervention for mathematics instruction that can enhance the mathematics performance of students with learning disabilities (Baroody, 1987). It is a three-part instructional strategy, with each part building on the previous instruction to promote student learning and retention and to address conceptual knowledge. The CRA sequence of instruction incorporates the use of hands-on manipulative in the concrete stage, followed by pictorial displays in the representations phase, and in the next phase facilitates abstract reasoning with numerical symbols. Learning disabled students learning basic mathematics facts with CRA instruction show improvements in acquisition and retention of mathematics concepts (Miller& Mercer, 1993). CRA supports understanding of underlying mathematical concepts before learning rules, and facilitates children moving from a concrete model of chips or blocks to an abstract representational (4×3=12). Thus CRA instructional sequence consists of three phases.

The first one is concrete phase. In the concrete phase children with learning disabilities in math are provided with manipulative and other material or physical learning tools that will provide them the opportunity to explore a mathematical concept or process by actually doing it with tools. This is the stage of 'getting their hands dirty' with the intent that having an actual experience will enable the construction of the knowledge being targeted. The second phase is the representational phase. In this phase, students with learning disabilities in math were trained to develop mental images of the mathematical manipulations by drawing on other means for understanding the target knowledge. Another way to think about this phase is to say that students with learning disabilities in maths are encouraged to step back form the manipulative and other concrete tools, and focus on the mathematical concept or process involved in performing actions with the tools. In the abstract phase, the third level, students with learning disabilities in math could manipulate concepts or processes in the absence of the tools that were important in the early phase of learning. The concrete-representational-abstract (CRA) teaching sequence has been found to facilitate maths learning in a variety of basic skills including addition (Miller, Mercer, & Dillon, 1992), place value (Peterson, Mercer, & O'Shea,1988), subtraction (Miller & Mercer, 1992), multiplication (Morin & Miller, 1998), division (Miller, Mercer, & Dillon, 1992), and fractions (Butler, 1999). In the present study the CRA approach and the lesson programme developed by Gowramma (2005), were used for remedial teaching of addition and subtraction and the effectiveness of the remediation was tested with the help of a control group.

Method

Participants

Participants were selected through screening more than 1,000 students studying in 4th and 5th grades in primary schools of Arak city in Iran for dyscalculia. Only 40 students who exhibited arithmetic disability were included in the present study. Their age range was 10-12 years. They were randomly divided into two groups—Experimental and Control groups (with 20 students in each group).

Measures

Key maths diagnostic arithmetic test: This test was meant for students from kindergarten through grade eight (Cannolley et al., 1997). It covers three aspects: (a) Basic concepts (numeration: 24 items, rational numbers: 18 items, geometry: 24 items). (b) Operations (Addition: 18 items, Subtraction: 18 items, Multiplication: 18 items, Division: 18 items, Mental Computation: 18 items). (c) Applications (Measurement: 24 items, Time and Money: 24 items, Estimation: 18 items, Problem Solving: 18 items). A correct response by the students received a score of one and a wrong response received a zero score. The students' final scores would correspond to total correct responses. This test was used as a criterion measure in both pre and post intervention testing.

Wechsler Intelligence Scale for Children-III): It is a battery of tests for 6 to 17 years old. The WISC-III consists of two sets scales, the verbal scale and the performance scale. Each of these scales has several subtests. The verbal scale measures include language expression, comprehension, and the ability to apply these skills to solving problems. The examiner presented the questions orally, and the participants gave spoken response. The performance scale assesses non-verbal problem solving, perceptual organization, and speed and visual-motor proficiency. The standard procedure of administration was followed.

Children's Behaviour Questionnaire (Proforma B): It consists of 26 items indicating the presence or absence of common behavioural and emotional problems as seen in school setting. The items describe behaviour against which the teacher is asked to indicate whether each description 'does not apply', 'applies to some extent' or 'definitely applies' to the child. Each of these responses is scored 0, 1, and 2 respectively. The scores on each item are added together to produce a total score. The scale has been shown to have a test-retest reliability of 0.89 over a 3-month period and inter rater reliability of 0.72.

DSM-IV (1994) suggests 12 item check list for identifying dyscalculia (mathematics disorder), which are completed by teachers. Teachers rate students on each of the items and decide whether an item can be definitely applied or not. The ratings are 0, and 1 (0 stands for "No" and 1 stands for "Yes"). The total score is the combination of the scores of all items. Standard procedure as mentioned in the manual was followed.

PROCEDURE

The study was carried out in there phases:

Phase I: Screening and pre-test: In the first phase, the investigator approached the primary school authorities and teachers in order to get their consent for conducting the study, and also to be directed to the students who don't have satisfactory performance in mathematics (meaning those who don't receive acceptable scores in mathematics). Out of the total population of 1,000, their teachers selected 300 students. Finally, 40 students out of 300 were found to be having dyscalculia and were selected for this study. The investigators put them randomly into control and experimental groups (20 students in each group). All the 40 students had the following characteristics:

1. Arithmetic disability (scored 70 and below in Key maths diagnostic arithmetic test, and scored above 5 in the checklist of DSM IV).
2. Adequate intelligence (IQ 90 and above as assessed by WISC-III).
3. No behavioural and emotional problems (scored 9 and below through as assessed by Rutter's Proforma B).

Phase II: After selection, the experimental group received remedial teaching based on CRA and Gowramma's lesson programme. Remedial teaching was done in Learning Disability Centre in Arak city, in 30 sessions (every second day). Each session was for 65 minutes. Gowramma's teaching module consisted of six broad units: Pre–requisite skills (26 lessons), Number concept (29 lessons), Addition (25 lessons), Subtraction (23 lessons), Multiplication (23 lessons), and Division (17 lessons). In this study we employed addition and subtraction lessons only (contents of lessons are given in tables 1 and 2). Worksheets designed on the basis of CRA with pictorial representations were given to experimental group during every session.

Phase III: Post-test was administered after two weeks of completing the intervention teaching. Key maths diagnostic arithmetic test, was given to participants of both experimental and control groups. Later, a master chart was prepared and the data were entered to the computer for further computations.

Table 1. Lesson Scheme for Teaching Subtraction

	SPECIFIC OBJECTIVES OF EACH LESSON IN SEQUENTIAL ORDER
Lesson 1	To learn the terms and symbol of subtraction
Lesson 2	To understand that subtraction means to take away things
Lesson 3	To make familiar with all terms used in subtraction
Lesson 4	To understand the concepts of subtraction
Lesson 5	To understand the procedure of subtraction
Lesson 6	To understand single digit numbers
Lesson 7	To subtract a number from the same number
Lesson 8	To subtract one from a number
Lesson 9	To make familiar with all terms used in subtraction
Lesson 10	To learn that subtraction is the reverse process of addition
Lesson 11	To subtract a one-digit number from a two-digit without borrowing
Lesson 12	To subtract a one-digit number from a two-digit with borrowing
Lesson 13	To subtract a two-digit number from a two-digit without borrowing
Lesson 14	To subtract a two-digit number from a two-digit number with borrowing
Lesson 15	To subtract horizontally
Lesson 16	To subtract a three-digit number from another three-digit number without borrowing
Lesson 17	To subtract a three-digit number from another three-digit number with borrowing from ten's place.
Lesson 18	To subtract a three-digit number from another three-digit number with borrowing from hundred's place
Lesson 19	To subtract a three-digit number from another three-digit number with borrowing from both ten's and hundred's place
Lesson 20	To subtract one-digit number from a three-digit number
Lesson 21	To subtract a two-digit number from a three-digit number
Lesson 22	To subtract any number from another number up to four-digit numbers.

Table 2. Lesson Scheme for Teaching Addition

SPECIFIC OBJECTIVES OF EACH LESSON IN SEQUENTIAL ORDER	
Lesson 1	To learn the terms and symbol of addition
Lesson 2	To undertstand that addition means putting together things
Lesson 3	To make familiar with all terms used in addition
Lesson 4	To understand the concept of addition
Lesson 5	To understand the procedure of addition
Lesson 6	To add single digit numbers (sum not exceeding 10)
Lesson 7	To understand that when the order of the addends change, the sum remains the same
Lesson 8	To familiarize addition if doubtless
Lesson 9	To add one to a number
Lesson 10	To add zero to a number
Lesson 11	To add single-digit number with another single-digit number
Lesson 12	To add three or more single-digit number
Lesson 13	To add a two-digit number to a one-digit number without carrying over
Lesson 14	To add a two-digit number to another two-digit number without carrying over
Lesson 15	To add a two-digit number to another two-digit number with carrying over
Lesson 16	To add three or more groups of two-digit numbers
Lesson 17	To add horizontally
Lesson 18	To add three or more groups of one and two digits
Lesson 19	To add a three-digit number to a three-digit number without carry over
Lesson 20	To add a three-digit number to a three-digit number with carry over the tens place
Lesson 21	To add a three-digit number to a three-digit number with carry over to hundred's place
Lesson 22	To add a three-digit number to a three-digit number with carry over to tens and hundred's place
Lesson 23	To add three or more groups of three-digit numbers
Lesson 24	To add three or more groups or four, three and two and one-digit numbers
Lesson 25	To solve simple daily life problems involving addition

Results and Discussion

Table 3 presents the means and standard deviation of both the groups in pre/post-tests for two mathematical operations, viz., addition and subtraction. Data were analyzed using analysis of covariance (ANCOVA) with the pre-scores considered as covariates, and by't' test.

ANCOVA revealed significant improvement in the addition test performance after remedial intervention for experimental group ($F=23.40$; $p<.000$). The mean pre- and post-test scores of experimental group were found to be 5.75 and 10.55 respectively, whereas for the control group they were 6.25 and 6.75. Table 4 presents the summary of t-tests.

There was no significant difference between experimental and control groups with respect to mean pre-test scores in addition ($t = .907$, $p< .370$). Also ANCOVA for subtraction showed significant improvement in the subtraction test performance after remedial intervention for experimental group ($F=30.91$; $p<.001$). The respective mean scores for pre and post-tests were 4.25 and 9.20, whereas the respective scores for the control group were 5.60 and 6.75. Table 4 shows that there was no significant difference between mean pre-intervention subtraction scores of experimental and control groups ($t = 1.742$, $p< .091$).

Thus the significant improvement observed in the experiment group that underwent remedial teaching proved the effectiveness of the remedial programme employed in the study. The results are in agreement with Gowramma (2005) and other researchers (Bahr & Rieth, 1989; Bolich, 1995; Chiang, 1986; Cook, Guzaukas, Pressley & Kerr,1993; Cybriwsky & Scuster,1990; Hasselbring, Goin & Bransford, 1988; Irish, 2002; Mcintry, Test, & Cooke, 1991; Mattingly & Bott, 1990; Morton & Flynt, 1997; Okolo, 1992; Ozaki, Williams, & Mclaughlin, 1996; Skinner, Beatty, Turco & Rasavage, 1989; Skinner, et. al., 1992; Stading, Williams & Mclaughlin, 1996; Van Houten & Rolider, 1990; VanLuit & Naglieri, 1999; Williams & Collins, 1994; Wilson & Majsterek, 1996; Wood, Frank & Wacker, 1998; Greene, 1999; Cook, & Reichard, 1996; Kroesbergen, VanLuit, & Naglieri , 2003).

Table 3. Group Means and Standard Deviations in Pre/Post-Tests for Addition and Subtraction

	Pre Test		Post Test	
Groups/Operation	Mean	SD	Mean	SD
Ex/Addition	5.75	1.33	10.55	3.44
Co/Addition	6,25	2.07	6.75	1.88
Ex/Subtraction	4.25	1.29	9.20	3.53
Co/Subtraction	5.20	2.06	5.60	2.43

Table 4. Summary of "t" Tests

Test/operation	Experimental Group		Control Group		t	p
	Mean	SD	Mean	SD		
Pre-test addition	5.75	1.33	6.25	2.07	.907	.370
Pretest subtraction	4.25	1.29	5.20	2.06	1.742	.091

Qualitative error analysis revealed the following pattern of errors in children with dyscalculia.

Addition

A1: Not being aware of the basic knowledge of the addition process.

A2: Not being aware of the basic knowledge of the addition of fraction with the same denominator.

A3: Missing a digit (number) during the addition of digits in the same column.

A4: Not being able to infer as well as possible during the addition process.

A5: Not being able to add the digits (number) which appear horizontally.

A6: Not being aware of the concept of 'zero' in addition.

A7: Not being able to add decimal digit.

Table 5 presents the errors in addition performance along with an example and frequency of each particular error in both pre- and post-tests. One can notice that there was a drastic decrease in number of errors committed in almost all of the categories after the intervention.

Table 5. Errors in Addition Performance along with an Example and Frequency of Each Particular Error in Both Pre- and Post-tests.

Errors	A1	A2	A3	A4	A5	A6	A7	Total
Example	9 + 6 14	½+2/5=3/10	261 40 + 751 992	5+8=13 5+18=23 5+28=?	18+5=68	26 +50 70	1.36 +2 1.38	
Pre test/f	28	2	2	2	4	3	0	41
Post test/f	5	1	0	2	2	1	3	14

Subtraction

The qualitative analysis of errors in subtraction resulted in the following categories of errors:

S1: Not being aware of the basic knowledge of the subtraction process.

S2: Subtracting the units of the first digits (number) from the units of the second digits.

S3: Not being aware of the concept of 'zero' in subtraction.

S4: Not being aware of the basic knowledge of the subtraction of fraction with the same denominator.

S5: Not being aware of the concept of the additive identity.

S6: Not being aware of the concept of the 'borrowing'

a) Not subtracting a digit from tens column after transmitting to the unit column.

b) Not subtracting a digit from hundreds column after transmitting to the tens column.

S7: Subtracting the units of tens.

S8: To leave the subtraction process incomplete.

Table 6 presents the errors in subtraction performance along with an example and frequency of each particular error in both pre- and post-tests. One can notice that there was a drastic decrease in number of errors committed in almost all of the categories after the intervention.

Table 6. Errors in Subtraction Performance along with an Example and Frequency of Each Particular Error in Both Pre- and Post-tests

Errors	S1	S2	S3	S4	S5-a	S5-b	S6	S7	S8	Total
Example	5 - 2 2	62 - 5 63	500 - 304 204	$\frac{7}{9}-\frac{2}{9}-\frac{5}{0}$	73 - 29 54	217 - 32 285	32 - 11 22	73 - 22 1	5.7 - 4 5.3	
Pre test/f	29	8	8	2	8	7	2	6	0	70
Pos test/f	7	2	3	4	3	4	0	3	5	31

It may be noted that the errors under the categories A7 and S8 (A7 stands for addition of decimal digits and S8 stands for subtraction of decimal digits) increased in post-test situation as compared to the pre-test condition. The reason behind such an unexpected performance of students was due to the fact that those topics were not covered in the classroom at the period of administrating of pre-test, and hence scored zero on them. Though these topics were taught in the class by the time of post-test, the students applied this knowledge wrongly. On the whole, it could be concluded that the remedial intervention improved significantly the basic knowledge of addition and subtraction.

References

American Psychiatric Association. (1994). *Diagnostic and statistical manual of mental disorders, fourth edition.* Washington DC: American Psychiatric Association, 48-55; 83-84.

Badian, N.A. (1983). Dyscalculia and non-verbal disorders of learning. In H.R. Myklebust (Ed.).*Progress in learning disabilities.* New York: Grune & Stratton, 5, 233-264.

Bahr, C.M, & Reith, H.J. (1989).The effects of instructional computer games and drill and practice software on learning disabled students' mathematics achievement. *Computer in the Schools, 6(3),* 87-101.

Baroody, A. (1987). *Children's mathematical thinking.* New York: Teachers College Press.

Bolich, B. (1995).The effects of a copy, cover, compare procedure and a token economy on the retention of basic multiplication facts by two midschool students with ADD and ADHD. *Journal of Special Education,* 1-10.

Behrad, B. (2006).Prevalence of learning disabilities in Iranian primary students: a meta- analysis. *Journal of Research on Exceptional Children 4,* 417-436.

Butler, M. (1999). *Fraction instruction for students with disabilities: Comparing two teaching sequences.* Unpublished doctoral dissertation, University of Nevada, Las Vegas.

Chiang, B. (1986). Initial learning and transfer effects of microcomputer drills on LD Students' multiplication skills. *Learning Disability Quarterly, 9,*118-23.

Christenson, S.L., Ysseldyke, J.E., &Thurlow, M.L. (1989).Critical instructional factors for Students with mild handicaps: An integrative review. *Remedial and Special Education,* 10, 21-31.

Connolly, A.J. (1997). *KeyMath Revised/NU: A diagnostic inventory of essential Mathematics.* Circle Pines, MN: American Guidance Service.

Cook, N.L., & Reichard, S.M. (1996).The effects of children interspersal drill rations on acquisition and generalization of multiplication and division facts. *Education and Treatment of Children, 19,* 124-142.

Cybriwsky, C.A., & Schuster, J.W. (1990). Using constant time delay procedures to teach multiplication facts. *Remedial and Special Education, 11,* 54-59.

Desoete, A., Roeyers, H., & DeClercq, A (2004). Children with mathematics learning disabilities in Belgium. *Journal of Learning Disabilities, 31,* 50-61.

Geary, D.C. (2004). Mathematics and learning disabilities. *Journal of Learning Disabilities, 37,* 4-15.

Ginsburg, H.P. (1997). Mathematics learning disabilities: A view from developmental psychology. *Journal of Learning Disabilities, 30,* 20-33.

Gowramma, I.P. (2005). *Development of remedial instruction program for children, With dyscalculia in primary school.* (1st Ed).Mysore: Chethana Book House.

Greene, G. (1999). Mnemonic multiplication fact instruction for student with learning disabilities. *Learning Disabilities Research and Practice, 14,*141-148.

Griffin, S., & Case, R. (1997).Wrapping up: Using peer commentaries to enhance models of mathematics teaching and learning. *Issues in Education, 3*,115-134.

Gross-Tsur, V., Manor, O., & Shalev, R.S. (1996). Developmental dyscalculia: Prevalence and demographic features. *Developmental Medicine and Child Neurology, 38*, 25-33.

Hanich, L.B., Jordan, N.C, Kaplan, D.Dick, J.'(2001). Performance across different areas of mathematical cognition in children difficulties .*Journal of Educational Psychology, 93*,615-619.

Harris, C.A., Miller, S.P., & Mercer, C.D. (1995).Teaching initial multiplication skills to Students with disabilities in general education classrooms. *Learning Disabilities Research & practice, 10*, 180-195.

_______________ ., Miller, S.P., & Mercer, C.D. (1995).Teaching initial multiplication skills to Students with disabilities in general education classrooms. *Learning Disabilities Research & practice, 10*, 180-195.

Hasselbring, T.S., Goin, L.I., & Bransford, J.D. (1988).Developing math automaticity in learning handicapped children: The role of computerized dill and practice. *Focus on Exceptional Children, 20*, 3-7

Irish, C. (2002).Using peg-and keyword mnemonics and computer assisted instruction to enhance basic multiplication performance in elementary students with Learning and cognitive disabilities. *Journal of Special Education Technology 17*, 29-40.

Kosc, L. (1974).Developmental dyscalculia. *Journal of Learning Disabilities.7* (3), 164-177.

Kroesbergen, E.V., VanLuti, J.E., & Naglieri, J.A. (2003). Mathematical learning difficulties and PASS cognitive processes. *Journal of Learning Disabilities, 36*,572-574.

Maccini, P. & Gagnon, J.C., (2000).Best practices for teaching mathematics to secondary students with special needs. *Focus on Exceptional Children, 32*, 1-22.

Mattingly, J.C., & Bott, D.A. (1990).Teaching multiplication facts to students with Learning Problems. *Exceptional Children, 56*, 438-439.

Mcintyre, S.B., Test, D.W., & Cook, N.L. (1991).Using count-bys to increase multiplication facts fluency. *Learning Disabilities Quarterly, 14*, 82-88

Meyer, M.S. (2000).The ability-achievement discrepancy: Dose it contribute to an understanding of learning disabilities? *Educational Psychology Revive 12*, 315-337.

Miller, S.P., & Mercer, C.D., (1992).Teaching students with learning problems in math to acquire, understand, and apply basic math facts. *Remedial and Special Education, 13,* 19-35.

_______________ ., & Mercer, C.D. (1993a). Using a graduated word problem sequence to promote problem-solving skills. *Learning Disabilities Research Practice, 8,* 169-174.

_______________ & Mercer, C.D. (1993b).Using data to learn about concrete-semi concrete- abstract instruction for students with math disabilities. *Learning Disabilities Research & Practice, 8,* 89-96.

_______________ , Mercer, C.D., & Dillon, A.S. (1992).CSA: Acquiring and retaining math skills. *Intervention in School and Clinic, 28,*105-110.

_______________ ., Mercer, C.D., Harris, C.A., Strawser, S., & Jones, W.P. (1998).Teaching multiplication to second graders in inclusive settings. *Focus on Learning Problems in Mathematics, 21*(4), 49-69.

Morin, V.A., & Miller, S.P. (1998).Teaching multiplication to middle school students with mental retardation. *Education and Treatment of children, 21,* 22-37.

Morton, R.C., & Flynt, S.W. (1997). A comparison of constant delay and prompt fading to teach multiplication facts to students with learning disabilities. *Journal of Instruction Psychology, 24,* 3-13.

Okolo, C.M. (1992). The effects of computer-based attribution retraining on the attributions, persistence, and mathematics computation of students with learning disabilities, *Journal of Learning Disabilities,* 25,327-334.

Ostad, S.A. (1998). Developmental differences in solving simple arithmetic word problems and simple number-fact problems: A comparison of mathematically disabled children. *Mathematical Cognition, 4,* 1-19.

Ozaki, C., Williams, R.L., & McLaughlin, T.F. (1996). Effects of copy cover compare drill and practice procedure for multiplication fact mastery with a sixth grade student with learning disabilitities.*B.C.Journal of Special Education, 20,* 65-74.

Peterson, S.K., Mercer, C.D., & O'shea, L. (1988).Teaching learning disabled students place value using concrete to abstract sequence. *Learning Disabilities Research, 4,* 52-56.

Ramaa, S. (1990). Study of neuropsychological processes and logico-mathematical Structure among dyscalculics, NCERT project Report, Regional College of Education, NCERT, Mysore, India.

Roberts, G.H. (1968).The failure strategies of third grade arithmetic pupils. *The Arithmetic Teacher, 15*,442-446.

Rutter, M. (1967). A children's behavior questionnaire for completion by teachers: Preliminary findings. *Journal of Child Psychology and Psychiatry, 8*, 1-11.

Shalev, R.S., Manor, O., Amir.N, & Gross-Tsur, V. (1993). Acquisition of arithmetic in normal children: Assessment by a cognitive model of dyscalculia. *DevMed Child Neurol, 35*,593-601.

Skinner, C.H., Beatty, K.L., Turco, T.L., & Rasavage, C. (1989) .Cover, copy & compare: a method for increasing multiplication performance. *School Psychology Review, 18*,412-420.

_____., Shapiro, E.S., Turco, T.L., & Cole, C.L. (1992). A comparison of self and peer-delivered immediate corrective feedback on multiplication performance *Journal of School Psychology, 30*, 101-116.

Stading, M., Williams, R.L., & McLaughlin, T.F. (1996). Effects of a copy, cover, and compare procedure on multiplication facts mastery with a third grad girl with learning disabilities in a home setting. *Education & Treatment of Children, 19*, 425-434.

Swanson, H.L., Hoskyn, & Lee, C. (1999).Intervention for students with learning disabilities: *A meta-analysis of treatment outcomes*. New York: Guilford Press.

Van Houten, R., & Rolider, A. (1990).The use of color mediation techniques to teach number identification and single digit multiplication problems to children with learning problems. *Education and Treatment of Children, 13*, 216-225.

VanLuti, J.E., & Naglieri, J.A. (1999).Effectiveness of the MASTER program for teaching Special children multiplication and division. *Journal of learning disabilities, 32*, 98-107.

Wechsler, D. (1997). *WAIS-III: Administration and Scoring Manual*, The Psychological Corporation, San Antonio, TX.

Williams, D.M., & Collins, B.C. (1994).Teaching multiplication facts to students with Learning disabilities: Teacher-selected versus student-selected material prompt within the delay procedure. *Journal of Learning Disabilities, 27*, 589-597.

Wilson, R., & Majsterek, D. (1996).The effects of computer-assisted versus teacher directed instruction on the multiplication performance of elementary students with learning disabilities. *Journal of Learning Disabilities, 29,* 382-390.

Wood, D.K., Frank, A.R., & Wacker, D.P. (1998).Teaching multiplication facts to Students with learning disabilities. *Journal of Applied Behavior Analysis, 31,* 323-338.

5

Impact of Life Skill Training on Self-esteem, Adjustment and Empathy among Adolescents

—Pooja Yadav and Naved Iqbal

The aim of the present study was to see the impact of life skill training on self-esteem, adjustment and empathy among adolescents. Total sample comprised of 60 students (30 males and 30 females) from the Hans Raj Model School, Punjabi Bagh who has received life skill training from the team of Expressions India. Self esteem inventory (school form), Adjustment inventory for school students (AISS) and the Empathy quotient (EQ) were administered in a group session one by one in two or three days both before training was given and after training. In the post condition, test scores were obtained after 5 months of training. The result showed that subjects improved significantly in post condition on self-esteem, emotional adjustment, educational adjustment, total adjustment and empathy. However, no significant difference was found on social adjustment in pre and post condition. Overall training was very effective as subjects improved in the post condition on all measures except one, thus showing that Life skill training do show positive results in bringing change in adolescent's attitude, thought and behaviour by providing supportive environment to them.

Keywords: Self-esteem, Adjustment, Empathy.

The present scenario of adolescents clearly shows that the condition of our youth has significantly deteriorated. Recent studies show that there is significant rise in the problems faced by the adolescents, for example, serious emotional disturbances

This paper originally appears in the Journal of the Indian Academy of Applied Psychology, October 2009, Vol.35, Special Issue, pp. 61-70.

has increased (WHO, 2001), increased sexual activity in schools, rise in AIDS cases in India and greater use of alcohol consumption has been found (BSS, 2007). Apart from the above, use of heavy drugs and youth dropouts have also increased in the recent years (UNICEF, 2001).

All these studies clearly illustrate the increase in aggressiveness, suicidal cases, drug use and depressive cases among adolescents. This gives us the clear image of the struggles that adolescents go through, the problems they face. So providing an experience that would strengthen adolescent's coping abilities to counter environmental stress and disadvantages with which they sometimes have to cope with while experiencing is an essential need.

One best practice model for contributing to the healthy development of adolescents is a life skills approach. A key aspect of human development—as important to basic survival as intellect—is the acquisition of socio-cognitive and emotional coping skills. This has been shown to have impact on behaviours. For more than a decade, research on interventions that address these specific skill areas has shown their effectiveness in promoting desirable behaviours, such as sociability, improved communication, effective decision making and conflict resolution, and preventing negative or high-risk behaviours, such as use of tobacco, alcohol and other drugs, unsafe sex, and violence. Developed by Dr. Botvin, a leading prevention expert, Life Skills Training is backed by over 20 scientific studies and is recognised as a model or exemplary programme by an array of government agencies including the U.S. Department of Education and the Centre for Substance Abuse Prevention.

Life skills are essentially those abilities that help promote mental well being and competence in young people as they face the realities of life. UNICEF and WHO agree that life skills are generally applied in various aspects of life. Such as in the context of health and social events like human relationships, learning about social influences on behaviour and learning about rights and responsibilities, as well as being taught in the context of health problems.

Life skills enable individuals to translate knowledge, attitudes and values into actual abilities, i.e., what to do and how to do it. Life skills are abilities that enable individuals to behave in healthy ways, given the desire to do so and given the scope and opportunity to do so. They are not a panacea: "How to do abilities" are not the only factors that affect behaviour. If the model were placed within a larger, more comprehensive framework there would be many factors that relate to the motivation and ability to behave in positive ways to prevent health problems. These factors include such things as social support, cultural and environment factors, etc.

It can be utilised in many content areas, issues, topics or subjects such as in prevention of drug abuse, sexual violence, teenage pregnancy, HIV/AIDS/STD prevention, suicide prevention, etc. UNICEF extends its use further into consumer education, environmental education, peace education or education for development, livelihood and income generation, among others. In short, it empowers young people to take positive actions to protect themselves and to promote health and positive social relationships.

Life skills education is an educational innovation that has spread in several countries since it was introduced in mid-1980, thus showing its effectiveness. Comprehensive life skills programmes developed in England, Canada, Australia and the United States have spread to over 30 countries. In our country, most of the initiatives have come from NGO's sector.

The current scenario of adolescents revealed by increased depression, increased suicidal rates, increased drug use is the clear indication of the challenges that adolescent's are facing. Information overload, mixed messages from media, press, teachers, and family and from society at large add to the confusing scenario of the assimilating young mind. No doubt that they are at risk because they lack social support to seek accurate information and services. Thus providing an experience that would strengthen adolescent's coping abilities to counter environmental stress and disadvantages with which they sometimes have to cope with while experiencing is an essential need. The purpose of this study is primarily to study the impact of life skill training on adolescents and to understand and explore what can be done at the grassroots level, starting from the school as school play crucial role in the development of cognitive, linguistic, social, emotional and moral function and competencies in a child. The present study therefore is an attempt to understand the effectiveness of this approach in the Indian setting on adolescent's self-esteem, adjustment level and empathy.

Method

Sample

The samples of the study comprised 60 students (30 males and 30 females). The age range was of 15-17 years. The sample was collected from the Hans Raj Model School, Punjabi Bagh.

Tools

Self-esteem inventory (Adult form): Self-esteem inventory by Coppersmith (1982) was used to measure the self esteem of the subjects. The SEI is designed to measure the evaluative attitude towards the self in social, academic, family and personal area of experience. It was developed in conjunction an extensive study of self-esteem on children and the major basis was the widely used belief that self-esteem is significantly associated with personal satisfaction and effective functioning. The adult form of the SEI was used in the study. This form consists of 25 items. The subject has to put a "x" in the column of either" LIKE ME", if he/she thinks that the item signifies what he feels or "UNLIKE ME", if he/she thinks the item does not signify what he/she feels. Reliability coefficients ranging from .71 to .80 have been reported when alternate forms were used. The concurrent validity and predictive validity of the SEI has been reported to be good. SEI scores are significantly correlated to creativity, academic achievement, perceived popularity and family adjustment. High personality adjustment scores accompany high SEI scores. SEI scores are also correlated with scores on achievement and intelligence. They are also predictive of school achievement.

Adjustment inventory for school students (AISS)

Adjustment inventory developed by Sinha and Singh (1984), for Hindi-knowing school students of India, was used to assess different areas of adjustment. The inventory seeks to segregate well-adjusted secondary school students (age group 14 to 18 years) from poorly adjusted students in three years of adjustment. In this scale, the scoring is done in a reverse direction, i.e., less score reveals better adjustment. A list of 100 questions indicating the significant problems of school students in the three areas was prepared. The questions were to be answered in "yes" or "no". The final inventory consisted of 60 items, 20 items in each area of adjustment. The meaning of the symbols and explanation of the areas: (a) *Emotional adjustment*: High scores indicate unstable emotion. Students with low scores tend to be emotionally stable. (b) *Social adjustment*: Individuals scoring high are submissive and tiring. Low scores indicate aggressive behaviour. (c) *Educational adjustment*: Individuals scoring high on third are poorly adjusted with their curricular and curricular programmes. Persons with low scores are interested in school programmes. Coefficient of reliability was determined by (i) Split – half method, (ii) Test retest method and (iii) K-R Formula- 20. Table I gives the reliability coefficients of the total test and of subtests by the different methods. In item analysis, validity coefficients were determined for each item by biserial correlation method and only such items were retained which yielded biserial correlation with both the criteria. (i) Total score and (ii) Area score, significant level being 0.01. Correlating inventory scores with high ratings by the hostel superintendent also validated this inventory. This was done on the data of 60 pupils living in the hostels of Patna Collegiate Multi-purpose higher secondary school. The hostel superintendent rated the pupils on a five point scale, namely, Excellent, Good, Average, Poor and Very poor in respect to their adjustments. The product moment coefficient correlation between inventory scores and superintendent's was found to be 0.51.

The EQ questionnaire

The empathy quotient by Cohen & Wheelwright (2004) was used to measure the empathy of the subjects. The EQ has a forced choice format, can be self aaministered, and is straightforward to score because it does not depend on any interpretation. It contains 40 empathy items and 20 filler/control items. On each empathy item a person can score 2, 1, or 0. The EQ comprises 60 questions, broken down into two types: 40 questions tapping empathy and 20 filler items. The 20 filler items were included to distract the participant from a relentless focus on empathy. Each of the items listed above scores 1 point if the respondent records the empathic behaviour mildly, or 2 points if the respondent records the behaviour strongly. Approximately half the items were worded to produce a "disagree" response and half to produce an "agree" response for the empathic response. This was to avoid a response bias either way. Following this, items were randomised. So, the EQ has a maximum score of 80 and a minimum of zero. Reliability-Cronbach's alpha was calculated for the EQ was 0.92, which is high.

Table 1 : Mean, SD and t value pre- and post-condition

Variable	*Condition*	*Mean*	*SD*	*t*
	Pre	53.93	18.87	9.97**
Self-esteem	Post	69.06	15.97	
Emotional	Pre	13.51	3.79	15.05**
Adjustment	Post	7.53	3.35	
Social	Pre	11.53	6.09	0.8
Adjustment	Post	10.93	1.74	
Educational	Pre	13.10	4.53	11.73**
Adjustment	Post	6.13	3.47	
Total	Pre	38.20	7.90	13.82**
Adjustment	Post	24.61	4.92	
Empathy	Pre	40.71	17.19	10.80**
	Post	54.26	13.08	

** $p< 0.01$

Table 1 shows that there was significant difference between pre- and post-condition on Self-esteem, Emotional, Educational, Total adjustment and Empathy. Significant differences were observed between all the pairs at .01 level of significance. In post condition, subjects have improved in all the above variables. However, significant difference was not found between pre and post condition on Social adjustment.

Comparison of adjustment scores before and after life skills training

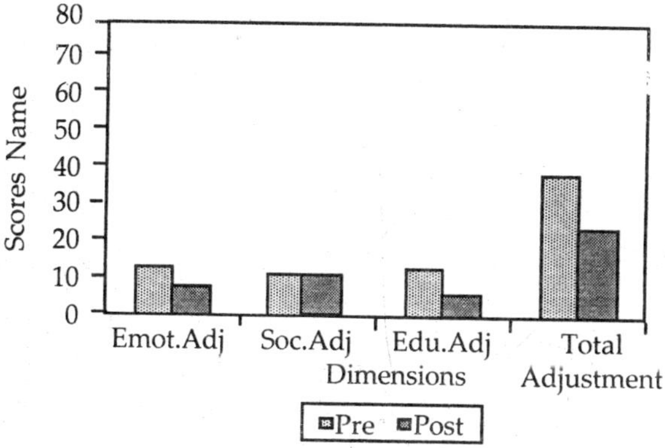

Figure 1: Depicts the gain in scores of all above dimensions among adolescents after LST.

Fig.1 clearly depicts the gain in scores of all above dimensions among adolescents after LST. It could be observed that there is decrease in case of adjustment, but as there is reverse scoring in the inventory used, lower score reveals better adjustment.

Discussion

Changes in society and environment surrounding young people have created various problems in their growth and development of health. For example, competitive examinations, reduction of free time, reduction of interpersonal relationship skills and low self-training skills are said to cause juvenile worries, anxiety and stress. Their low tolerance and inappropriate management toward stress are highlighted and have made health issues surrounding them varied and more serious. The trend is expected to become more complex. Under these circumstances, valued skills to survive in healthy conditions are life skills, with which we can subjectively and positively solve various everyday problems and requirements. The World Health Organisation (WHO) has defined life skills as "necessary skills to constructively and effectively manage various issues and needs arising in daily life." They are regarded as skills for people to act in a flexible and positive way. The present study focuses on these life skills as youth survival skills in healthy conditions and, using the framework of WHO's definition of three aspects in health: physical, psychological, and social aspects, aims to understand the skills that are useful in enhancing health in daily life (health-related life skills, hereafter).

Comparison of self-esteem, adjustment and empathy among adolescents before and after life skill training

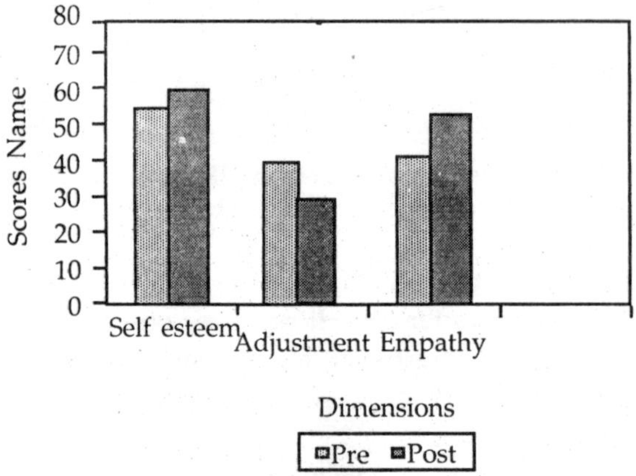

Figure 2. Depicts the decrease in adjustment scores in adolescents after life skill training, thus proving the efficiency of the technique. As, in the case of adjustment, lower score reveals better adjustment.

The present study was aimed at studying the impact of life skill training on self-esteem, adjustment and empathy among adolescents. For this purpose, the total sample of the study taken was 60 students, out of these 30 were males and 30 were females. The sample was collected from the Hans Raj Model School, Punjabi Bagh. Scores of the subjects in the two conditions, i.e., pre- and post-training were compared.

It was found that in the present investigation, there was significant difference at .01 level between pre- and post- condition on self-esteem of adolescents .The mean score obtained by the subjects was found to be 53.93 before training and 69.06 after training. This indicates that the subjects had scored higher on the self-esteem dimension. The t-ratio obtained was 9.97, which was significant at .01 level of significance. Thus, life skills' training is effective in increasing self-esteem of adolescents.

This result has been supported by various studies (Morgan et al. 1996, Friesenhahn 1999, Winkleby et al 2004). Morgan et.al., (1996) found that LST have significant effects on attitudes and beliefs regarding substance use but rather less effects on actual behaviour. An analysis of how these effects were mediated suggests that the enhancement of self-esteem and the learning of assertiveness skills played an important role in the outcomes. Winkleby et al (2004) also obtained Similar results. Friesenhahn (1999) study also confirm that there is significant difference in the self-esteem of adolescents after LST, along with improved ability to interact with others, strengthened communication skills, gain in creative thinking skills, enhanced ability to make their own decisions and manage their resources, and greatly improved their ability to effectively work in groups to accomplish group goals.

The self-esteem of an adolescent is an important contributor of his growth and dealing with difficulties. Studies have found that one-third to one-half of adolescents struggle with low self-esteem, especially in early adolescence (Harter, 1990; Hirsch & Dubois, 1991). The results of low self-esteem can be temporary, but in serious cases can lead to various problems including depression, delinquency, self-inflicted injuries, suicide (Battle, 1990; Bhatti, 1992), and anorexia nervosa.

Miller (1988) demonstrated that a programme to increase self-esteem significantly changed the attitudes of students regarding their alcohol and drug use.

The results of these studies clearly illustrate the positive effect of life skills training on adolescents and importance of self-esteem as an important personality variable that needs to be strengthened as it is directly related to negative behaviours. If adolescents develop some life skills, then positive feelings of self worth will follow—or if such youth have positive feelings of self-worth, they will be more likely to develop and practice new life skills. It could be said that group learning provides opportunity for social skills by encouraging social interaction and thus promotes self-esteem in the subjects.

Present investigation also revealed that there was significant difference at .01 levels between pre- and post-condition on emotional adjustment. In post-condition, subject's emotional adjustment has improved significantly.

Emotionally adjusting can be interpreted as emotionally stable. To be stable in emotions, to handle emotions well is an important skill that adolescents must learn, as this seems to be major cause of their involvement in high-risk behaviours. Effectiveness of LST has been supported by various researches like Deffenbacher, et al, (1986) reported that LST teach anger control.

LST thus teaches social and emotional skills that have positive effects in multiple realms, such as decreasing aggression in boys, decreasing suspensions and expulsions, decreasing drug use and delinquency, increasing academic test scores, and increasing positive attachments to school and families (Hawkins et al, 1992). Concisely, life skills programmes address and have an impact on multiple behaviours. Skills for coping with emotions through learning self-management and controlling stress (often incorporating social problem solving skills) are a critical dimension of most life skills programmes.

On social adjustment, significant difference was not found between pre- and post-condition. This shows that there is no impact of LST on the part of social adjustment among subjects.

The reason for getting this result could be chance factors or may be due to individual differences and could be because of small sample size. Whereas it promote positive social adjustment is supported by study of Elias, et.al (1991). Mize and Ladd (1990) have also researched that LST Prevent peer rejection.

The importance of social adjustment has been seen in the behaviour of adolescents in dealing with people, having control on aggressiveness and to deal with different situations.

Apart from this, recent findings in behavioural epidemiology indicate that mental health problems, social problems, and health-risk behaviours often co-occur as an organised pattern of adolescent risk behaviours (Greenberg et al, 1999). It focuses on increasing positive social skills with which to handle inevitable social disagreement and conflict, on the ability to generate alternative solutions to an interpersonal problem and on the ability to conceptualise the consequences of different behaviours. Relationships between these problem solving skills and social adjustment were found not only in preschool and kindergarten children, but also in adolescents and adults. So, it can be said that social-cognitive skills, social competence, and problem-solving skills serve as mediators for behaviours, both positive and negative.

As for the third type of adjustment, i.e., educational adjustment, Table I reveals that mean of subjects in pre condition, 13.10 is higher than mean in post condition, 6.13, thus showing difference between the two mean values. The t value obtained is 11.73 that is significant at .01 level and thus again proves the effectiveness of LST. It is known that individuals having good adjustment in context of educational are at better pace in their adjustment with curricular and curricular programmers. One of such study is that of Hawkins et al (1992), who found that LST has been found to increase academic test scores. Significant difference was also observed between pre- and post-condition on total adjustment. Total adjustment improved significantly in post condition. Because adjustment is inevitably tied in with issues of independence, sufficiency and control and will vary from person to person influenced by their character, previous experiences and support network.

Hence, we can conclude that there is significant difference on adjustment of adolescents before and after life skill training in the area of emotional, educational and total adjustment, only in social adjustment findings does not support the expectations.

Another result that has been produced in this study is that there was significant difference on empathy level of adolescents before and after life skill training. The mean score obtained by the subjects was found to be 40.71 before training and 54.26 after training. This indicates that the subjects had scored higher on the dimension of empathy. The t-ratio obtained was 10.80, which was significant at .01 level of significance. The result indicated that a significant difference exists on the ability of adolescents to empathise before and after life skill training.

Empathy is a verbal response, which reflects emotional content of the other person's talk and the causes of emotions. Empathy has an affective component (for example, feeling an appropriate emotion triggered by another's emotion), a cognitive component (for example, understanding and/or predicting what someone else might think, feel, or do), and a mixed component (cognitive and affective).

Sympathy is clear instance of the affective component of empathy. Sympathy is said to occur when the observer's emotional response to the distress of another leads the observer to feel a desire to take action to alleviate the other person's suffering (Davis, 1994). The observer may not actually act on this desire, but at the very least the observer has the emotion of wanting to take appropriate action to reduce the other's distress.

Empathy is a component of communication and can only be improved with appropriate training (Winefield and Chur-Hansen 2000). It allows us to understand the intentions of others, predict their behaviour, and experience an emotion triggered by their emotion.

Perspective taking and empathy are two critical social skills. Programmes in violence prevention have successfully taught specific skills that link perspective taking and empathy to appropriate behaviours. Young people are found to show increased skill in identifying and relating to another person's feelings if a real-life role model demonstrates empathy for a character in a distressful situation (Feshbach, 1982). Guiding children to practise these empathic responses within conflict situations can build habits of thinking and caring about other people's perspectives and feelings and help them to come up with non-violent solutions instead of resorting to aggression (Slaby and Guerra, 1998).

The reason for getting such a result could be summarised in this way. Life skills applied to drug/substance use prevention are supposed to facilitate the practice and reinforcement of psychosocial skills that contribute to the promotion of personal and social development such as self awareness, empathy, communication skills, interpersonal skills, creative thinking, critical thinking, coping with emotions and coping with stress.

Empathy and interpersonal sensitivity may be turned simply into useful 'tools' for adjusting delinquent or disturbed young people to schooling. Lack of empathic concern, poor communicative responsiveness and high emotional contagion significantly contributed to reduced personal accomplishment (Orndahl and O'Donnell 1999).

Thus, it is an important variable to be considered and the ability of subjects empathising has been found to be greater after LST.

In the light of above discussion, it could be said that life skill training can specifically address the needs of children growing up in disadvantaged environments that lack opportunities to develop these skills. Health promotion and prevention programmes focusing only on transferal of information are less effective than programmes incorporating skills development.

The social, cognitive and emotional coping skills targeted by life skills programmes are shown to be mediators of problem behaviours and there lies the success of LST.

There are research indications that teaching skills in this way, as part of broad-based life skills programmes, is an effective approach for primary prevention education (Errecart et al., 1991; Caplan et al., 1992). Apart from this, the most important point for its effectiveness is in its delivery method that was most effective emphasized sharing, cooperating and contributing. The conclusions drawn were that interactive educative programmes were 'statistically superior' (Black et al., 1998) to non-interactive interventions in preventing drug misuse as the style was not didactic, but highly interactive and participatory. A similar study of Tobler et al. (2000) also indicated that non-interactive lecture-oriented programmes have minimal impact, whereas interactive programmes like LST, that enhance the development of interpersonal skills have greater impact. LST includes training in refusal skills, goal setting, assertiveness, communication, and coping and therefore greater benefits were also achieved.

The other point to be mention is that life skills are taught using an interactive, problem-solving approach that arranges activities as a series of steps. First, the students identify the problem, and then they brainstorm all possible solutions. They then examine the advantages and disadvantages of each solution, and the best solution is agreed upon. Students next devise plans for carrying out selected solutions. Thus, nothing is forced upon subjects. Concisely it could be said that the learning activities offer numerous opportunities for participants to provide their own input into the nature and content of the situations addressed during the learning activities (e.g., creating their own case studies, brainstorming possible scenarios, etc.).

But one obvious limitation of this type of prevention approach is that it addresses a limited set of etiological factors within school settings. More research is therefore needed either to extend this approach to other intervention modalities (e.g., approaches targeting the family or community) or to integrate it within a more comprehensive intervention strategy targeting a broader array of etiological factors.

Thus although considerable progress has been made in the past decade, the present study would be an important contribution in this field but still further research is needed.

References

Battle, J. (1990), *Self-Esteem: The New Revolution*. Alberta, Canada: James Battle & Associates.

Baron-Cohen, S. & Wheelwright, S. (2004), The empathy quotient: an investigation of adults with Asperger syndrome or high functioning autism, and normal sex differences, *Journal of Autism and Developmental Disorders, 34*,163-175.

Bhatti, B., Derezotes, D., Seung O. & Specht, H. (1989), *Association Between Child Maltreatment and Self-Esteem: The Social Importance of Self-Esteem,* Berkeley: U.C.

Black, D. R., Tobler, N. S. & Sciacca, J. P. (1998), Peer helping/ involvement: an efficacious way to meet the challenge of reducing alcohol, tobacco and other drug use among youth? *Journal of School Health, 68,* 87-93.

Botvin, G.J., Eng, A. & Williams, C.L. (1980), Preventing the Onset of Cigarette Smoking through Life Skills Training, *Preventative Medicine, 9*,135-143.

Botvin, G. J & Griffin K.W. (2004), Life Skills Training: Empirical Findings and Future Directions, *The Journal of Primary Prevention, 25,* 211-232.

Caplan, M., Weissberg, R., Grober, J., Sivo, P., Grady, K. & Jacoby, C. (1992), Social Competence Promotion with Inner City and Suburban Young Adolescents: Effects on Social Adjustment and Alcohol Use, *Journal of Consulting and Clinical Psychology, 60,* 56-63.

Coopersmith, S. (1967), *The Antecedents of Self-Esteem,* San Francisco: Freeman.

Coopersmith, S. (1981), *The antecedents of self-esteem,* Palo Alto, CA: Consulting Psychologists Press.

Coopersmith, S. (1981), *Manual for self esteem inventory (SEI)*, Palo Alto, California: consulting psychologist press.

Davis, M. H. (1994), *Empathy: A social psychological approach*, Colorado: West view Press

Deffenbacher, J., Lynch, R., Oetting, E., & Kemper, C. (1996), Anger reduction in early adolescents, *Journal of Counselling Psychology, 41,* 149-157

Eisenberg, N., & Strayer, J. (1987), *Empathy and its development,* Cambridge: Cambridge University Press.

Elias, M., Gara, M., Schulyer, T., Brandon-Muller, L., & Sayette, M. (1991), The promotion of social competence, *American Journal of Orthopsychiatry, 6,* 409-417.

Errecart, M.T., Walberg, H.J., Ross, J.G., Gold, R.S., Fiedler, J.L., & Kolbe, L.J. (1991), Effectiveness of teenage health teaching modules, *Journal of School Health, 61,* 26–30.

Expressions India, (2004), *School Mental Health Programmes in India: Introduction and Rationale,* New Delhi: CDAHC, VIMHANS.

Friesenhahn, K. (1999), *An analysis of leadership life skills development at the 1998 Texas 4-H Congress,* Kingsville, TX: Texas A&M University.

Greenberg, M. T., Domitrovich, C., & Bumbarger, B. (1999), *Preventing mental disorders in school-age children: A review of the effectiveness of prevention programmes,* PA: Pennsylvania State University, Prevention Research Centre for the Promotion of Human Development.

Gallo, D. (1989), Educating for Empathy, Reason and Imagination, *The journal of creative behaviour, 23,* 98-115.

Gibbs, J.C. (1987), Social processes in delinquency: The need to facilitate empathy as well as sociomoral reasoning, In W.M. Kurtines & J.L. Gewirtz (Eds.), *Moral development through social interaction.* New York: John Wiley.

Harter, S. (1990), Identity and self development, In S. Feldman and G. Elliott (Eds.), *At the threshold: The developing adolescent.* Cambridge, MA: Harvard University Press. 352-387.

Harter, S. (1999), *The construction of the self,* New York: Guilford.

Hawkins, J., Catalano, R., & Miller, J. (1992), Risk and Protective Factors for Alcohol and Other Drug Problems in Adolescence and Early Adulthood: Implications for Substance Abuse Prevention. *Psychological Bulletin, 112,* 64-105.

Hawkins, J., Catalano, R., Morrison, D., O'Donnell, J., Abbott, R. & Day, L. (1992), The Seattle Social Development Project. In J. McCord & R. Tremblay (eds), *The Prevention of Antisocial Behaviour in Children.* New York: Guilford Publications.139-161.

Hirsch, B., & DuBois, D. (1991), Self-esteem in early adolescence: The identification and prediction of contrasting longitudinal trajectories, *Journal of Youth and Adolescence, 20,* 53-72.

Hoffman, MS. (2000), *Empathy and Moral Development: Implications for Caring and Justice,* Cambridge, Mass: Cambridge University Press.

Marilyn A.., Winkleby , Ellen F., Meredith D., Sara K., David A.& Joel D. K. (2004). Effects of an Advocacy Intervention to Reduce Smoking Among Teenagers, *Arch Pediatr Adolesc Med, 158,* 269-275.

Miller, R.L. (1988), Positive self-esteem and alcohol/drug related attitudes among school children, *Journal of Alcohol and Drug Education, 33,* 26-31.

Mize, J. & Ladd, G. (1990), A cognitive-social learning approach to social skill training with low-status preschool children, *Developmental Psychology, 26,* 388-397.

Morgan, M., Morrow, R., Sheehan, A.M. & Lillis, M. (1996). Prevention of substance misuse: Rationale and effectiveness of the programme 'On My Own Two Feet'. *Journal of the Department of Education,* (Ireland), 44, 5-26.

O'Donnell, L., Stueve, A., Doval, A., Duran, R., Haber, D., Atnafou, R., Johnson, N., Grant, U., Murray, H., Juhn, G., Tang, J. & Piessens, P. (1999), The effectiveness of the Reach for Health Community Youth Service Learning Programme in reducing early and unprotected sex among urban middle school students, *American Journal of Public Health, 89,* 176-181.

Rogers, C.R. (1957), The necessary and sufficient conditions for therapeutic personality change, *Journal of Consulting Psychology, 21,*97-103.

Sinha, A.K.& Singh, R.P. (1984), *Manual for adjustment inventory for school students (AISS),* Agra: National Psychological corporation.

Slaby, R. & Guerra, N. (1988), Cognitive mediators of aggression in adolescent offenders, *Developmental Psychology,* 24, 580-588.

Tobler, N.S., Roona, M.R., Ochshorn, P., Marshall, D.G., Streke, A.V. & Stackpole, K.M. (2000), School-Based Adolescent Drug Prevention Programmes: 1998 Meta-Analysis, *The Journal of Primary Prevention, 20,* 275-336.

UNAIDS, UNICEF & The department of Mental Health, Thai ministry of public health (2004), *Report of the regional Forum on life skills based education for behaviour development change,* Bangtok: UN office.

UNICEF (2001), *The Participation rights of adolescents: A strategic approach.* Prepared by R. Rajani. Commissioned paper for UNICEF, Retrieved from http://www.unicef.org/ programme/youth_day/ assets/participation.pdf

Winefield, H.R.&Chur-Hansen, A. (2000), Evaluating the outcome of communication skills teaching for entry level medical students: does knowledge of empathy increase? *Medical Education, 34*, 90-94.

WHO (1999), *Partners in Life Skills Education. Conclusions from a United Nations Inter-agency Meeting,* Geneva: World Health Organisation.

WHO (1997). Programme *on Mental Health - Life Skills Education in Schools,* Geneva: World Health Organisation.

6

Impact of Rational-emotive Behaviour Therapy (REBT) on Adolescents with Conduct Disorder (CD)

—*G. Venkatesh Kumar*

The present study is to examine the impact of Rational-Emotive Behaviour Therapy on adolescent students with conduct disorder. It was hypothesized that the REBT Psychotherapy would have a positive impact on adolescents' conduct disorder symptoms. The Youth Self Report (YSR) was distributed to 1142 students and they were instructed to fill the forms. The sample included 200 students (100 girls and 100 boys), which 100 was taken as control group (50 girls and 50 boys), and other 100 was taken for experimental group (50 girls and 50 boys) from the schools and colleges in Mysore. The intervention program was given on experimental group for 7 sessions, in seven weeks. There were 10 groups, with 10 subjects in each group. The intervention program consisted of Cognitive, Emotive and Behavioural techniques of REBT. Subjects were thought the techniques of REBT and how to apply it on their problems. One month later the last intervention program and the post test, to assess the impact of REBT. Data analysis involved the use of GLM repeated measure of ANOVA to measure the impact of REBT on Conduct Disorder Symptoms of subjects. Significant impacts were found on the reduction of conduct disorder symptoms experienced by subjects. The results

This paper originally appears in the Journal of the Indian Academy of Applied Psychology, October 2009, Vol.35, Special Issue pp. 103-111.

revealed that the treatment decreased the symptoms of conduct disorder. The results showed that REBT has a positive impact on conduct disorder and other emotional and behavioural disorders co morbid with conduct disorder experienced by adolescents.

Keywords: REBT, Conduct disorder.

Adolescence is the stage in a person's life between childhood and adulthood. It is the period of human development during which a young person moves from dependency to independence, autonomy and maturity, from being part of a family group to being part of a peer group and to be independent as an adult (Mabey & Sorensen, 1995). With the onset of adolescence the nature and behaviour of the adolescent also changes. Many of the behaviours of adolescents appear unsocial and unsympathetic. Buhler (1927) defined this period as a negative phase. Chronologically, adolescence comes roughly in between the years from 12 to the early 20s. The World Health Organisation defines adolescence as the period between 10 and 19 years. The onset of adolescence varies from culture to culture depending on the socio economics of the country. During adolescence great changes occur in all developmental aspects of the individual.

Children and youngsters with emotional and behavioural disorders (EBD) are a vulnerable group in society. Their disorder proves to be stable and long-term (Fergusson & Horwood 1992). These children run a high risk of being placed in special education (Lyon 1996) or in semi-residential specialised care (Eme & Kavanaugh, 1995). More boys than girls are affected (3:1 or 4:1) (American Psychiatry Association 1987; Fagot & Leve 1998) and boys show a more violent behaviouristic pattern and more externalising behaviour (Eme & Kavanaugh 1995).

The types of mental, emotional, and behavioural disorders that may occur during adolescence are generally known as: Anxiety Disorders, Severe Depression, Bipolar Disorder, Attention Deficit Hyperactivity Disorder, Autism, Schizophrenia, Learning Disorders, Conduct Disorder, Eating Disorders and so on. All can have a serious impact on overall health of adolescent. Some disorders are more common than others, and conditions range from mild to severe. Often, an adolescent has more than one disorder (U.S. Department of Health and Human Services, 1999).

Although adolescent health has gained increasing prominence in India's national health policies, the focus has been on reproductive and sexual health concerns. Despite reports showing that suicide is a leading cause of death in young people in India (Aaron, Joseph, Abraham, Muliyil, George, Prasad, Minz, Abraham, & Bose, 2004), mental health has been a low priority in health policy for adolescents. The few published studies from India have reported prevalence of mental disorders from 2.6 per cent to 35.6 per cent (Srinath, Girimaji, Gururaj, Seshadri, Subbakrishna, Bhola, & Kumar, 2005); (Verghese & Beig, 1974) . Although comparability between the findings of these studies is limited owing to methodological factors (Ford, Goodman, & Meltzer, 2003), one reason for the wide variation in rates could be the strong influence of social, cultural and environmental factors on the risk of mental disorders in adolescents.

The term conduct disorder (CD) refers to a persistent pattern of antisocial behaviour in which the individual repeatedly breaks social rules and carries out aggressive acts that upset other people. DSM-IV mentions CD as one of the most frequently diagnosed conditions in outpatient and inpatient mental health facilities for children. CD has been separated from the adult diagnosis of antisocial personality in order to acknowledge what psychiatrists believe to be a greater potential for change in the young. CD has been classified along with oppositional defiant disorder and attention-deficit hyperactivity disorder (ADHD) in the attention-deficit and disruptive behaviour disorders section of DSM-IV-TR. The essential feature of CD is a repetitive and persistent pattern of behaviour in which the basic rights of others or major age-appropriate societal norms or rules are violated. Since its inception in DSM-III, the diagnosis of CD has undergone several modifications. DSM-IV-TR lists 15 criteria grouped into four major categories: (i) aggression to people and animals; (ii) destruction of property; (iii) deceitfulness or theft; and (iv) serious violations of rules. Three (or more) of the criteria should have been present for the last 12 months, with at least one criterion present in the past six months.

The disturbance in behaviour should cause clinically significant impairment in social, academic, or occupational functioning. If the individual is 18 years or older, the criteria for antisocial personality disorder should not be met. Since the criteria for the diagnosis of CD vary widely, its manifestations at different developmental stages differ and because the databases of different studies are not uniform, the prevalence estimates reported in various studies vary widely. At one end lies the study of Esser and colleagues (1990), reporting a prevalence of 0.9 per cent, while at the other end is the study by Kashani *et al* (1987), reporting a prevalence of 8.7 per cent. DSM-IV reports prevalence in males of 6 per cent-10 per cent and in females of 2 per cent-9 per cent.

Among Indian studies, Deivasigamani (1990), has reported the prevalence of CD to be 11.13 per cent, Sarkar, Kapur and Kaliaperumal *(1995)*, reported the prevalence rate of antisocial behaviour to be 7.1 per cent while recently Srinath *et al* (2005), have reported prevalence as low as 0.2 per cent.

Several common childhood psychiatric conditions have features similar to those of conduct disorder, and comorbid conditions are also common. The differential diagnosis should include attention-deficit/hyperactivity disorder (ADHD), oppositional defiant disorder, mood disorder (major depression, dysthymia, and bipolar disorder), substance abuse and intermittent explosive disorder.

Rational emotive behaviour therapy (REBT) is an active-directive, solution-oriented therapy which focuses on resolving emotional, cognitive and behavioural problems in clients, originally developed by the American psychotherapist Albert Ellis. REBT views that emotional suffering result primarily, though not completely, from our evaluations of a negative event, not solely by the events *per se*. In other words, human beings on the basis of their belief system actively, though not always consciously, disturb themselves, and even disturb themselves about their disturbances.

REBT helps clients to replace absolutist philosophies, full of 'musts' and 'shoulds', with more flexible ones; part of this includes learning to accept that all human beings (including themselves) are fallible and learning to increase their tolerance for frustration while aiming to achieve their goals. Although emphasizing the same 'core conditions' as person-centred counselling—namely, empathy, unconditional positive regard, and counsellor genuineness—in the counselling relationship, REBT views these conditions as neither necessary nor sufficient for therapeutic change to occur.

Conduct disorder in adolescents is a serious and common mental disorder. There are very limited data on adolescents with conduct disorder in India and no adequate research studies have been reported on the treatment of adolescents with conduct disorder and other emotional and behavioural problems experienced by them.

This study was designed to assess the effectiveness of Rational Emotive Behavioural Therapy (REBT) on the treatment of adolescent students suffering from conduct disorder and other emotional and behavioural problems they experience along with conduct disorder. The findings may help us develop a better treatment for adolescents with conduct disorder.

Hypotheses

H1. Rational Emotive Behaviour Therapy (REBT) has a positive impact on treatment of Conduct Disorder.

H2. Rational Emotive Behaviour Therapy (REBT) has a positive impact on the treatment of additional variables of DSM Scale.

Method

Sample

A stratified random sample of 200 (100 boys and 100 girls) students with conduct disorder between the age group of 11 and 18 years was selected. They were from different schools and colleges located in Mysore City.

Me.

Youth Self-Report for Ages 11-18 (2001), to measure conduct

disorder, Designed by ASEBA (Achenbach System of Empirically Bused Assessment, 2001), research centre for children, youth, and families (using YSR DSM-Oriented Scales for Boys and Girls and YSR Syndrome Scales). The "Youth Self-Report" (YSR) (Achenbach, 2001) is a well-known psychopathological instrument designed to obtain adolescent reports of their competencies and behavioural/ emotional problems. The emotional/behavioural part contains 112 items, scored from 0 ("not true") to 2 ("very true or often true"), according to the behaviour displayed during the last six months. From this set of items a "Total problem" score (103 specific problem items) can be derived. The total problem scale is a measure of perceived general maladjustment level.

Procedure

A sample of 1,142 students, boys and girls, aged 11 to 18 years old, was administered to complete the Youth Self Report (YSR). Out of this sample 200 adolescents diagnosed of conduct problems by the help of DSM-Oriented Scale, were selected for the study. Out of 200 students, 100 were taken as experimental group (consisting of 50 boys and 50 girls), and another 100 (50 boys and 50 girls) were taken as control group. Following the selection, a teachers report on students' behaviour was given by the teachers. Each experimental group went under seven sessions of REBT in duration of seven weeks. Four stages were presented in systematic order:

Stage 1: Introductory session:

Stage 2: Using Cognitive Techniques of REBT

I: Active Disputing; II: Rational Coping Self Statements; III: Cognitive Homework.

Stage 3: Using Emotive Techniques of REBT

I: Rational Emotive Imagery; II: Role-Playing; III: Reverse-Role Play.

Stage 4: Behavioural Techniques of REBT

I: Skill Training; II: Use of Reinforcement; III: Use of Pena'

No treatment was given to control group but it was kept under observation. One month after the last REBT session, post-test is taken from experimental and control group. Results were analysed and hypothesizes were tested.

RESULTS

Table 1 : Mean scores on conduct problems of male and female subjects in experimental and control groups in pre- and post-test sessions

Groups	*Gender*	*Age*	*Pre-Test*		*Post-Test*		*Change*
			Mean	*S.D*	*Mean*	*S.D*	
Experimental	Male	Early	10.71	2.06	8.86	2.27	1.85
		Late	11.86	2.32	9.33	2.63	2.53
		Total	11.7	2.30	9.26	2.56	2.44
	Female	Early	10.3	3.45	7.47	3.92	2.83
		Late	9.15	1.66	6.70	3.33	2.45
		Total	9.84	2.90	7.16	3.68	2.68
Total		Early	10.38	3.21	7.73	3.68	2.65
		Late	11.00	2.47	8.49	3.09	2.51
		Total	10.77	2.77	8.21	3.33	2.56
Control	Male	Early	12.49	2.68	12.87	2.65	0.38
		Late	11.09	1.70	11.27	2.10	0.18
		Total	12.18	2.55	12.52	2.60	0.34
	Female	Early	9.98	1.95	10.29	2.14	0.31
		Late	8.00	0.00	8.00	0.00	0.00
		Total	9.90	1.95	10.2	2.15	0.30
Total		Early	11.1	2.61	11.45	2.70	0.35
		Late	10.62	1.94	10.77	2.28	0.15
		Total	11.04	2.53	11.36	2.65	0.32
Total	Male	Early	12.22	2.66	12.26	2.95	0.04
		Late	11.70	2.21	9.72	2.63	1.98
		Total	11.94	2.43	10.89	3.05	1.05
	Female	Early	10.10	2.61	9.21	3.24	0.89
		Late	9.05	1.62	6.82	3.19	2.23
		Total	9.87	2.46	8.68	3.36	1.19
Total		Early	10.89	2.81	10.34	3.46	0.55
		Late	10.93	2.38	8.88	3.08	2.05
		Total	10.91	2.65	9.79	3.39	1.12

Table 1 shows that between pre-test and post-test scores a significant difference was observed (F=26.939; P=.000) in conduct disorders where a decrease of 1.12 (pre-10.91, post-9.79) scores was noticed irrespective of the groups.

Table 2: Mean scores on affective disorders of male and female subjects in experimental and control groups in pre- and post-test sessions

Groups	*Gender*	*Age*	*Pre-Test*		*Post-Test*		*Change (Pre-post)*
			Mean	*S.D*	*Mean*	*S.D*	
Experi-mental	Male	Early	6.57	3.21	5.14	2.12	1.43
		Late	10.51	3.49	8.91	3.35	1.60
		Total	9.96	3.69	8.38	3.45	1.58
	Female	Early	11.07	3.3	8.67	3.06	2.40
		Late	10.7	2.47	9.75	2.99	0.95
		Total	10.92	2.97	9.28	3.02	1.64
Total		Early	10.22	3.7	8.24	3.25	1.98
		Late	10.57	3.18	9.17	3.24	1.40
		Total	10.44	3.37	8.83	3.26	1.61
Control	Male	Early	9.97	4.76	10.41	5.00	0.44
		Late	7.64	5.14	7.73	5.41	0.09
		Total	9.64	4.89	9.82	5.16	0.18
	Female	Early	9.94	2.98	10.19	3.42	0.25
		Late	6.5	0.71	6.50	0.71	0.00
		Total	9.8	3	10.40	3.43	0.60
Total		Early	9.65	3.85	10.29	4.18	0.64
		Late	7.46	4.72	7.54	4.96	0.08
		Total	9.63	4.04	9.93	4.36	0.30
Total	Male	Early	9.46	4.69	9.61	5.04	0.15
		Late	9.93	4	8.67	3.83	1.26
		Total	9.71	4.32	9.10	4.43	0.61
	Female	Early	10.37	3.13	9.72	3.32	0.65
		Late	10.32	2.66	9.45	3.00	0.87
		Total	10.36	3.02	9.66	3.24	0.70
Total		Early	10.03	3.8	9.68	4.03	0.35
		Late	10.04	3.65	8.89	3.61	1.15
		Total	10.04	3.73	9.38	3.88	0.66

However, when the decrease in conduct disorders were analysed group wise, (experimental v/s control) again a significant F value (F=38.782; P=.000) was obtained. From the mean scores it is evident that experimental group decreased its mean by 2.56 (Pre-10.77 – Post-8.21) scores compared to control group, which changed its scores by only 0.32 scores (pre 11.04 – Post 11.36).

Table 3 : Mean scores on anxiety problems of male and female subjects in experimental and control groups in pre- and post-test sessions

Groups	*Gender*	*Age*	*Pre-Test*		*Post-Test*		*Change (Pre-post)*
			Mean	*S.D*	*Mean*	*S.D*	
Exp.	Male	Early	0.40	1.63	3.57	1.51	0.43
		Late	4.67	2.26	4.16	2.27	0.51
		Total	4.58	2.19	4.08	2.17	0.50
	Female	Early	5.17	1.78	4.57	1.85	0.60
		Late	5.50	1.76	0.50	1.81	0.50
		Total	5.30	1.76	4.74	1.83	0.56
Total		Early	4.95	1.79	4.38	1.82	0.57
		Late	4.94	2.14	4.43	2.15	0.51
		Total	4.94	2.01	4.41	2.03	0.53
Control	Male	Early	4.18	1.99	4.54	2.42	0.36
		Late	0.40	2.65	4.27	2.90	0.27
		Total	4.14	2.12	4.48	2.50	0.34
	Female	Early	4.98	1.71	5.15	2.04	0.17
		Late	0.80	1.41	0.80	1.41	0.00
		Total	5.10	1.79	5.26	2.09	0.16
Total		Early	4.62	1.87	4.87	2.22	0.25
		Late	4.62	2.87	4.85	3.02	0.23
		Total	4.62	2.01	4.87	2.33	0.25
Total	Male	Early	4.15	1.92	4.39	2.31	0.24
		Late	4.54	2.34	4.19	2.38	0.35
		Total	4.36	2.15	4.28	2.34	0.08
	Female	Early	5.05	1.73	4.92	1.98	0.13
		Late	5.73	1.86	5.27	1.96	0.46
		Total	5.20	1.77	0.50	1.97	0.20
Total		Early	4.72	1.85	4.73	2.12	0.01
		Late	4.88	2.26	4.50	2.31	0.38
		Total	4.78	2.01	4.64	2.19	0.14

Table 2 shows that between pre-test and post-test scores a significant difference in affective problems was observed (F=16.164; P=.000) where a decrease of 0.66 (pre-10.04, post-9.38) scores was noticed irrespective of the groups. However, when the decrease in affective problems were analysed group wise, (experimental v/s control) again a significant F value (F=27.015; P=.000) was obtained. From the mean scores it is evident that experimental group reduced its mean by 1.61 (Pre- 10.44 – Post-8.83) scores compared to control group, which changed its scores by only 0.3 scores (pre 9.63 – Post 9.93).

Table 3 shows that in anxiety problems a non-significant difference was observed (F=2.134; P=.146) where a decrease of 0.14 (pre-4.78, post- 4.64) scores was noticed irrespective of the groups. However, when the decrease in anxiety problems were analysed group wise, (experimental v/s control) a significant F value (F=11.148; P=.001) was obtained. From the mean scores it is evident that experimental group reduced its mean by 0.53 (Pre-4.94 – Post-4.41) scores compared to control group, which changed its scores by only 0.25 scores (pre 4.62 – Post 4.87).

Table 4 : Mean scores on somatic problems of male and female subjects in experimental and control groups in pre- and post-test sessions

Groups	*Gender*	*Age*	*Pre-Test*		*Post-Test*		*Change*
			Mean	*S.D*	*Mean*	*S.D*	
Experi-mental	Male	Early	2.43	2.30	2.26	2.06	0.17
		Late	3.60	2.65	3.33	2.36	0.27
		Total	3.44	2.61	3.18	2.33	0.26
	Female	Early	4.33	2.70	4.24	2.64	0.09
		Late	3.05	2.24	3.05	2.24	0.00
		Total	3.82	2.58	3.76	2.53	0.06
Total		Early	3.97	2.70	3.86	2.63	0.11
		Late	3.43	2.52	3.24	2.31	0.19
		Total	3.63	2.59	3.47	2.43	0.16
Control	Male	Early	0.40	2.87	4.31	2.90	0.31

(Contd...)

(Contd...)

		Late	3.82	2.57	4.18	2.96	0.36
		Total	3.96	2.81	4.28	2.89	0.32
	Female	Early	3.15	2.27	3.23	2.28	0.08
		Late	0.10	1.41	0.10	1.41	0.00
		Total	3.06	2.27	3.14	2.29	0.08
Total		Early	3.53	2.57	3.71	2.62	0.18
		Late	3.38	2.75	3.69	2.98	0.31
		Total	3.51	2.58	3.71	2.65	0.20
Total	Male	Early	3.76	2.82	0.40	2.87	0.24
		Late	3.65	2.64	3.5	2.49	0.15
		Total	3.70	2.71	3.73	2.67	0.03
	Female	Early	3.60	2.49	3.62	2.46	0.02
		Late	2.86	2.23	2.86	2.23	0.00
		Total	3.44	2.45	3.45	2.42	0.01
Total		Early	3.66	2.61	3.76	2.61	0.10
		Late	3.42	2.54	3.32	2.42	0.10
		Total	3.57	2.58	3.59	2.54	0.02

Table 4 shows that between pre-test and post-test scores a non-significant difference was observed (F=.145; P=.704) in somatic problems where a decrease of 0.02 (pre-3.57, post-3.59) scores was noticed irrespective of the groups. However, when the decrease in somatic problems were analysed group wise, (experimental v/s control) a significant F value (F=4.371; P=.038) was obtained. From the mean scores it is evident that experimental group reduced its mean by 0.16 (Pre- 3.63 – Post-3.47) scores compared to control group, which increased its scores by 0.20 scores (pre 3.51 – Post 3.71).

Table 5 shows that In ADHD, the intervention did not have any significant change from pre- to post-test situation irrespective of the groups, as the obtained F value of .084 was found to be non-significant (P=.772). No differential change for both groups—experimental and control groups—were observed from pre- to post-test session (F=.300; P=.584). The changes for both the groups were found to be statistically same.

Table 5 : Mean scores on ADHD of male and female subjects in experimental and control groups in pre- and post-test sessions

Groups	*Gender*	*Age*	*Pre-Test*		*Post-Test*		*Change*
			Mean	*S.D*	*Mean*	*S.D*	
Experi-mental	Male	Early	0.60	0.10	0.60	0.10	0.00
		Late	6.86	2.78	6.79	2.56	0.07
		Total	6.74	2.62	6.68	2.41	0.06
	Female	Early	6.67	2.32	6.43	2.25	0.24
		Late	5.50	2.01	5.45	2.06	0.05
		Total	6.20	2.26	6.04	2.21	0.16
Total	Male	Early	6.54	2.14	6.35	2.07	0.19
		Late	6.43	2.63	6.37	2.48	0.06
		Total	6.47	2.45	6.36	2.32	0.11
Control	Male	Early	0.60	2.48	6.21	2.85	0.21
		Late	6.73	2.87	6.82	3.16	0.09
		Total	6.16	2.26	6.34	2.90	0.18
	Female	Early	5.88	2.55	5.69	2.42	0.19
		Late	5.50	0.71	5.50	0.71	0.00
		Total	5.86	2.50	5.68	2.38	0.18
Total		Early	5.93	2.50	5.92	2.62	0.01
		Late	6.54	2.67	6.62	2.93	0.08
		Total	6.01	2.52	6.01	2.66	0.00
Total	Male	Early	0.60	2.31	6.17	2.64	0.17
		Late	6.83	2.77	6.80	2.66	0.03
		Total	6.45	2.59	6.51	2.66	0.06
	Female	Early	6.18	2.48	5.97	2.37	0.21
		Late	5.50	1.92	5.45	1.97	0.05
		Total	6.03	2.38	5.86	2.29	0.17
Total		Early	6.11	2.41	6.05	2.47	0.06
		Late	6.45	2.61	6.41	2.54	0.04
		Total	6.24	2.49	6.18	2.50	0.06

Table 6 : Mean scores on ODD of male and female subjects in experimental and control groups in pre- and post-test sessions

Groups	*Gender*	*Age*	*Pre-Test*		*Post-Test*		*Change*
			Mean	*S.D*	*Mean*	*S.D*	
Experi-mental	Male	Early	4.29	2.21	4.14	2.41	0.15
		Late	4.65	2.27	4.40	2.08	0.25
		Total	04.6	2.24	4.36	2.11	0.24
	Female	Early	03.9	2.12	3.70	1.60	0.20
		Late	03.7	1.26	3.45	1.19	0.25
		Total	3.82	1.81	3.60	1.44	0.22
Total		Early	3.97	2.11	3.78	1.75	0.19
		Late	4.35	2.04	4.10	1.89	0.25
		Total	4.21	2.07	3.93	1.84	0.28
Control	Male	Early	3.79	1.73	4.10	2.01	0.31
		Late	4.91	2.39	5.27	2.10	0.36
		Total	4.04	1.93	4.36	2.07	0.32
	Female	Early	3.81	2.12	3.94	2.53	0.13
		Late	06.5	2.12	6.50	2.12	0.00
		Total	3.92	2.17	4.04	2.37	0.12
Total		Early	03.8	1.95	4.01	2.19	0.21
		Late	5.15	2.34	5.46	2.07	0.31
		Total	3.98	2.04	4.20	2.22	0.22
Total	Male	Early	3.87	1.80	4.11	2.05	0.24
		Late	04.7	2.27	4.57	2.10	0.13
		Total	4.32	02.1	4.36	2.08	0.04
	Female	Early	3.85	2.11	3.85	2.08	0.00
		Late	3.95	1.53	3.73	1.52	0.22
		Total	3.87	1.99	3.82	1.97	0.05
Total		Early	3.85	1.99	3.94	2.07	0.09
		Late	4.49	2.10	4.33	1.98	0.16
		Total	4.10	2.05	4.09	2.04	0.01

Table 6 shows that between pre-test and post-test scores a non-significant difference was observed (F=.005; P=.942) in ODD where a decrease of 0.01 (pre-4.10, post-4.09) scores was noticed irrespective of the groups. However, when the ODD were analysed group wise, (experimental v/s control) a significant F value (F=5.153; P=.024) was obtained. From the mean scores it is evident that experimental group reduced its mean by 0.28 (Pre- 4.21– Post-3.93) scores compared to control group, which increased its scores by 0.22 scores (pre 3.98 – Post 4.20).

Discussion

The results clearly indicate that REBT is highly effective in reducing emotional and behavioural problems of the adolescents in affective problems, anxiety problems, somatic problems, Oppositional defiant problems and conduct problems except for ADHD.

The main findings of the present study are:

1. Experimental groups showed a reduction of 8.61 per cent on conduct disorder. The finding supports hypotheses #1 that states Rational Emotive Behaviour Therapy (REBT) has a positive impact on treatment of Conduct Disorder. The finding is consistent with the study by Morris (1993), who conducted an experiment to compare adolescents diagnosed with Conduct Disorder (CD) and adolescents diagnosed with Attention Deficit Hyperactivity Disorder (ADHD) for group effectiveness. He used a 12-weeks treatment programme based on the principles underlying REBT and designed for 'at risk' adolescents (Morris, 1993). Significant differences were found for the CD subjects, who overall reported higher levels of anger and frustration at the outset of the study. There are very limited studies on the effectiveness of REBT on conduct disorder.
2. Considering the sub-variables on DSM-Oriented Scale, REBT had the highest effectiveness of reduction in Affective Problems with 6.57 per cent after the Conduct Disorder. The third effect was on Anxiety Problems with 2.92 per cent of reduction. REBT also had a 0.56 per cent of reduction on scores with Somatic Problem and 0.24 per cent with ODD Problems. This finding supports the hypothesis # 2 that states Rational Emotive Behaviour Therapy (REBT) has a positive impact on treatment of additional variables of DSM Scale.

Conclusion

Over time, the consequences of conduct disorder are severe and pervasive. When identified in childhood, this condition can be a predictor for chronic problems in many areas of adolescent and adult functioning (Kazden, 1996; Kazden, 1993; Kazden, 1987). For example, many conduct disordered children as they develop over the lifespan tend to: be at greater risk for becoming juvenile delinquents than their non-conduct disordered peers; be at high risk for exhibiting chronic antisocial behaviour and criminality as adults; experience poor interpersonal functioning and marital difficulty; dropout of school; remain chronically unemployed; become financially dependent as adults; developmental and/or physical health problems with greater frequency; have higher rates of alcoholism and drug abuse as adults; (as parents) be likely to pass along antisocial behaviours to their children who continue this cycle, (Srorm-Mathisen and Vaglum, 1994; Kazdin, 1996, 1993, 1987).

Literature from Indian studies shows a high level of emotional and behavioural problems among adolescents. Deivasigamani (1990) has reported the prevalence of conduct disorder to be 11.13 per cent, further, Sarkar, kapur and Kaliaperumal (1995) reported the prevalence rate of antisocial behaviour to be 7.1 per cent, while recently Srinath *et al* (2005) have reported a prevalence as low as 0.2 per cent. In a study in the state of Goa, by Pillai *et al* (2008) out of 2684 adolescents, they found the most common diagnosis which was anxiety disorder (1.0%), depressive disorder (0.5%), behavioural disorder (0.4%) and ADHD (0.2%). Paul (2006) in his study on Delhi adolescents using the YSR scale reported that social problems (34.41%) rank the highest compared to the other problems, such as anxiety/ depression (19.74%), somatic complaints (19.12%), thought problems (14.13%), delinquent behaviour (10.75%), attention behaviour (10.52%), aggressive behaviour (8.29%) and withdrawn behaviour (6.91%). The present study also revealed the emotional and behavioural disorders, adolescents are facing. Considering the literature it should be concluded that majority of adolescents are struggling with emotional and behavioural problems. For these reasons alone, the development of more effective methods of treatment for conduct disordered children is indicated as a means of preventing such negative outcomes. For Rational Emotive Behaviour Therapy (REBT), a host of studies were compiled by Engles, et al (1993) and Lyons and Woods, (1991) in their meta-analysis report which examined the efficacy of REBT. Results indicate that REBT is useful for a large range of clinical diagnosis and clinical outcomes; REBT is equally efficient for clinical and non-clinical populations, for a large age range (9-70), and for males and females. It is high time now the counsellors, social workers, psychiatrists, psychologists, and sociologists to plan proper treatment packages to avoid psychological morbidity among adolescents since it is a serious mental health concern.

References

Aaron, R., Joseph, A., Abraham, S., Muliyil, J, George, K., Prasad, J., Minz, S,, Abraham, V.J., & Bose, A., (2004), Suicides in young people in rural southern India, *Lancet; 363*,1117–18.

Achnebach, T. M., (2001), *Manual for the ASEBA School Age Forms & Profiles.* Burlington, VT: University of Vermont.

Buhler, C. (1927), Die ersten sozialen Verhaltungsweisen des Kindes. In C. Buhler, H. Hetzer and B. Tudor-Hart (Eds.), *Soziologische und Psychologische Studien uber das Erste Lebensjahr,* Jena: Gustav Fischer.

Deivasigamani, T.R. (1990), Psychiatric morbidity in primary school children: An epidemiological study, *Indian Journal of Psychiatry,* 32, 235-40.

Eme, R. F., & Kavanaugh, L. (1995), Sex differences in conduct disorder, *Journal of Child Clinical Psychology, 24,* 406-426.

Engels, G. I., Garnefski, N., & Diekstra, R.F.W. (1993), Efficacy of rational-emotive psychotherapy outcome studies, *Journal of Consulting and Clinical Psychology, 61,* 1083-1090.

Esser, G, Schmidt, M.H., & Woerner, W. (1990), Epidemiology and course of psychiatric disorders in school-age children-results of a longitudinal study, *Journal of Child Psychology and Psychiatry, 31,* 243-63.

Fagot, B., & Levy, L. (1998), Gender identity and play. In D.P. Fromberg & D. Bergen (Eds.), *Play from birth to twelve an beyond* (pp. 187-192), New York: Gartland.

Fergusson, D.M. & Horwood, L.J. (1992), Attention deficit and reading achievement, *Journal of Child Psychology and Psychiatry*, 33, 375 – 385.

Ford, T, Goodman, R., & Meltzer, H. (2003), The British Child and Adolescent Mental Health Survey 1999: the prevalence of DSM–IV disorders, *Journal of American Academy of Child Adolescent Psychiatry*, 42, 1203 –11.

Kashani ,J.H., Daniel, A.E, & Sulzberger, L.A., (1987), Conduct disordered adolescents from a community sample, *Canadian Journal of Psychiatry*, *32*, 756-60.

Kazdin, A.E. (1987), Treatment of antisocial behaviour in children: Current status and future directions, *Psychological Bulletin*, 102, 187-203.

Kazdin, A.E. (1993), Treatment of conduct disorder: Progress and directions in psychotherapy research, *Developmental and Psychopathology*, 5, 277-310.

Kazdin, A.E. (1996), *Conduct Disorders in Childhood and Adolescence/ Second Edition, Developmental Clinical Psychology and Psychiatry Volume 9*, Thousand Oaks, Calf: Sage Publications.

Lyon, G.R. (1996), Learning disabilities, *Future Child*. 6, 54-76.

Lyons, L.C., & Woods, P.J. (1991), The efficacy of rational-emotive therapy: A quantitative review of the outcome research. *Clinical Psychology Review*, 11, 357 369.

Mabey, J., & Sorensen, B. (1995), *Counselling for Young People*, Buckingham, Open University Press.

Morris, G.B. (1993), The Rational Emotive Approach: A Critique, *Canadian Counsellor, 10*, 52-59

Paul, D. (2006), Establishment of Adolescent Guidance Centre At NIPCCD – Some Experiences in Vol. 31

Pillai, A., Patel, V., Cardozo, P., Goodman, R., Weiss, H.A., & Andrew, G. (2008), Non-traditional lifestyles and prevalence of mental disorder in adolescents in Goa, *International Journal of Epidemiology*.

Sarkar, A.B., Kapur, M, & Kaliaperumal, V.G. (1995), The prevalence and pattern of psychological disturbance in school going middle childhood children, *NIMHANS Journal*, 13, 33-41.

Srinath, S, Girimaji, S.C., Gururaj, G., Seshadri, S, Subbakrishna, D.K., Bhola P, & Kumar, N. (2005), Epidemiological study of child and adolescent psychiatric disorders in urban and rural areas of Bangalore, *Indian Journal of Medicine* , 122, 67 –79.

Srorm-Mathisen, A., & Vaglum, P. (1994), Conduct disorder patients twenty years later, *Acta-Psycjiatrical-Scandanavica, 89,* 416-420.

U.S. Department of Health and Human Services. (1999), *Mental Health: A Report of the Surgeon General*. Rockville, MD: U.S.A.

Verghese A, & Beig A., (1974), Psychiatric disturbances in children: an epidemiological study, Indian J Med Res 62: 1538 –42.

7

Resilience, Metacognition and Complexity

—*Annalakshmi Narayanan*

The present study is to investigate the relationship between resilience and certain cognitive variables. Resilience was assessed by using Resilience Scale for Adolescents (READ). The Attributional Complexity Scale purports to measure the complexity of the attributional schemata people used to explain human behaviour. The scale assessed the individuals with reference to measured seven attributional constructs including a motivational component, preference for complex rather than simple explanations, metacognition concerning explanations, awareness of the extent to which people's behaviour is a function of interaction with others, a tendency to infer abstract or causally complex internal attributions, a tendency to infer abstract, contemporary, external causal attributions, and a tendency to infer external causes operating from the past. The sample consisted of 114 high school students in the age group 15-16 years. Both male and female students were included in the study. Criterion groups on resilience were formed using the median scores of the distribution of scores of subjects on READ. Findings showed that among the aspects of attributional schemata investigated in this study, complex explanation and metacognition had significant effect on resilience. The highly resilient had higher preference for complex rather than simple explanations for explaining human behaviour and used metacognition concerning explanations more than those who had low resilience.

This paper originally appears in the *Journal of the Indian Academy of Applied Psychology*, October 2009, Vol.35, Special Issue, pp. 112-118.

To describe the children who were exposed to negative conditions of life and yet not succumbed to their ill effects Werner (1971; 1982) introduced the term resilience to psychological literature. Resilience is regarded as the human capacity to face, overcome and even be strengthened by experiences of adversity. It is developed from and nurtured by external supports and resources, inner personal strengths and, interpersonal social skills (Grotberg, 1995), as the positive capacity of individuals to cope with stress and catastrophe psychological resilience which indicates characteristic resistance to future negative events. Resilience is analogous to cumulative protective factors and stands in contrast to cumulative risk factors.

Resilience connotes a dynamic process that people exhibit in positive behavioural adaptation when they encounter significant adversity or trauma (Luthar et al, 2000). As a two-dimensional construct it has reference to both exposure of adversity and positive adjustment outcomes of that adversity (Luthar and Cicchetti, 2000). Adversity is construed by any risks associated with negative life conditions that are statistically related to adjustment difficulties. Poverty, children being of schizophrenic mothers, and experiences of the terrorist attacks are a few of the negative life conditions that drastically challenge adjustment. Behaviour reflecting social competence or success at meeting any particular tasks in spite of exposure to negative life conditions at a specific life stage construes positive adaptation.

Research on resilience received a fillip from studies on children of schizophrenic mothers (Masten, 1989; Masten et al, 1990). The research on resilience specifically focused on discovering the protective factors that explain people's adaptation to adverse conditions including maltreatment, (Cicchetti & Rogosch, 1997) catastrophic life events (Fredrickson et al, 2003) or urban poverty (Luthar, 1999). Attempts to appreciate the underlying protective process are also reported in literature.

In order to understand the world around them people constantly seek and create explanations for others' behaviour. They perceive events and occurrences as having strong cause-effect relationship. In addition they tend to presume that the relationship can be understood in a few brief moments.

Occasionally one may contemplate others' actions for hours. The process of seeking causes to events is considered as being helpful to predict or control the behaviour of others. The process of 'attributing behaviour' involves seeking explanation, gaining understanding, making a meaningful prediction and eventual control of some phenomena (Heider 1958; Jones 1965; Kelley 1967). In reality we miss or skip parts of the model.

Research in recent times has focused on use of schemata in the individual (Fletcher, 1986). Schemata refer to general knowledge constructs that help one to streamline stimuli preference, information gathering, cognitive organisation, and decision making. Individuals differ in the relative sophistication of their schemas for organising and interpreting social stimuli. Attributional complexity (AC) is considered as a personality variable that refers to the extent that one prefers complex explanations of behaviour. It is a construct designed to describe individual differences in the motivation and preference for complex attributions for behaviour. It describes the degree to which an individual is interested in understanding the causes of other's behaviour and considers many different possible causes (Fletcher et al., 1986).

Individuals with higher level of AC are theoretically more likely to consider dispositional factors, situational factors, and factors operating from the past (Fletcher et al., 1986). On the contrary, those with lower level of AC are theorised to be less likely to think about the causes of behaviour or to consider multiple causes. Attributionally complex individuals are relatively less prone to errors and bias in social judgement. This could be chiefly because when one is interested in understanding behaviour, able to think about several possible causes of behaviour, and given time to deeply process social information he is less given to errors and bias (Fletcher et al., 1990; Follett & Hess, 2002; Stalder & Baron, 1998).

The Attributional Complexity Scale of Fletcher et al. (1986) (ACS) reconciles these two views of attribution. It combines the view that attributional process proposes that people are cognitive misers who rely on simple heuristics when attributing the cause of other's behaviour (Tversky & Kahneman, 1974) and another view is that the attributional process is complex and that people generate and consider multiple causes (Ross & Fletcher, 1985). The ACS views that individuals may vary in the extent to which their attributions are sophisticated. While some individuals are 'simpletons' some are 'experts' (Fletcher et al., 1986). ACS purports to measure the complexity of the attributional schemata that people use to explain human behaviour.

An attributionally complex individual shows a preference for thinking deeply about the causes of behaviour. He/she is able to use complex to simple attributions depending on the restrictions of the situation. On the contrary, an attributionally simple individual is limited to elementary and uncomplicated explanations for behaviour. High scorers on ACS are found to be socially astute because they are less prone to make a variety of classic attributional errors. Scores on the ACS have been found to be related to a lesser propensity to error and greater accuracy in social judgement. Attributionally complex individuals are less likely to form erroneous group stereotypes in conditions where participants do not have to justify their impressions (Schaller, Boyd, Yohannes, & O'Brien, 1995).

High scorers on ACS spontaneously generate a larger number of causes for behaviour, prefer complex rather than simple attributions, and take more time in processing difficult problems than their lower scoring counterparts (Fletcher et al., 1992; 1986). Severe depression is associated with reduced AC (Flett & Hewitt, 1990). AC has been shown to predict job performance among employed students (Townsend et al, 2006).

Studies correlating AC with self-reported personality characteristics show a mixed picture of the attributionally complex: some evidence suggest that they may have a positive reputation and behave in a socially skilled man and some other evidence suggest that they may be socially detached and awkward. Individuals higher in AC are observed to be relatively open, positive, expressive and socially skilled (Fast et al, 2007). AC was unrelated to academic achievement or SAT scores. Individuals higher in AC were described by peers as having social wisdom, thoughtfulness, empathy, and openness. AC has a near zero correlation with locus of control (Fletcher et al., 1986).

AC is associated with significant reductions in committing the fundamental attribution error (Blumberg & Silvera, 1998; Devine, 1989; Follett & Hess, 2002). Individuals high on AC follow attributional rules better than those low on AC. When given problems in which one needs to determine whether a behaviour was caused by the person, circumstance, or stimulus, individuals higher in AC make more correct attributions. This trend is seen even when the problems increase in difficulty (Fletcher et al., 1992). With those high on AC having enhanced ability to follow attributional rules and reductions in error, they also show increased accuracy in social judgment as well.

Objectives

The research question mooted in this study is "whether Attributional Complexity has significant effect on Resilience?"

The objective of the present study is to investigate the relationship resilience and the complexity of the attributional schemata that people use to explain human behaviour.

Method

Sample

The sample consists of 114 students studying in higher secondary classes. Both males and females were included. The age group ranged from 15 to 16 years.

Instruments

The Attributional Complexity Scale (Fletcher, 1986) was used to measure the complexity of the attributional schemata (that people use to explain human behaviour) was used to assess attributional variables. The scale measured seven attributional constructs. The subscales delineate the various ways in which one's attributions may be complex. The subscales focus on the degree to which an individual is motivated to understand behaviour, prefers complex rather than simple explanations for behaviour, thinks about his own thinking processes involved in attribution, is aware of the influence of interactions with others on behaviour, tends to infer internal causes of behaviour, tends to infer external causes of behaviour, and (Fletcher et al., 1986). While the scores on the subscales can be combined into a total attributional complexity score (ACS), each subscale also can be treated as separate scales focusing on specific aspect of AC.

Resilience Scale for Adolescents (READ) was used to assess the resilience of the subjects (Friborg, 2005). Five factors of resilience, namely, Personal Competence, Social Competence, Structured Style, Social Resources and Family Cohesion are assessed by this scale.

RESULTS

The criterion groups on resilience were compared with regard to their various aspects of attributional complexity using one way analysis of variance. The various constructs of attributional complexity used in the analysis are motivational component, preference for complex rather than simple explanations, metacognition concerning explanations, awareness of the extent to which people's behaviour is a function of interaction with others, a tendency to infer abstract or causally complex internal attributions, a tendency to infer abstract, contemporary, external causal attributions, and a tendency to infer external causes operating from the past. The mean for the scores of the criterion groups on attributional complexity are presented in Table 1.

The test of homogeneity of variance of the criterion groups on various aspects of attributional complexity was carried out.

The F-ratio relating to complex versus simple explanations {$F = 6.18$ at (1,112), $p<0.01$} and the F-ratio relating to metacognition {$F= 3.07$ at (1,112), $p<0.08$} are significant. As may be seen in Table 1 the high group on resilience are significantly lower on complex explanations and higher on metacognitions aspects of attributional complexity as compared to the high group on resilience.

The F-ratios relating to motivational component, awareness of behaviour as a function of interaction, abstract versus concrete, external causal attributions, and past causes are not significant. The low group on resilience does not differ significantly from the high group on resilience with regard to motivational component, awareness of behaviour as function of interaction, abstract versus concrete, external causal attributions, and past causes aspects of attributional complexity. Similarly, the criterion groups do not differ significantly from each other with regard to their overall score on attributional complexity.

Table 1

Mean for the scores of the criterion groups on attributional complexity.

Variable	*Criterion Groups on Resilience*	*N*	*Mean*	*SD*
Motivational component	Low Resilience Group	57	–.18	5.90
	High Resilience Group	57	.98	5.65
	Total	114	.40	5.78
Complex vs simple explanation	Low Resilience Group	57	-1.21	4.56
	High Resilience Group	57	-3.19	3.93
	Total	114	-2.20	4.35
Metacognition	Low Resilience Group	57	4.02	5.04
	High Resilience Group	57	5.53	4.11
	Total	114	4.77	4.64
Awareness of behaviour as function of interaction	Low Resilience Group	57	1.77	4.49
	High Resilience Group	57	2.04	4.94
	Total	114	1.90	4.70
Abstract vs concrete	Low Resilience Group	57	2.84	3.71
	High Resilience Group	57	3.60	3.99
	Total	114	3.22	3.85
External causes	Low Resilience Group	57	2.98	4.00
	High Resilience Group	57	2.26	4.48
	Total	114	2.62	4.24
Past causes	Low Resilience Group	57	2.95	4.65
	High Resilience Group	57	3.32	5.43
	Total	114	3.13	5.04
Total Attributional Complexity	Low Resilience Group	57	13.18	21.21
	High Resilience Group	57	14.53	19.13
	Total	114	13.85	20.12

Discussion

The findings show that the high and low resilient do not differ from each other with regard to certain aspects of attributional complexity like motivational component, awareness of behaviour as function of interaction, abstract versus concrete, external causal attributions, and past causes in addition to showing similarity in their overall attributional complexity. However, certain aspects of attributional complexity seem to be significantly contributing to resilience: highly resilient seems to employ more complex explanations to behaviour than simple explanations. They also employ more metacognition concerning causal attributions. Metacognition is a type of thinking that is oriented to the underlying framework of mental processes.

The findings imply that attributional complexity is a complex variable and perhaps, only a few aspects of it significantly effect on resilience. Individuals high on resilience prefer more simple attributions rather than complex ones. Perhaps, the resilient individuals are satisfied with a straight-forward explanation to others' behaviour than being sceptic in comprehending the causes behind others' behaviours. Similarly individuals high on resilience are found to use more of metacognitions in explaining behaviours. They have a higher need to use metacognitive thinking to resolve the varying cognitive elements involved in an issue. High resilience group has greater need for understanding than that of the low resilience group (Annalakshmi, 2008). Perhaps being oriented towards understanding one's thought process helps an individual to avoid attributional errors and bias. This eventually leads to enhanced judgement which helps one to stay alert to available resources. Being aware of resources available to him may induce optimism in the individual and hence helps him to bounce back during times of trouble.

The highly resilient and less resilient do not differ with regard to the level of interest in attributions, understanding that one's behaviour is a product of dealings with other people, frequent use of abstract internal attributions and abstract external attributions, external causes operating from the past. Motivational component related to attributions did not influence resilience. Resilience could be seen as predominantly a personality variable with motivation playing a less significant role. The highly resilient and the less resilient did not differ from each other with regard to using abstract attributions, be it internal attributions or external attributions. Earlier studies have shown that resilience is linked with higher level abstract thinking (Bernard, 1997). This relationship, however, is not reflected in the present findings. This is intriguing. More studies may be needed to clarify this deviation of the present finding from the trend of results already reported.

As far as the present findings are concerned, constructs like understanding that ones behaviour is a product of dealings with other people, abstract external attributions and external causes operating from the past are not found to be differentiating the highly resilient from the less resilient.

References

Annalakshmi, N. (2008), The Resilient individual - A Personality Analysis, *Journal of the Indian Academy of Applied Psychology, 34,* 110-118.

Bernard, B. (1991), *Fostering resiliency in kids: Protective factors in the family, school and community,* Portland, OR: Northwest Regional Educational Laboratory.

Benard, B. (1997). Drawing forth resilience in all our youth. *Reclaiming Children and Youth, 6* , 29-32.

Block, J. H., & Block, J. (1980), The role of ego-control and ego-resiliency in the organisation of behaviour. In W. A. Collins (Ed.), *Development of cognition, affect, and social relations: Minnesota Symposia on Child Psychology* (pp.39-101), Hillsdale, NJ: Erlbaum.

Blumberg, S., & Silvera, D. (1998), Attributional Complexity and cognitive development: A look at the motivational and cognitive requirements for attribution, *Social Cognition, 16,* 253–266.

Cicchetti, D., & Rogosch, F. A. (1997), The role of self-organization in the promotion of resilience in maltreated children, *Development and Psychopathology, 9,* 797-815.

Cicchetti, D., Rogosch, F. A., Lynch, M., & Holt, K. D. (1993), Resilience in maltreated children: Processes leading to adaptive outcome, *Development and Psychopathology, 5,* 629-647.

Crano, W., & Schroder, H. (1967), Complexity of attitude structure and processes of conflict resolution, *Journal of Personality and Social Psychology, 5,* 110–114.

Crockett, W. H. (1965), Cognitive complexity and impression formation, In B. A. Maher (Ed.). *Progress in experimental personality research* (pp. 47–90), New York: Academic Press.

Devine, P. G. (1989), Overattribution effect: The role of confidence and attributional complexity, *Social Psychology Quarterly, 52,* 149–158.

Fast, L.A., Reimer, H.M. & Funder, D.C. (2008), The social behaviour and reputation of the attributionally complex, *Journal of Research in Personality. 42,* 208–222.

Fletcher, G. (1983), The analysis of verbal explanations for marital separation: Implications for attribution theory, *Journal of Applied Social Psychology, 13,* 245–258.

Fletcher, G. J., Danilovics, P., Fernandez, G., Peterson, D., & Reeder, G. D. (1986), Attributional Complexity: An individual differences measure, *Journal of Personality and Social Psychology, 51,* 875-884.

Fletcher, G. J., Reeder, G. D., & Bull, V. (1990), Bias and accuracy in attitude attribution: The role of attributional complexity, *Journal of Experimental Social Psychology, 26,* 275–288.

Fletcher, G. J., Rosanowski, J., Rhodes, G., & Lange, C. (1992), Accuracy and speed of causal processing: Experts versus novices in social judgment, *Journal of Experimental Social Psychology, 28,* 320–338.

Flett, G.L., & Hewitt, P.L. (1990), Clinical depression and attributional complexity, *British Journal of Clinical Psychology. 29,* 339-340.

Follett, K. J., Hess, T. M. (2002), Aging, cognitive complexity, and the fundamental attribution error, *Journal of Gerontology: Psychological Sciences, 57,* 312-323.

Fredrickson, B. L., Tugade, M. M., Waugh, C. E., & Larkin, G. (2003), What good are positive emotions in crises?: A prospective study of resilience and emotions following the terrorist attacks on the United States on September 11th, 2001, *Journal of Personality and Social Psychology, 84,* 365-376.

Friborg et al. (2005), Resilience in relation to personality and intelligence, *International Journal of Methods in Psychiatric Research. 14,* 29-42.

Grotberg, E. (1995), *The International Resilience Project: Promoting resilience in children,* ERIC ED 383424.

Heider, F. (1944), Social perception and phenomenal causality, *Psychological Review, 51,* 358–374.

Heider, F. (1958), *The psychology of interpersonal relations,* New York: John Wiley & Sons.

Jones, E., & Davis, K. (1965), From acts to dispositions: The attribution process in person perception, In L.Berkowitz (Ed.), *Advances in experimental social psychology* (pp. 220–266). New York: Academic Press.

Kelley, H.H. (1973), The process of causal attribution, *American Psychologist, 28,* 107–128.

Kelley, H. H. (1967), Attribution theory in social psychology, In D. Levine (Ed.), Nebraska symposium on motivation. Lincoln: University of Nebraska Press.

Luthar, S. S. (1999), *Poverty and children's adjustment,* Newbury Park, CA: Sage.

Luthar, S. S., & Cicchetti, D. (2000), The construct of resilience: Implications for interventions and social policies, *Development and Psychopathology, 71,* 543-562.

Luthar, S.S., Cicchetti, D., & Becker, B. (2000), The Construct of Resilience: A Critical Evaluation and Guidelines for Future Work, *Child Development, 71,* 543-562.

Masten, A. S. (1989), Resilience in development: Implications of the study of successful adaptation for developmental psychopathology, In D. Cicchetti (Ed.), *The emergence of a discipline: Rochester symposium on developmental psychopathology* (pp. 261 294). Hillsdale, NJ: Erlbaum.

Masten, A. S., Best, K. M., & Garmezy, N. (1990), Resilience and development: Contributions from the study of children who overcome adversity, *Development and Psychopathology, 2,* 425-444.

Ross, M. & G. J. O. Fletcher (1985), Attribution and Social Perception. In G. Lindzey and A. Aronson (eds.), *The Handbook of Social Psychology,* volume 3, pp. 73-122. Reading, MA: Addison-Wesley,

Schaller, M., Boyd, C., Yohannes, J., & O'Brien, M. (1995), The prejudiced personality revisited: Personal need for structure and formation of erroneous group stereotypes, *Journal of Personality and Social Psychology, 68,* 544-555.

Stalder, D. R., & Baron, R. S. (1998), Attributional complexity as a moderator of dissonance-produced attitude change, *Journal of Personality and Social Psychology, 75,* 449–455.

Townsend, J.C., Silva, N.D., Mueller, L., Curtin, P. & Tetrick, L.E. (2006), Attributional Complexity: A Link Between Training, Job Complexity, Decision Latitude, Leader–Member Exchange, and Performance, *Journal of Applied Social Psychology.*

Tversky, A., & Kahneman, D. (1974). Judgment under uncertainty: Heuristics and biases, *Science, 185,* 1124-1131.

Wang, M.C., Haertel, G.D., & Walberg,H.J. Educational Resilience in Inner City, In *Educational Resilience in Inner-City America – Challenges and Prospects,* Edited by Wang, M.C., Gordon, E.M

Werner, E. E. (1971), The children of Kauai : a longitudinal study from the prenatal period to age ten, *Honolulu: University of Hawaii Press.*

Werner, E.E. & Smith, R.S. (1982), *Vulnerable but invincible: A longitudinal study of resilient children and youth,* New York: McGraw-Hill.

The Effect of Obsession Thoughts on Intelligences Achievement Relationship of Late Adolescents

—*Partha Malakar, Jayanti Basu* and *Anindita Chaudhuri*

The present study was conducted to explore whether there is any difference in intelligence-achievement relationship between low and high Obsessional thought groups among late adolescent students. The aims of the study were to determine (i) whether there is any sex difference in obsessional thoughts (ii) whether there is any sex difference in achievement scores and (iii) whether there exist any difference in intelligence-achievement relationship between low and high Obsessional thought groups. The sample consisted of 103 Bengali girls and 92 Bengali boys selected randomly from Class XI (16-18 years). Raven's Standard Progressive Matrices and Leyton Obsessional Inventory by Cooper and an information schedule were administered. The achievement level of the students was measured from the Madhyamik mark-sheet. The analyses revealed significant differences between high and low Obsessional thought groups indicating substantial loss in intelligence-achievement relationship attributable to obsessional thought. The results have been discussed in terms of future research directions and therapeutic implications.

Keywords: Obsession thoughts, Intelligence, Achievement, Late Adolescents.

This paper originally appears in the *Journal of the Indian Academy of Applied Psychology*, July 2009, Vol.35, No.2, pp. 277-282.

Literature reveals that Obsessive-compulsive symptoms in children and adolescents have characteristics common to, as well as different from, the adult stage. Their biological, psychological, social and cognitive resources shift throughout childhood and adolescence (Rangaswami, 1998). Normal children often display obsessive ideas and compulsions at certain stages of development, which later fades away (Judd, 1965). Yet, like the adult Obsessive Compulsive Disorder (OCD) patient the principal problem among child OCD is also cognitive in nature (Rangaswami, 1999). Various cognitive models like 'thought action fusion model' (Rachman, 1976), cognitive behaviour model (Salkovskis, 1985; 1989), Clark and Pardon model (1993), meta cognitive model (Wells and Mathews, 1997), general working model (Wells, 1997) and developmentally based cognitive model (Rangaswamy, 1998) have been used to explain cognitive deficit associated with obsessive compulsive symptoms.

Obsessive-compulsive tendencies result in a number of functional impairment in the child. Studies have revealed that usually the greatest difficulties occur in execution of those areas, which are of greatest significance to the adolescent, that is, in academic performance, and various aspects of social interaction (Sukhodolsky et al., 2005). A study by Piacentini et al (2003) surveyed the complaints reported by 151 OCD children and adolescents and their parents. They observed that parents of clinic referred OCD children and adolescents identified the most significant problems as trouble with concentrating on schoolwork (47%), doing homework (46%), and getting ready for bed (42%). The children and adolescents themselves complained more of difficulties relating to concentrating on schoolwork (37%), doing homework (32%), and doing household chores (30%).

The present study focuses on the investigation of one particular functional deficit, that is the loss of academic achievement among late adolescents due to obsessive-compulsive characteristics. This is particularly relevant, since late adolescence is the phase of preparing for subsequent career. Particularly, in countries like India, where grades are given much importance, poor achievement in examination may result in damage of both career and self-esteem. Academic achievement, the crux of this study has been variously defined: as level of proficiency attained in academic work or as formally acquired knowledge in school subjects which is often represented by percentage of marks obtained by students in examinations (Kohli, 1975). There is an overwhelming evidence establishing intelligence as the most significant predictor of academic achievement, although role of non-cognitive variables is also well known (Eysenck 1960; Karnes et al 1984). The present study argues that the presence of obsessive traits in an adolescent, particularly at the time of important examinations, would impair proper utilisation of one's intellectual functioning and would therefore have impact on expression of intellectual potential on academic achievement. Indeed, it has been observed that there is little significant difference in intelligence between the obsessive and normal adolescents and adults, but the potential may not be unfolded or utilised in time of need (Purcell et al, 1998).

Some studies indicate that among children, OCD is greater among boys, but in adults, it is more prominent in women. The research about gender difference in OCD prevalence and contents among adolescents remain an area of continued interest, since conclusive indications are not available. Indeed OCD among children and adolescents had been a neglected issue for decades and has started being probed by the researchers only since the early nineties (Presta et al., 2003). Therefore, the present study took into consideration both girls and boys and assessed the gender difference. The objective of the study is to determine (i) whether there is any sex difference in obsessional thoughts, (ii) whether there is any sex difference in achievement scores and (iii) whether there exist any difference in intelligence-achievement relationship between low and high Obsessional thought groups.

Method

Sample

Hundred and three girls and 92 boys studying in Class XI of four different schools of South Kolkata participated in the study. Their age ranged from 16 to 18 years. All of them were from Bengali Hindu middle class families and living with their parents in Kolkata. All of them had passed Madhyamik examination (school-leaving examination) in the previous year.

Tools

Raven's Standard Progression Matrices (SPM) was used to assess their intelligence level. (Raven et al., 2000).

The Leyton Obsessional Inventory was used to assesses their obsessional tendency (Cooper, 1970). This is a 69-item scale applicable on non-clinical population for assessing obsessive tendency.

The achievement level was measured from the mark sheet of Madhyamika examination (secondary examination). The marks of language group, science group, arts group, additional subject and total marks were considered. The full marks in language group and science group is was 300, and in social science group was 200. Besides, an additional subject was also taken up which was of 100 marks.

RESULTS

The means and standard deviations of all the variables of obsessional thought and achievement in different subject domains in Madhyamika examination were recorded for males and females separately in Table 1. The significance of difference between the sexes was estimated by 't' test.

Results indicated that there was no gender difference in obsessional thought. The girls were somewhat better than boys in social science group and boys better than girls in additional subject. Since there was no significant difference in total marks between the sexes, it was decided to treat the total group as a whole for subsequent analyses.

To determine whether intelligence–achievement relation differs across high and low obsessive thought groups, the sample was split according to the median value of obsessional thought scores.

Table 1 : Mean, SD and t values for all variables with 92 boys and 103 girls

Variables	*Male*		*Female*		
	Mean	*SD*	*Mean*	*SD*	*t- value*
Obsessional thought scores	23.50	5.83	23.10	5.57	–0.49
Intelligence	42.10	10.56	43.32	7.97	0.92
Language group marks	167.31	22.93	171.10	24.24	1.12
Science group marks	166.29	35.59	172.83	41.19	1.18
Social science group marks	111.42	18.40	117.32	20.28	2.12 *
Additional subject marks	75.18	9.93	68.34	11.35	–4.46 **
Total marks	488.45	69.81	497.81	79.41	0.87

**p <.01, *p <.05.

The means and standard deviations of scores in intelligence, language group, science group, social science group, additional and total marks were determined for these two groups. Then t tests were done to determine whether there was any significant difference between adolescents with high and low obsession in the results of the Madhyamika examination in various subjects. The results are presented in Table 2.

Table 2. Mean, SD and t value of high and low obsessive thought groups

Variables	*Groups*	*N*	*M*	*SD*	*t values*
Intelligence	Low obsession	90	43.36	8.06	0.80
	High obsession	105	42.29	10.20	
Language group marks	Low obsession	90	173.12	25.59	2.10 *
	High obsession	105	166.05	21.43	
Science group marks	Low obsession	90	178.32	41.51	2.92 **
	High obsession	105	162.38	34.63	
Social Science Group marks	Low obsession	90	120.40	20.45	4.02 **
	High obsession	105	109.51	17.41	
Additional Subject marks	Low obsession	90	70.42	12.58	–1.33
	High obsession	105	72.55	9.85	
Marks (total)	Low obsession	90	508.73	83.84	2.69 **
	High obsession	105	480.24	64.01	

** p< 0.01 * p< 0.05

Subsequently the Pearson product moment correlation was computed between intelligence and achievement for low and high obsessional thought groups and t test for significance of difference between correlations was computed. The results are presented in Table 3.

Table 3 : Pearson Product Moment Correlations between intelligence and achievement for low and high obsessional thought groups and t values

Variables of Achievements	*Obsessional thought group*		
	Low obsessional	*High obsessional*	*t values*
Language group marks	0.47 ***	0.10	2.92 ***
Science group marks	0.44 ***	0.20 **	1.85 *
Social science group marks	0.25 ***	0.19 *	0.57
Additional subject marks	0.02	–0.01	1.32
Total marks	0.42 ***	0.20 ***	1.78 *

*** $p<0.01$ (2-tailed). ** $p<0.05$ (2-tailed). *$p<0.10$ (2-tailed).

Results indicated that there was no significant difference between the low and high obsessional thought groups in terms of intellectual ability. But significant differences existed between the high and low obsessional thought groups in the marks of language group, science group, arts group and total marks. The low obsessional thought group performed significantly better than the high obsessional thought group.

The difference was also observed in intelligence-achievement relationship between groups with high and low obsessional thoughts in the variables language group, science group and total marks. Intelligence-achievement relationship was high in low obsessional thought group in comparison to high obsessional group.

Discussion

The fact that no gender difference was found in case of obsessional thought is in line with that of Castle et al. (1995). The findings of the study further reveal that, as expected, both low obsessional and high obsessional thought groups have significant positive correlation of intelligence with the variables of achievement. However, the two groups differed in the overall achievement, the low obsessional thought group having higher achievement in comparison to the high obsessional thought group. The low obsessional thought group is also found not only higher in absolute achievement, but also higher in intelligence-achievement relationship than high obsessional thought group. It is probably due to the fact that students with high obsession are busy with thinking intrusive trifle things, and cannot easily switch over from one topic to another as obsessional thoughts forcibly engulf their consciousness.

The general findings of the study corroborate earlier findings (Mather & Cartwright, 2004; Mrdjenovich, & Bischiof, 2003). Poor achievement of high obsessional thought group may be attributed to their intrusive thoughts, which are key sources of cognitive disturbance. People with high obsessional thought pay more attention to the dysfunctional beliefs (Clark and Purdon, 1993), which, coupled with the schemas concerned with the need to control them produces distress. Obsessional thoughts are known to impair cognitive performance on domains like visuo-spatial memory, verbal fluency (Roh et al., 2005), spatial working memory, spatial recognition (Purcell et al., 1998), and executive functions (Andres-Perpina et al., 2002). These faculties are required for achievement in different subjects in differing amount, and therefore may serve as moderators between obsessional thought and poor performance.

Conclusion and Implications

It can be concluded from the study that obsessional thought impairs the function of intelligence to lead an adolescent to the academic achievement one deserves. Therefore, future research needs to be directed at further probing of specific cognitive elements that may be disturbed, as well as toward pragmatic intervention. Studies reveal that obsessional symptoms express themselves as problems in thinking and decisionmaking, and therefore, cognitive restructuring seems to be the most acceptable mode of intervention (Shafran, 2001). However, obsessive compulsive disorder is a spectrum disorder, and there are various ranges of difficulty. It also needs to be remembered that often failure to achieve is connected with punitive measures at school and home in our country and a permanent loss of self-esteem may result. The parents and teachers need to be educated about the early recognition of the problem and a need-based referral system for pharmacotherapy and cognitive-behavioural therapy needs to be developed (Storch et al., 2007).

References

Andres-Perpina, S., Lazaro-Garcia, L., Canalda- Salhi, G. & Boget-Lucia, T (2002), Neuropsychological aspects of obsessive-compulsive disorder, *Rev Neurol, 35,* 959-963.

Castlem, D. J., Deale, A. & Marks, M. (1995), Gender differences in obsessive compulsive disorder, *Aust NZ Journal of Psychiatry, 29,* 114-117.

Clark, D.M. & Purdon, C. (1993), New perspective of cognitive therapy of obsessions, *Australian Psychologist, 28,* 161-167.

Cooper, J. (1970), Leyton obsessional Inventory, *Psychological Medicine, 1,* 48-64.

Eysenck, H.J. (1960), *Structure of Human Personality,* London, Routledge & Kegan Paul.

Judd, L.L. (1965), Obsessive compulsive neuroses in children, *Archives of General Psychiatry, 12,* 136-143.

Karnes, F.A., Whorton, J.E., & Curries, B.B. (1984), Correlations between WISC-R IQs and wide range Achievement Test grade equivalents for Intellectually Gifted Students, *Psychological of Reports, 54,* 69-70.

Kohli, T.K. (1975), *Characteristic Behavioural and Environmental Correlates of Academic Achievement of Over and Under-Achievers of Different Levels of Intelligence,* Punjab University, unpublished Ph. D. Thesis.

Mather, A. & Cartwright–Hatlon S. (2004) Cognitive predictors of obsessive-compulsive symptoms in Adolescents, *Journal of Clinical Child and Adolescent Psychology, 33,* 743-749.

Mrdjenovich, A.J. & Bischiof, G.A. (2004). Obsessive-Compulsive Complaints and Academic Performance. *College Student Journal, 37,* 145-155.

Piacentini, J., Bergman R L., Keller M., McCracken J., (2003), Functional impairment in children and adolescents with obsessive-compulsive disorder, *Journal of child and adolescent psychopharmacology, 13,* 61-69.

Purcell, R., Maruff, P., Kyrios, M. & Pantelis, C. (1998), Cognitive deficits in obsessive-compulsive disorder on tests of frontal-srtiatal function, *Biological Psychiatry, 43,* 348-357.

Rachman, S.J. (1976), Obsessive-compulsive checking, *Behaviour Research and Therapy, 14,* 269-277

Rangaswami, K. (1998), Developmentally based cognitive model of obsessive compulsive disorder in children and adolescence, *Indian Journal of Clinical Psychology: 25,* 188-193

Rangaswami, K (1999), Cognitive disturbances in obsessive compulsive disorders: A Review, *Indian Journal of Clinical Psychology: 26,* 148-155.

Raven, J.C., Court, J.H. & Raven, J. (1992). Manual for Standard Progressive Matrices. Oxford Psychologists Press:Oxford

Roh, K.S., Shin, M.S., Kim, M.S., Ha, T.H., Shin, Y.W. Lee, K.J. & Kwon, J.S. (2005), Persistent cognitive dysfunction in patients with obsessive compulsive disorder: A naturalistic study, *Psychiatry Clinical Neuroscience, 59,* 539-45

Presta, S., Marazziti, D., Dell'Osso, L., Pfanner, C., Pfanner, P., Marcheschi, M., Masi, G., Muratori, F., Mucci, M,, Millipiedi, S. & Cassano, G. B. (2003), Obsessive-Compulsive Disorder in Childhood and Adolescence. *Psychopathology;* 36:55-64 Salkovskis, P.M (1985), Obsessional-compulsive problems: A cognitive behavioural analysis, *Behaviour Research Therapy, 23,* 571-583.

Salkovskis, P.M (1989), Cognitive-behavioural factors and the persistence of intrusive thoughts in Obsessional problems, *Behaviour Research Therapy, 27,* 677-682.

Shafran, R. (2001), Obsessive-compulsive disorder in children and adolescents, *Child Psychology and Psychiatry Review, 6,* 50-58.

Storch, E. A.. Geffken, G. R. & Murphy, T. K. (Eds.) (2007), *Handbook of Child and Adolescent Obsessive-Compulsive Disorder,* NY. Routledge.

Sukhodolsky, D. G., do Rosario-Campos, M.C., Scahill, L., Katsovich, L., Pauls, D. L., Peterson, B. S., King, R. A., Lombroso, P. J., Findley,

D. B., and Leckman, J. F. (2005), Adaptive, Emotional, and Family Functioning of Children With Obsessive-Compulsive Disorder and Comorbid Attention Deficit Hyperactivity Disorder, *American Journal of Psychiatry, 162,* 1125-1132.

Wells, A., (1997), *Cognitive therapy of anxiety disorders: A practical manual and conceptual guide,* New York: John Wiley and sons.

Wells, A & Mathews, G. (1997), Modelling cognition in emotional disorders: The SREF Model, *Behavioural Research and Therapy, 35,* 473-475.

9

Self-esteem and Emotional Stability of Visually Challenged Students

—Majda Tarannum and Naima Khatoon

The present paper attempts to study certain demographic variables as determinants of self-esteem and emotional stability of visually challenged students. The sample constitutes 100 visually challenged students of Ahmadi School for Blinds, Aligarh Muslim University, Aligarh, out of which 63 are boys and 37 girls belonging to the age range of 5-18 years. The tools self-esteem inventory and emotional stability test for children were used for the study. The data collected were analysed statistically by using stepwise regression analysis. Out of the demographic variables of gender, age, class, family system and area of living, only gender emerged as the significant predictor of emotional stability of visually challenged students and none of the demographic variables emerged as predictors of self-esteem of these students.

Keywords: Self-esteem, Emotional Stability, Visually Challenged Students.

In the past, challenged children were generally excluded from the purview of nominal experience. They have been treated as defective beings and believed that these children will not profit from regular schools and their facilities. In the early nineteenth century as the idea of democracy, individual freedom and

This paper originally appears in the *Journal of the Indian Academy of Applied Psychology,* July 2009, Vol.35, No.2, pp. 245-250.

egalitarianism swept in the West, advancement in learning theory and technology contributed to the emergence of optimistic attitude towards challenged pupils. UNESCO envisaged the most positive response to this section of population in the year 1946.

In India educational provisions for challenged children has become a priority as a result of the National Policy on Education 1986. All these attempts brought the galore of publicity on the needs of the blind in the world and in India as well.

The population of visually challenged people in India is approximately 40.5 million. An individual whose normal learning and development is impaired by visual conditions and who therefore, need specific conditions and related services in order to develop their abilities can be identified as visually challenged (Whitmore, 1981). Demographic data refers to selected population characteristics as used in government, marketing or opinion research, or the demographic profile in such research. Commonly used demographic include: Gender refers to an individual's "psychological type", it is acquired through experience. An individual can be viewed as either masculine or feminine. It refers to the differences between men and women. Age may refer to the length of time that an organism has lived. Education is a broad concept; it refers to all the experiences in which children can learn something. The nuclear family or conjugal family is the basic unit of family organisation in virtually every society. It is generally defined as a married couple and their children (including adopted and fostered children, as well as the couple's natural children). A joint family consists of a man, his wife, their adult sons, their wives and children, younger children of parental couple (Gore, 1968).

Over the past few decades, self-esteem has been the theme of numerous conferences and the subject of many books. The topic has huge exposure, and parents and teachers have been endlessly instructed about how important it is to build a child's self-esteem. Self-esteem is a widely used concept both in popular language and in psychology. It refers to an individual's sense of his or her value or worth, or the extent to which a person values, approves of, appreciates, prizes, or likes him or herself (Blascovich & Tomaka, 1991).

Emotional stability is considered as one of the important aspects of human life. It is one of the effective determinants of the personality patterns. An emotionally stable individual has the capacity to withstand delay in satisfaction of needs, the capability to tolerate a reasonable amount of frustration, the belief in long-term planning and is capable of delaying or revising his expectations in terms of demands of the situations.

Kling, Hyde, Showers and Buswell (1999) conducted a study to examine gender differences in global self-esteem. The result indicated that males scored higher on standard measure of global self-esteem than females but the difference is small. Mullis and Chapman (2000) studied the relationship between coping, gender, age and self-esteem in adolescents and found that adolescents with higher self-esteem used more problem-focused coping strategies and adolescents with lower self-esteem used more emotion focused coping strategies. Vasuki and Reddy (1997) explored the self-esteem of single children using an *ex-post facto* design, which revealed that most of the children had high self-esteem and no gender differences in the self-esteem of 12-15 years olds were found. Overall all boys showed high self-esteem, and also indicated significant differences in the self-esteem of boys of the two age groups whereas the same was not observed in the case of girls.

Hay and Ashman (2003) investigated gender differences associated with the development of adolescents' sense of general self-concept and emotional stability and 655 adolescents were investigated. Relationships with parents were important for males' emotional stability, but not females'. Peer relations were more influential in the formation of adolescents' emotional stability than parental relationships. Aleem (2005) examined the difference between the mean scores of male and female students on emotional stability and revealed that male students are found to be more emotionally stable than female students.

Objectives

1. To find out whether demographic variables, e.g., gender, age, class, family system and area of living, predicts self-esteem of visually challenged students.

2. To identify whether demographic variables, e.g., gender, age, class, family system and area of living, predicts emotional stability of visually challenged students.

METHOD

Sample

The sample of 100 visually challenged students was selected from Ahmadi School for Blinds, Aligarh Muslim University, Aligarh. The sample consists of 63 boys and 37 girls. All the students range in age between 5 and 18 years.

Tools

Self-esteem inventory

The self-esteem of students is measured through self-esteem inventory, developed by Prasad and Thakur (1977). It consists of 30 items. Of the thirty items, 17 were socially desirable and 13 were socially undesirable. The scale was developed with a view to assess personally perceived self and socially perceived self. Split-half reliability co-efficient of both sets of the inventory is .82 and .78 for personally perceived self and socially perceived self, respectively. Retest reliability coefficient found for both the tests were .69 and .66 respectively for personally perceived self and socially perceived self.

Emotional stability test for children

Emotional stability of children is measured through Emotional Stability Test for Children, developed by Sengupta and Singh (1985). This scale contains 15 items for testing emotional stability of children. The maximum possible score of this test is 15. Test-retest reliability was .70 which was significant beyond .01 level and split-half reliability was .55.

Table 1 projects that 6 per cent variation in self-esteem can be explain on the basis of the five predictor variables, i.e., gender, age, class, family system and area of living, but all the five predictors do not contribute significantly in explaining self-esteem of visually challenged students.

Results

Table 1. Self-Esteem Regressed on Gender, Age, Class, Family System (FS) and Area of Living (AL) of Visually Challenged Students

Variables	*Standardised Coefficient*	*t-Value*
Gender	-.159	1.502
Age	-.224	1.549
Class	.040	0.277
FS	-.014	0.135
AL	.047	0.455
R^2	.060	

Table 2: Emotional Stability Regressed on Gender, Age, Class, Family System (FS) and Area of Living (AL) of Visually Challenged Students

Variables	*Standardised Coefficient*	*t-Value*
Gender	.557	6.580
Age	–.185	1.598
Class	–.098	0.846
FS	.096	1.174
AL	–.045	0.545
R^2	.400	

Table 2 describes that 40 per cent variation in self-esteem can be explain on the basis of the five predictors, i.e., gender, age, class, family system, and area of living, but only gender emerged as a significant predictor in explaining emotional stability of visually challenged students. Age, class, family system and area of living have no significant emergence as the predictor of emotional stability of visually challenged students.

Discussion

Table 1 shows that the five predictor variables, i.e., gender, age, class, family system and area of living, do not contribute significantly in explaining self-esteem of visually challenged students. Munford (1994) conducted a study and found no significant gender differences in the levels of self-esteem. The majority of studies found that during adolescence, females report lower self-esteem (Cairns, McWhirter, Duffy, & Barry, 1990; Chubb, Fertman, & Ross, 1997; Martinez & Dukes, 1991; Quatman & Watson, 2001) and greater depressive mood (Marcotte, Fortin, Potvin, & Papillon, 2002) in comparison to males. Some research has also shown that not only do adolescent females report lower self-esteem, but their self-esteem decreases and depressive symptoms increase over time when compared with males (e.g., Robins, Trzesniewski, Tracy, Gosling, & Potter, 2002). Peterson, Sarigiani and Kennedy (1991) indicated that blind men had more positive and realistic self-concept than blind women. Rothemburg (1997) also noted these differences and found that women scored higher on personal identity, physical, family and social self-concept and men scored higher on self satisfaction and moral self-concept. Alfered-Liro and Sigelman (1998) found that male college students fare better in the transition between secondary and tertiary education in terms of their self-concept. Male and female students start with same level of self concept, and female decline over the first 18 months of studies before starting to catch up with their male counterpart. Marsh (1990) suggests that it is possible that the female students will exhibit lower levels of self-concept than their male peers.

Kling, Hyde, Showers, and Buswell (1999) found that males scored higher on standard measure of global self-esteem than females but the difference is small. A study done by Seifert and Miller (1988) states that males judge less harshly than females, which in turn causes female performance and behaviour to be evaluated negatively which decreases their self-esteem. Marjoribanks and Mboya (2001) found that male participants had significantly higher score on perceptions of their physical, emotional stability and relations with their peers, whereas the female participants had significantly higher scores on perceptions of their music abilities.

Kaminski, Shafer, Neumann, and Ramos (2005) found that boys reported higher self-concept than girls on the physical ability and physical appearance subscales, but girls had higher self-concept than boys on the reading subscale. Cheng and Puge (1989) found that males tended to have higher self-esteem than the females. Maehr and Nicholls (1980) suggested that some gender differences in self-esteem might be due to a response bias, in that girls have been found to be more modest in self-report measures than boys. Furthermore, some research has shown that gender differences in adolescent self-esteem may be linked to gender differences in the perception of physical appearance. For example, a longitudinal study of students in the 3rd through 11th grades indicated that in elementary school, boys and girls viewed their physical appearance equally, but at the end of high school, girls' views of their physical appearance was significantly lower than those of boys (Harter, 2000). Connor, Poyrazli, Ferrer-Wreder, and Grahame (2004) found that age is not significantly correlated with self-esteem.

Findings on age as a predictor of self-esteem have been inconsistent. Various longitudinal studies (Bergman & Scott, 2001; Block & Robins, 1993; Chubb, Fertman, & Ross, 1997; Wade, Thompson, Tashakkori, & Valente, 1989) and a cross-sectional study (Mullis & Chapman, 2000) found that self-esteem levels remained constant with increased age, and therefore increased age was not a significant predictor of self-esteem. Other longitudinal researches indicated a gradual increase in self-esteem across adolescence (Hirsch & Rapkin, 1987; O'Malley & Bachman, 1983; Wigfield, Eccles, Mac Iver, Reuman & Midgley, 1991). Conversely, Robins and his colleagues (2002) provided a comprehensive picture of age differences in self-esteem from age nine to 90 years. Self-esteem levels were high in childhood, dropped during adolescent, rose gradually throughout adulthood, and declined sharply in old age.

Hoppe (1995) reported in his study that the correlation between self-esteem and age was 0.6. He found that age determines self-esteem. Old people tend to have a higher level of self-esteem than do younger people. Some research indicated that self-concept remains stable over the lifespan. While others indicate that it can increase with experience. It is therefore possible that older students will exhibit higher level of self-concept than the younger students (Marsh, 1990). When children were younger they rarely thought about self-esteem and what it meant or even how it could possibly shape them as a person. As they got older, self-esteem gradually became important and determined how they viewed themselves especially when their peers started to have an influence or impact on their life. Age, as a predictor of self-esteem, has yielded varied findings.

Table 2 shows that only gender emerged as a significant predictor in explaining emotional stability of visually challenged students. Age, class, family system and area of living do not play any significant role in describing the self-esteem of visually challenged students. Arora (2002) found in his study that visually challenged girls are emotionally less stable than boys. Gramer and Imaike (2002) proposed that females are less emotionally stable than males. Budaev (1999) found that females have higher agreeableness and lower emotional stability than males. Gramer and Imaike (2002) also reported that men's emotions are stable than women. Brabner (2003) indicated that females tend towards affection and sadness, and males incline to pride. Affection and sadness are categorised negative emotions (low emotional stability); pride is classified low agreeableness (Gomez, 2006). In addition, Wolfradt and Dalbert (2003) found that females tend to neuroticism (low emotional stability). Aleem (2005) reported that male students are more emotionally stable than female students.

Conclusion

The results indicate that out of the above demographic variables only gender predicts significantly emotional stability of visually challenged students. None of the demographic variables predict self-esteem of visually challenged students. However, the size of the sample, the environmental set-up and some other variables may be playing some role for such findings.

References

Aleem, S. (2005), Emotional Stability among College Youth, *Journal of the Indian Academy of Applied Psychology, 31,* 100-102

Alfered-Liro, C., & Sigelman, C. K. (1998), Sex differences in self-concept and symptoms of depression during the transition to college, *Journal of Youth and Adolescence, 27,* 219-244.

Arora, S. (2002). *Personality and Creativity of Blind,* New Delhi, Anmol Publications,

Bergman, M. M., & Scott, J. (2001), Young adolescents' well-being and health-risk behaviours: Gender and socioeconomic differences, *Journal of Adolescence, 24,* 183-197.

Blascovich, J., & Tomaka, J. (1991), Measures of self-esteem, In J. P. Robinson, P. R. Shaver, & L. S. Wrightsman (Eds.), *Measures of Personality and Social Psychological Attitudes,* Volume 1.San Diego, CA: Academic press.

Block, J., & Robins, R. W. (1993), A longitudinal study of consistency and change in self-esteem from early adolescence to early adulthood, *Child Development, 64,* 909-923.

Brebner, J. (2003), Gender and emotions, *Personality and Individual Differences, 34,* 387-394.

Budaev, S. V. (1999), Sex differences in the big five personality factors: Testing an evolutionary hypothesis, *Personality and Individual Differences, 26,* 801-813.

Cairns, E., McWhirter, L., Duffy, U., & Barry, R. (1990), The stability of self-concept in late adolescence: Gender and situational effects, *Personality and Individual Differences, 11,* 937-944.

Cheng, Hsiao-Ping., & Puge, R. C. (1989), The relationship among sex, academic performance, anxiety and self-esteem of junior high school in Taiwan, *Journal of Multicultural Counselling and Development, 17,* 123-133.

Chubb, N. H., Fertman, C. L., & Ross, J. L. (1997), Adolescent self-esteem and locus of control: A longitudinal study of gender and age differences, *Adolescence, 32,* 113-129.

Connor, J. M., Poyrazli, S., Ferrer-Wreder, L., & Grahame, K.M. (2004), The relation of age, gender, ethnicity, and risk behaviours to self-esteem among students in nonmainstream schools, *Adolescence, 39,* 457-473.

Gomez, R. (2006), Gender invariance of the five factor model of personality among adolescents: A mean and covariance structure analysis approach, *Personality and Individual Differences, 41*, 755-765.

Gore, M. S. (1968), *Urbanisation and Family Change*. Bombay, Popular Prakashan.

Gramer, K.M., & Imaike, E. (2002), Personality blood type and the five-factor model, *Personality and Individual Differences, 32*, 621-626.

Harter, S. (2000), Is self-esteem only skin-deep? *Reclaiming Children and Youth, 9*, 133-138.

Hay, I., & Ashman. A.F. (2003), The development of adolescents' emotional stability and general self-concept. The interplay of parents' peers and gender, *International Journal of Disability, Development and Education, 50*, 77-91.

Hirsch, B. J., & Rapkin, B. D. (1987), The transition to junior high school: A longitudinal study of self-esteem, psychological symptomatology, school life, and social support, *Child Development, 58*, 1235-1243.

Hoppe, H. M. (1995), *The effects of self-esteem on education*, Missouri Western State College.

Kaminski, P. L., Shafer, M. E., Neumann, C. S., & Ramos, V. (2005), Self-Concept in Mexican American Girls and Boys: Validating the Self-Description Questionnaire-I, *Cultural Diversity and Ethnic Minority Psychology. 11*, 321-338.

Kling, K. C., Hyde, J. S., Showers, C. J., & Buswell, B. N. (1999), Gender differences in self-esteem: A meta analysis, *Psychological Bulletin, 125*, 470-500.

Maehr, M. L., & Nicholls, J. G. (1980), Culture and achievement motivation: A second look. In N. L. Warren (Ed.), *Studies in cross-cultural-psychology*, pp, 221-267. San Diego, CA: Academic Press.

Marcotte, D., Fortin, L., Potvin, P., & Papillon, M. (2002), Gender differences in depressive symptoms during adolescence: Role of gender-typed characteristics, self-esteem, body image, stressful life events, and pubertal status, *Journal of Behavioural and Emotional Disorders, 10*, 29-42.

Marjoribanks, K., & Mboya, M. (2001), Age and gender differences in the self-concept of South African students, *Journal of Social Psychology, 141*,148-149.

Marsh, H. W. (1990), The structure of academic self-concept. The Marsh/ Shavelson model, *Journal of Educational Psychology, 82,* 623-636.

Martinez, R., & Dukes, R. L. (1991), Ethnic and gender differences in self-esteem: *Youth & Society, 22,* 318-338.

Mullis, R. L., & Chapman, P. (2000), Age, gender, and self-esteem differences in adolescent coping style, *Journal of Social Psychology, 140,* 539-541.

Munford, M. B. (1994), Relationship of Gender, Self-Esteem, Social Class, and Racial Identity to Depression in Blacks, *Journal of Black Psychology, 20,* 157-174.

O'Malley, P. M., & Bachman, J. G. (1983), Self-esteem: Change and stability between ages 13 and 23, *Developmental Psychology,* 19, *257-268.*

Peterson, A., Sarigiani, P., & Kennedy, R. (1991), Adolescents depression; why more girls? *Youth Adolescent, 20,* 247-271.

Prasad, M. S., & Thakur, G. P. (1977), *Manual and Directions for Self-Esteem Inventory,* Agra Psychological Research Cell, Agra.

Quatman, T., & Watson, C. M. (2001), Gender differences in adolescent self-esteem: An exploration of domains, *The Journal of Genetic Psychology, 162,* 93-117.

Robins, R. W., Trzesniewski, K. H., Tracy, J. L., Gosling, S. D., & Potter, J. (2002), Global self-esteem across the lifespan, *Psychology and Aging, 17,* 423-434.

Rothemburg, D. (1997), *Supporting girls in early adolescence,* Wahington, DC: Office of Educational Research and Improvement.

Seifert, C., & Miller, C. E. (1988), Subordinates perceptions of leaders in task-performing dyads: Effects on sex of leader and subordinate, method of leader selection, and performance feedback, *Sex Roles, 19,* 13-28.

Sengupta, A., & Singh, A. K. (1985), *Manual of the Emotional Stability Test for Children,* National Psychological Corporation, Agra.

Vasuki, R., & Reddy, V. (1997), Self-esteem of single children, *Journal of Community Guidance and Research, 14,* 181-188.

Wade, T. J., Thompson, V., Tashakkori, A., & Valente, E. (1989), A longitudinal analysis of sex by race differences in predictors of adolescent self-esteem, *Personality and Individual Differences, 10,* 717-729.

Whitmore, J. R. (1981), Gifted children with handicapping conditions: A new frontier, *Exceptional Children, 48,* 106-11.

Wigfield, A., Eccles, J. S., Mac Iver, D., Reuman, D. A., & Midgley, C. (1991), Transitions during early adolescence: Changes in children's domain-specific self-perceptions and general self-esteem across the transition to junior high school, *Developmental Psychology, 27,* 552-565.

Wolfradt, U., & Dalbert, C. (2003), Personality, values and belief in a just world, *Personality and Individual Differences, 35,* 1991-1981.

10

Cognitive Behaviour Group Therapy in Mathematics Anxiety

—Ayatollah Karimi and S Venkatesan

The present study investigated whether the CBGT has any impact on mathematics anxiety of high school students. The sample consisted of 16 subjects in the experimental group and 17 subjects in the control group who had high level of Mathematics anxiety on Mathematics anxiety rating scale (MARS). After the pre-test of two groups, the intervention by CBGT was given to the experimental group in (15 sessions) for 1.5 hours – two time in a week and at the end of intervention, again the Mathematics anxiety evaluated. Analyses of data of pre- and post-test by repeated measures ANOVA has shown that CBGT was highly effective in reducing Mathematics anxiety and two subscales of this scale (test anxiety and numerical anxiety). More over with respect to gender, there is a significant difference between boys and girls in mathematics anxiety in post test of experimental group.

Keywords: Intervention, CBGT, Mathematics, Anxiety and High School Students.

Many learners experience mathematics anxiety in our schools today. Reported consequences of being anxious toward mathematics include the avoidance of mathematics and the decline in mathematics achievement. Suinn, Taylor and Edwards (1988) suggested that it affects many people and threatens both performance and participation.

This paper originally appears in the *Journal of the Indian Academy of Applied Psychology*, July 2009, Vol.35, No.2, pp. 299-304.

This kind of 'anxiety' was first detected in the late 1950s. Dreger and Aiken (1957) noticed undergraduate college students reacting emotionally to arithmetic and mathematics. Although this reaction appeared to be similar to test anxiety in general; they found that mathematics anxiety has an existence of its own. They labelled it 'number anxiety'. It is often assumed that the high level of anxiety impairs performance. A moderate amount of anxiety may actually facilitate performance. Beyond a certain degree, however, anxiety hinders performance particularly in the case of higher mental activities and conceptual process (Shemp, 1986).

Psychological literature provides a number of conceptualisations of mathematics anxiety (Rabalise, 1988). Richardson and Suinn (1972) defined mathematics anxiety in terms of its (debilitating) effect on mathematical performance. They observed that the feeling of tension and anxiety interferes with manipulation and solving of mathematical problems in a wide variety of ordinary life and academic situations. Many students who suffer from mathematics anxiety have little confidence in their ability to do mathematics and tend to take the minimum numbers of required mathematics courses, greatly limiting their career choice options (Garry, 2005). Mathematics anxiety is an outcome of low self-esteem and fear of failure. It causes problems for processing the next oncoming information as well as in using previously learned information for problem solving. Such students tend to avoid mathematics whenever or wherever possible (Daane, Judy, & Tina, 1986).

Mathematics anxiety may be a critical factor in the educational and vocational choices students make and may influence whether or not they achieve their educational or career goals (Betz, 1978). Identifying individuals suffering from mathematics anxiety and gaining a better understanding of the domains that contribute to such anxiety is a start to addressing the problem of mathematical illiteracy today. A number of studies pertaining to mathematics anxiety and attitudes towards mathematics have been conducted. But instead of working together, the majority of these studies are against each other. Results of this study can help us to understand the real scene of mathematics anxiety determine the level of effectiveness of the CBGT intervention in reducing Mathematics anxiety in a group of Iranian students.

A different teaching methodology has been used to reduce Math's anxiety. Vacc (1993) believes that a personal and process-orientated teaching method which emphasizes understanding rather than drill and practice reduces mathematics anxiety. Moreover, few studies have considered the use of psychological interventions in the treatment of mathematics anxiety. Relaxation training resulted in significantly lower mathematics anxiety and significantly higher mathematics performance (Sharp, Colthar, Hurford, & Cole, 2000). Moreover, Schneider and Nevid (1993) found that systematic desensitisation and stress management training with college students lowered math's anxiety but did not change performance on an aptitude test. Cognitive behavioural therapy (CBGT) also is an effective treatment of anxiety in the general population and in the school, and there is some indication that it may be effective for mathematics anxiety. The aim of the present study was to evaluate the effect of CBGT as a treatment in mathematics anxiety.

Method

Sample

The study was carried out on two independent groups of subjects. Participants were selected through screening of more than 400 students in the age range of 13–16 years and randomly assigned to two groups. The control group consisted of 16 subjects (eight girls and eight boys) and the experimental group also consisted of 17 subjects (nine girls and eight boys).

Measures

Mathematics Anxiety Rating Scale (MARS), developed by Alexander and Martray (1989), consisted of 25 items in two subscales. This version was designed with the belief that "Math anxiety is defined primarily by a Maths test anxiety (with 12 items) and secondarily by anxiety about executing Maths tasks or taking Maths courses (with 13 items). The correlation between scores on the 25 item of this scale and 69 items MARS Richardson and Suinn (1972) was computed 0.93 and internal consistency alpha coefficient was 0.86. For each item there are five options (1- not at all anxious, 2- not anxious, 3- slightly anxious, 4-anxious, 5-very much anxious) and the ranges of scores is between 25 and 125.

Procedure

The study was carried out in three separate but interconnected phases, viz., pre- test, intervention and post-test as described below.

Phase 1: Pre- test. In this phase Mathematics Anxiety Rating Scale (MARS) was administered to 400 students and 25 of them with high level of mathematics anxiety were selected and assigned randomly to two groups (control and experimental).

Phase 2: Intervention. This phase consisted of adapting a Cognitive Behavioural Group Therapy (CBGT) treatment manual which has proven to reduce mathematics anxiety. The CBGT therapy contains 15 sessions for 1.5 hours, two times in a week and was co-led by two doctoral level psychologists using the adapted CBGT treatment manual. Participants were given a workbook with a summary of the material presented in each session and worksheets used in sessions and for home practice assignments. All sessions were carried out each week - on Monday and Thursday in school. Intervention programme, consisted of identify negative thoughts NAT, coping with NAT, assertiveness and modelling parts (The purpose of the programme and CBGT was explained for students in three sessions, identify negative automatic thoughts (N.A.T.) and training the students on how to cope with N.A.T. has done in six sessions. Assertiveness training and modelling methods in six sessions].

Phase 3: Post-test. After five days from phase 2, MARS was administered on two groups and data has given for computing by SPSS. In this study, testing was done in a quiet atmosphere. The instruction was given clearly without any ambiguity and there was no time limit for answering the questionnaire.

Results

Table 1 presents the various domains of MA in control and experimental groups. The results of repeated measures ANOVA are described below.

Total scores: In total mathematics anxiety scores a significant decrease was observed from pre- to post-test session in the high school students irrespective of the groups (f = 36.123 p <.000). In the pretest, both groups had mean MA scores of 108.35 which had reduced to 91.45. Moreover the reduction in MA scores with

Table 1 Mean, SD, pre- and post-test scores of experimental and control groups on various domains of MA.

Group/ Gender	*Domains of mathematics anxiety*											
	Maths test and course				*Numerical task*				*Total MA scores*			
	Pre		*Post*		*Pre*		*Post*		*Pre*		*Post*	
	M	*SD*	*M*	*SD*	*M*	*SD*	*M*	*SD*	*M*	*SD*	*M*	*SD*
Experimental												
Male	87.10	6.10	55.70	6.58	19.70	4.16	13.00	3.01	106.70	9.36	68.40	10.01
Female	88.40	6.415	66.10	4.72	22.70	3.12	18.70	3.46	111.10	6.98	84.80	4.93
Total	87.75	6.129	60.90	7.718	21.20	3.90	15.85	4.308	108.90	8.35	76.60	11.39
Control												
Male	88.10	8.65	90.30	8.60	19.70	4.27	20.20	3.93	105.30	10.27	107.00	10.51
Female	87.60	6.88	82.50	10.98	22.10	3.84	22.70	3.65	110.30	7.36	105.60	13.17
Total	87.85	7.61	86.40	10.40	20.90	4.14	21.45	3.91	107.80	9.07	106.30	11.62
Male	87.60	7.04	73.00	6.42	19.70	4.19	16.60	3.098	106.00	9.61	87.70	9.342
Female	88.00	6.54	74.30	6.83	22.40	3.33	20.70	2.94	110.70	7.13	95.20	7.72
Total	87.80	6.62	73.65	6.49	21.05	3.94	18.65	3.61	108.35	8.58	91.45	9.18

respect to group was also found to be significant (f = 66.57 p <. 000). The mean values also show us that the experimental group had a reduction from 108.90 to 76.60 and the control group had a reduction from 107.80 to 106.30. In terms of percentages 81 per cent of the reduction in the scores was observed in the experimental group.

With respect to gender and gender group, there were no significant differences in pre-test of total scores. But the differences was significant in post-test of experimental group (f = 21.57 p <. 000). In the post-test mean scores of boys was 87.70 but for girls it was 95.20.

Maths test domain: As it has shown, there is a significant decrease from pre-test to post-test in math test domain, irrespective of the groups (f = 46.57 p <. 000). In the pre-test the total sample had mean 87.80 which had reduced to 73.65. The reduction of maths test domain with respect to groups also was significant (f = 77.49 p<.000). In an experimental group, the mean scores reduced from 87.75 to 60.90. But in the control group the reduction was only from 87.85 to 86.40 and it was not significant.

Moreover, with respect to gender and gender group, there was not significant differences in pre-test of maths test scores. But it was significant in the post-test of the experimental group (f = 16.471 p <. 001). In the post-test mean scores of boys was 55.70 but for girls it was 66.10.

Numerical domain: In numerical domain a significant decrease was observed from pre- to post-test sessions irrespective of the groups. (f = 4.27 p <. 05). In the pre-test the mean scores of two groups was 21.05 which had reduced to 18.65. (in this domain also the reduction in the experimental group (from 21.20 to 15.85) was significantly more than the control group (from 20.90 to 21.45). The change in the numerical domain, with respect to gender, and group and gender were all found to be non-significant.

With respect to gender and gender group, in this domain also there was not significant differences in pre-test of numerical domain. But the differences was significant in post-test of the experimental group (f = 15.382 p <. 001). In the post-test mean scores of boys was 13.00 but for girls it was 18.70.

Discussion

The objective of the study was to explore the effectiveness of CBGT therapy on mathematics anxiety among high school students in Iran. The finding revealed that CBGT was highly effective in reducing mathematics anxiety in the two domains—test and numerical anxiety. The results of this study have approved the hypothesis and are in agreement with previous studies. Hembree (1990) found that psychological treatments such as systematic desensitisation, anxiety management training and cognitive behavioural therapy (CBGT) are highly successful in reducing mathematics anxiety levels.

Other researchers also have shown that cognitive factors should be taken into account in the treatment of maths anxiety. Hadfield & Maddux (1988) found that CBGT treatments can help students to overcome their cognitive difficulties in the learning of mathematics which may be associated with an appreciable reduction in maths anxiety. Genshaft (1982) also suggests that cognitive-behavioural therapy (CBGT) is an effective first-line strategy for the treatment of mathematics anxiety.

In addition with respect to gender and gender group, there was no significant differences in total mathematics anxiety scores between boys and girls and the differences was significant only in post-test of experimental group. For that reason the results of this study doesn't support the previous studies by Frankensteini (1984); Juliet (2000), that has shown the significant difference between boys and girls in total scores of Mathematics anxiety.

References

Alexander, L., & Maratray, C. (1989), The development of an abbreviated version of the Mathematics anxiety rating scale, *Measurement and Education in counselling and development, 22,* 143-150.

Betz, N.E. (1978), Prevalence, distribution and correlates of math anxiety in college students, *Journal of counselling psychology. 25,* 441-448.

Daane, C.J., Judy, G., & Tina, S. (1986), "Mathematics Anxiety and learning styles: What is the Relationship in the Elementary pre service Teachers?" *School Science & Mathematics*: 84-88.

Dreger, R. M., & Aiken, L. R. (1957), The identification of number anxiety in a college population, *Journal of Educational Psychology, 47,* 344-351.

Frankensteini, M. (1984), Overcoming math anxiety by learning about learning, *Mathematics and computer education, 18,* 169-180.

Garry, V.S. (2005), The effect of mathematics anxiety the course and career choice of high school vocational-technical education students. PhD Thesis (Unpublished), Philadelphia: Drexel University

Genshaft, J.L. (1982), The use of cognitive behaviour therapy for reducing Math anxiety. *School Psychology Review, 11,* 32-34.

Hadfield, O.D., & Madux, C. (1988), Cognitive style and math anxiety among high school students, *Psychology in the schools, 25,* 75-83.

Hembree, R. (1990), The nature, effects and relief of Mathematics anxiety. *Journal of research in Mathematics education, 21,* 33-46.

Juliet, H. M. (2000). Gender differences in Mathematics anxiety and achievement. *Rowan University.*

Rabalise, A. (1988), Identification of math anxiety subtypes. *Thesis submitted for degree master of clinical psychology in West Virginia University.*

Richardson, F.C. & Suinn, R.M. (1972), "The Mathematics Anxiety Rating Scale: Psychometric Data". *Journal of Counselling Psychology, 19,* 39-47.

Schneider, W.J. & Nevid, J.S. (1993), Overcoming math anxiety: A comparison of stress inoculation training & systematic desensitisation, *Journal of college student's development, 34,* 283-288.

Sharp, C., Colthar, H., Hurford, D., & Cole, A. (2000), Increasing mathematical problem- solving performance through relaxation training, *Mathematics Education Research Journal, 12,* 53-61.

Shemp. R.R. (1986), "The psychology of learning", *Mathematics. Penguin: Harmondsworth.* 95-112.

Suinn, T., & Edwards (1988), The measurement of mathematics anxiety: The mathematics anxiety rating scale for adolescents - MARS-A. *Journal of Clinical Psychology, 38,* 576-580.

Vacc, N.N. (1993), Teaching and learning mathematics through classroom discussion, *Arithmetic teacher,* 227-227.

11

Intervention as an Adjunct to Drug Therapy for Childhood Depression

—R. Kannappan

The sixty female children who had the symptoms of depression such as tension, irritability, social withdrawal, weeping spells, sleep disturbance, loss of appetite, forgetting, fear of examination, low activity level, palpitation, and diminished ability to concentrate came for treatment. Children's Depression Rating Scale (CDRS) was used at the assessments of before, after, and follow-ups of the therapeutic intervention. Pharmacotherapy (PT) and combination of Pharmaco and Psychological Therapies (PPT) - Parental counselling, cognitive behavioural program - were used for 18 sessions, each 50 minutes for the improvement of depressive disorder. Statistics such as percentage, and t-test were calculated for analysing the data. Results indicate a significant reduction of depressive symptoms in female children and better maintained at follow-ups in Pharmacotherapy (PT) and combination of Pharmaco and Psychological Therapies. Further the combination of Pharmaco and Psychological Therapies is significantly more effective than the PT in treating the depressive features of children.

Keywords: Depressive disorder, Cognitive behaviour therapy, Drug therapy.

Experiences of "ups" and "downs" are common in one's life. Some people have the "downs" over two weeks causing problems

This paper originally appears in the *Journal of the Indian Academy of Applied Psychology*, January 2009, vol.35, no.1, pp. 57-62.

with everyday activities such as eating, sleeping, working, and getting along with friends. They indicate the temporary sadness, loneliness, or blues that everyone feels from time to time and lead a medical condition called depression. The condition affects a person's physical health, as well as feeling, thinking, and acting toward others. It brings about a combination of feelings and thoughts which leads one to depart from his usual behaviour. Such symptoms of depression are treatable (Johnstone, Cunningham Owens, Lawrie, Sharpe, & Freeman, 2004; Sarason, & Sarason, 2002; Kaplan, & Sadock, 1999) and it is the most common psychiatric problems in primary care (Mc Daniel, Mussleman, & Proter, 1995). This appears at an earlier age, even young children (Lash & Weissman, 1990). A new episode can occur abruptly with same symptoms or more severe symptoms (Hales, Yudofsky & Talbott, 2003). Its recurrence is most common and 6.5 per cent women and 3.3 per cent men suffer from depression each year. The illness affects all people, regardless of sex, race, ethnicity, or socioeconomic standing.

Depressed children tend to be socially withdrawn (France, Cristoff, Crimmins, & Kelly, 1983) and have minimal conversational skills, no friends and long-standing socially isolated lifestyle (France, Cristoff, Crimmins, & Kelly, 1983). Their peers do not accept depressed children as non-depressed children (Faust, Baum, & Forehand, 1998). The present study attempts to examine the remission of depressive symptoms using by the use of drug therapy and the combination of drug and psychological therapies for depressed children.

Objectives

They were (i) to use appropriate intervention strategies for the management of disorder (ii) to use psychological scales to assess disorder and (iii) to assess the qualitative changes in depressive patient after the intervention and at follow-ups.

Method

Design

Pre- and post-research designs were used for the study. The

children who had depressive features for one month came to the hospital. Anti-depressants and psychological therapies— parental counselling, cognitive behavioural programme—were given. The duration of the therapies was 18 sessions, each for 50 minutes session. Data were collected before, after and follow-ups by using the Children's Depression Rating Scale (CDRS).

Sample

Sixty female children out of 250, who had the symptoms of depressive disorder, were randomly classified into two groups, namely, Pharmacotherapy (PT) group (n=30), and combined Pharmaco and Psychological therapy (PPT) group (n=30). The former group received only drugs and the latter group received both drugs and cognitive behaviour therapy with parental counselling. The duration of the therapies was 18 sessions, each comprising 50 minutes. The follow-ups were done once in a month by using the CDRS.

A majority of them belonged to the age group of 11-12 years (53%) followed by the age group of 9-10 years (47%), and belonged to Hindu (83%) followed by Christians (13%). A majority of them were studying in 6th standard and they had moderate depression (70%). A majority of the children's father had education less than 8th standard followed by 10th standard (25%). Five per cent of the fathers had no formal education, and 15 per cent of the children had suicidal risk.

Measures

Description of the scales: Children Depression Rating Scale (CDRS), developed by Ponznanski, Cook and Carroll (1979) is a 16-item scale used to evaluate the severity of depression in children in the age group of 6 to 12 years. Each item is rated on either a 0-3 spectrum (0 = no information and 3 = most severe) except the last item which was answered by a yes or no. The total score of the CDRS consists of the sum of the items. Statistics such as percentage and t-test were calculated for analysing the data.

Pharmacological Management

Antidepressant drugs-capsules. Fluoxetine 20 mg 1-0-0 and tablet Imipramine 25 mg 0-0-1 were given to all the patients by the psychiatrists for the entire sessions to arrest the symptoms of the depressive disorder. After a couple of days, the patients found relief from the symptoms, such as pain, insomnia and loss of appetite. Later on they were relieved from all other symptoms.

Psychological Management

It was primarily a psychosocial intervention used for the parent(s) to understand the child's depressive features and related problems. The parents' point of view and of their hardship of living with the child was crucial for therapeutic intervention. Parental serious problems merged into the way for individual treatment of the parent and to modify practices that seemed to be contributing to the current difficulties. Parents deserved education in selecting treatment and management difficulties. They spent far more time with their children and powerfully assisted or impeded treatment. In therapeutic sessions, the parents learned about normal development and understood their child's adjustment and difficulties.

Initially the patient was assigned reading material on coping with depression and a weekly activity schedule (self-report) of homework assignment emphasizing on an active learning approach. Carefully selected reading materials were extremely useful to parents (Lytryn, McKnew, & Cytryn, 1996; Beck, Rush, & Shew, 1979). Parents became skilled to cope with depression and they observed the child while engaging in selected activities like reading, writing, doing homework, not refusing to do something, etc., and these observation made the parents feel good. Parents had active learning *in vivo* exposure such as doing homework, checking progress and assisting her, giving feedback, teaching and enhancing coping skills, encouraging play and parental communication training. They increased the frequency of parental positive reinforcements, reducing punishment and teaching social skills which had been used to improve behaviour associated with depression.

Cognitive behavioural programme: The children selectively perceived the world as harmful while overlooking evidence to the contrary. They emphasized on thinking processes and cognitive modalities to reframe, restructure and solve problems and therapy devoted to recognise and modify their distorted thoughts. Children's distortions were addressed by generating alternative ways of dealing with problematic situation. They were involved in pleasurable activities (Hughes, 1988). Besides, study skills training was taught for improving study habits and they practised skills.

Results and Discussion

Table 1 : Mean, SD, and t-value for the scores of the Children's Depression Rating Scale (CDRS) of the two PT and PPT groups.

Groups	*Sample*	*Scale*	*Assessment*	*Mean*	*S.D*	*t-value*
PT	n=30	CDRS	Before	27.60	4.20	
PPT	n=30		Before	27.61	2.54	0.01
			Before	27.60	4.20	
PT	n=30		After	20.36	2.07	8.62 **
			Follow-up	119.24	1.84	2.24 *
			Follow-up	218.70	1.70	.46 **
PPT	n=30		Before	27.61	2.54	
			After	18.27	3.31	17.51 **
			Follow-up	116.90	2.78	.91 **
			Follow-up	216.70	2.60	2.04 *

PT-Pharmacotherapy group, and PPT- Pharmaco and psychological therapy group.

**$p < 0.01$; * $p < 0.05$

Mean and standard deviation were calculated for each of the group, i.e., the Pharmacotherapy (PT) group and the combined

Pharmaco and Psychological Therapy (PPT) group to facilitate the comparison of repeated assessments by Children's Depression Rating Scale (CDRS) (Ponznanski, Cook, & Carroll, 1979). The main analysis of the data was to determine the significance of mean difference between before and after, after and follow-up1, and after and follow-up2 assessments of each group, i.e., PT and PPT groups. Besides, these two groups were compared between after and after, after and follow-up1, and after and follow-up2 for significant differences t-test was applied in the scores of the children to determine the significant difference between before and before assessments the two groups -(PT) and (PPT), which showed no significant difference. On comparison, the PT group showed a significant difference between before and after assessments ($t = 8.62$, $p < 0.01$) and no significant difference between after and follow-up1 ($t = 2.24$, $p < 0.05$) as well as between after and follow-up2 ($t = 3.46$, $p < 0.01$). These showed that the PT group had maintenance of improvement even after two months.

Table 2: Mean, SD, and t-value for the scores of the Children's Depression Rating Scale (CDRS) of the two PT and PPT groups after intervention.

Groups	*Sample*	*Scale*	*Assessment*	*Mean*	*S.D*	*t-value*
PT	n=30	CDRS	After	20.36	2.07	
PPT	n=30		After	18.27	3.31	2.94*
PT	n=30		Follow-up1	19.24	1.84	
PPT	n=30		Follow-up1	16.90	2.78	3.90**
PT	n=30		Follow-up2	18.70	1.70	
PPT	n=30		Follow-up2	16.70	2.60	3.51**

PT-Pharmacotherapy group, and PPT- Pharmaco and Psychological Therapy group.

**$p < 0.01$; * $p < 0.05$

The PPT group was compared between before and after assessments and it had a significant difference ($t = 17.51$, $P < 0.01$) and significant difference between after and follow-up1 ($t = 2.91$, $P < 0.01$) as well as between after and follow-up2 ($t = 2.04$, $P < 0.05$).

The findings showed that the PPT group also had significant improvement of depressive disorder.

When PT and PPT groups were compared, the groups had significant differences between after and after ($t = 2.94$, $p < 0.01$), between follow-up1 and follow-up1 ($t = 3.90$, $p < 0.01$), and between follow-up2 and follow-up2 ($t = 3.51$, $p < 0.01$). The follow-ups1 of the two groups had significant difference but there was no significant difference between follow-up2 and follow-up2. The significant differences between these two groups showed that the PPT group was significantly more effective than the PT group. These findings imply that a therapist/clinician could use PPT for relieving the symptoms and making changes in the depressive patients.

The present study confirms the finding of the previous studies (Conte & Karasu, 1992; Scott, 1998; Scott, 1992; Kocsis, Frances, Voss, & Mason, 1988) for the treatment of depressive disorder by pharmacotherapy. The earlier studies (Kendell, & Panichelli-Mindel, 1995; Kovacs, Rush, Bech, & Akiskal, 1981; Simons, Murphy, Levines, & Garfield, 1996; Dobson 1989; Murphy, Simons, Wetzel, & Lustman, 1984; Blackburn, Bishop, & Glen, 1981)) support the present finding that the combined Pharmaco and Psychological Therapy (PPT) is significantly more effective in improving depressive disorder and better maintenance at the assessment of follow-ups. The findings reveal that a therapist/ clinician can use PPT for relieving the patient's symptoms and changing their pattern of coping.

Report of the Family Members

The children's emotional state of sadness changed as they had shown interest in moving freely with family members and friends. They laughed and played with others. They had not shown irritability, and were alert and energetic. There had been no impairment in social and academic areas of functioning. They managed situations successfully.

Limitation

The present study did have a control group to compare with the PT and the PPT groups as the patients needed immediate care and treatment due to their suffering of depression. The sample was limited to n= 30 focusing only on female depressed children.

Conclusion

The symptoms of the depressive disorder are arrested significantly by the two therapies, i.e. the Pharmacotherapy (PT) and the combined Pharmaco and Psychological Therapy (PPT) but the PPT is significantly more effective in treating female children. The implication of the findings is that the PPT can be used to change the depressive patients in order to relive their symptoms and change their pattern of coping.

References

Beck, A. T., Rush, A. J., & Shew, B.F. (1979), *Cognitive therapy of Depression,* New York: Guilford

Blackburn, J. M., Bishop, S., & Glen, A. M. (1981), The efficacy of cognitive therapy in depression: a treatment trail using cognitive therapy and Pharmaco-therapy, each alone and in combination, *British Journal of Psychiatry, 139,* 181-189.

Conte, H. R. & Karasu, T. B. (1992), A review of treatment of minor depression, *American Journal of Psychotherapy, 46,* 58-74.

Dobson, K. S. (1989), A Meta analysis of the efficacy of cognitive therapy for depression, *Journal of Consulting and Clinical Psychology, 57,* 414-419.

Faust, J., Baum, C.G., & Forehand, R. (1998), An examination of the association between social relationships and depression in early adolescence, *Journal of Applied Developmental Psychology, 6,* 291-297.

France, D.P., Cristoff, K.A., Crimmins, P.B., & Kelly, J.A. (1983), Social skills training for an extremely shy young adolescent: A case study, *Behaviour Therapy, 14,* 568-575.

Hales, R.E., Yudofsky, S.C., & Talbott, J.A. (2003), *Text book of psychiatry,* 3rd Ed, New Delhi: Jaypee Brothers Medical Publishers (p) Ltd.

Hughes, J.N. (1988), *Cognitive behaviour therapy with children in schools*, New York: Pergamon press.

Johnstone, E.C., Cunningham Owens, D.G., Lawrie, S.M., Sharpe, M., & Freeman, C.P.L. (2004), *Companion to psychiatric studies*, London, Churchill Livingstone.

Kaplan, H.J., & Sadock, B.J. (1999), *Concise Text Book of Clinical Psychiatry*, London: Williams and Wilkins.

Kendell, P.C., & Panichelli-Mindel, S.M. (1995), Cognitive behavioural treatment, *Journal of Abnormal Child Psychology, 23,107.*

Kocsis, J. H., Frances, A. H., Voss, C., & Mason, B.J. (1988), Imipramine treatment for chronic depression, *Archives of General Psychictry*, 35, 253-57.

Kovacs, M., Rush, A.J., Bech, A.T., & Akiskal, H.S. (1981), Depressed outpatient treatment with cognitive therapy or pharmacotherapy: a one year follow-up, *Archives of General Psychiatry, 38*, 33-39.

Lasch, K., & Weissman, M. M. (1990), Birth cohort changes in the rate of mania, *Psychiatry Research, 33*, 31-37.

Lytryn, McKnew, D.H., & Cytryn, L.W. (1996), *Growing up sad: childhood depression and its treatment*, New York: WW Norton.

Mc Daniel J.S., Mussleman, D.L. & Proter, M.R. (1995), Depression in patients with cancer, Achieves *of general psychiatry, 52*, 89-99.

Murphy, G. E., Simons, A D., Wetzel, R. D., & Lustman, P.J. (1984), Cognitive therapy and pharmacotherapy, singly and together in the treatment of depressive disorder, *Archives of General Psychiatry, 41*, 33-41.

Ponznanski, E.O., Cook, S.C., & Carroll, B. J. (1979), A depression rating scale for children, *Paediatrics, 64*, 442-50.

Ponznanski, E.O., Cook, S.C. & Carroll, B. J. (1983), Use of the children's depression's depression rating scale in an inpatient psychiatric population, *Journal of Clinical Psychiatry, 44*, 200-03.

Sarason, I.G., & Sarason, B.R. (2002), *Abnormal psychology; The Problem of Maladaptive Behaviour*, 3rd Ed, Delhi: Pearson Education.

Scott, J. (1992), Chronic depression: can cognitive therapy succeed when other treatment fail? *Behavioural Psychotherapy, 20*, 25-36.

Scott, J. (1998), Cognitive therapy for depression, *German Journal of Psychiatry*. *1*, 15-30.

Simons, A. D., Murphy, G. E., Levines, J. E., & Garfield, S.L. (1996), Cognitive therapy and pharmacotherapy or depression: sustained improvement over a year, *Psychiatric Annals, 43*, 43-49.

12

Alienation and Emotional Intelligence of Adolescents with Internalising Symptoms

—Anupama Shrivastava and Anjana Mukhopadhyay

Present investigation has assessed the levels of alienation and emotional intelligence of adolescents with internalising symptoms. Multi-dimensional Assessment of Personality (form-t) test was used as screening tool in the first phase. Total 510 adolescents in the age group of 14-18 years studying in various schools of Varanasi were screened for internalising symptoms. Those who scored above the cut-off point were identified as the "affected group" having internalizing symptoms showing more than 6 symptoms, the sample showing 4-5 symptoms as "moderate group", sample showing 1-2 symptoms as "mild group" and adolescents without internalising symptoms were identified as "normal group". Student Alienation Scale and Mangal Emotional Intelligence Inventory were then administered on all the four groups each having 15 subjects for the final study. The result obtained from ANOVA revealed that the affected group is significantly alienated and emotionally immature in awareness and management compared to their comparative normal group.

Keywords: Alienation, Emotional Intelligence, Internalising Symptoms.

'Adolescence' in human life is a stage when rapid change takes place. Bower (1982) opined that children with emotional problems

---

This paper originally appears in the *Journal of the Indian Academy of Applied Psychology*, January 2009, Vol.35, No.1, pp. 99-106.

may manifest behaviour patterns, like inability to learn without adequate explanation, inability to build or maintain satisfactory interpersonal relation, immature types of behaviour, general pervasive mood of happiness or depression etc. A type of emotional and behavioural problem that is often misunderstood and frequently overlooked is internalising disorders (Merrell, 2001). Internalising disorders are common in adolescents. It is considered to be constituted of over controlled behaviours, denoting that the individual suffering from the symptoms often attempts to maintain a maladaptive high level of control of his or her emotions, behaviours and thought processes. The term internalising indicates that problems like depression, loneliness, guilt-feeling, anxiety, social withdrawal, suicidal behaviour etc. are developed and maintained to a great extent within the individual.

Hodges, Boivin, Vitaro, and Bukowski (1999) observed symptoms such as being worried and fearful, working alone, or appearing sad or close to tears to be common internalising symptoms among the adolescents who are deprived of close friends and victimised by being bullied from peers. It has been observed that incidents of parental hostility, rejection and neglect are more frequent than acceptance, love and trust in the history of adolescents with behaviour problem (Scott, Scott, & McCobe, 1991). Marchand and Hock (2003) identified avoidance behaviour of parents to be as significant predictors of children's internalising behaviours. Muris, Merckelbach, Moulaert, and Gadet (2000) argued that the more frequently children reported anxiety disorder, the more often they reported emotional problems. Both anxiety and depression can lead to other serious problem such as an elevated risk of suicide and self-harm (Lewinson, Rohde, & Seeley, 1994), and, if they attempt self- medication, they may expose themselves at an increased risk of substance misuse (Kushner, Sher, & Beitman, 1990).

In the recent years emotions are increasingly being viewed as signals that provide information, direct attention and facilitate attainment of goals and are seen as organising processes that enable people to think and behave adaptively. Knowing one's emotions, managing emotions, motivating oneself, persistence and social deftness are the key components of emotional intelligence (EI). The EI involves the ability to monitor one's own and other's emotions, to discriminate among them, and to use the information to guide one's thinking and actions (Mayer & Salovey, 1993). So, emotional intelligence refers to an ability to recognise the meaning of emotions and their relationships to solve problems on the basis of them (Mayer, Caruso, & Salovey, 2000). Conversely, emotional dysregulation (for instance, the inability to manage hostile or negative emotion) can lead to work and relationship difficulties and is associated with clinical problems such as anxiety and mood disorders (Gross, 1998).

Alienation usually refers to describe a social state in which conditions of normlessness or the breakdown of social rules is identifiable. The phenomena of alienation are slow and systematic at the affective level. Psychologists observe that alienation grows as soon as the feeling of significant others in comparison to one's own feelings of insignificance emerge. Alienation as a psychosocial phenomenon is growing among students of almost all levels of educational institutions. It has been reported that the outcome of alienated behaviour is so serious and harmful that it not only obstruct the growth of the institution but damages the personality of the individual also. Wilkerson, Protinsky, Maxwell, and Lentner (1982) investigated the relationship between ego identity and alienation and concluded that when scores on the ego identity increase; there was a moderate decrease in alienation. The result implies that young people who have successfully resolved the Eriksonian crises and conflicts will feel a sense of mastery over their environment and control of their destiny.

Available literature suggests that many adolescents who are in need of psychiatric assessment do not receive appropriate help as their problems remain unnoticed or unrecognised by adults including teachers and their parents. It is important to detect and then resolve their problems which may lead to other serious problems, such as, suicide, substance abuse, alcoholism and other severe emotional disorders. The present study is aimed to detect adolescents having internalising symptoms and examine the level of alienation and emotional intelligence

Objectives

1. To screen out adolescents with high internalising symptoms on the basis of crucial personality dimensions and designates the clinical and non clinical sample into four categories, i.e., affected, moderate, mild and normal.
2. To explore various dimensions of alienation and emotional intelligence of the adolescent with internalising symptoms.

Hypotheses

1. Adolescents with internalising symptoms will report of low emotional intelligence compared to their normal counterparts.
2. Adolescents with internalising symptoms will report of high alienation compared to their normal counterparts.

Method

Sample

The initial sample comprised 510 students (both males and females) studying in various schools of Varanasi. The age range of the subjects was 14-18 years studying in IX to XII standards. The screening tool, i.e., Multi-dimensional Assessment of Personality (form-t) test was administered to select the adolescents with internalising symptoms. The final target sample selected out of the group and divided into four sub groups each having 15 students, i.e., affected, moderate, mild and normal.

Tools

Multidimensional Assessment of Personality (Form-Teenagers) (MAP, FORM-T) (PSY-COM Services, 1996). It consists of 147 items, which cover 20 normal personality dimensions, e.g., adaptability, academic achievement, boldness, competition, creativity, enthusiasm, excitability, general ability, guilt proneness, individualism, innovation, leadership, maturity, mental health, morality, self-control, sensitivity, self-sufficiency, social warmth and tension. Each item has three choices.

Student Alienation Scale (SAS) (Sharma, 1988). It contains 54 items and measures the alienation tendency of student in five areas: powerlessness, isolation, self-estrangement, meaninglessness and normlessness.

Mangal Emotional Intelligence Inventory (MEII) (Mangal & Mangal, 2004). It consists of 100 items in four areas, i.e., intra-personal awareness (own emotions), inter-personal awareness (others emotions), intra-personal management (own emotions) and inter-personal management (others emotions). Twenty-five items each for the four areas are to be answered as 'Yes' or 'No'.

Procedure

The sample was screened out on the basis of low scores in adaptability, boldness, enthusiasm, maturity, mental health, morality, self-control, self-sufficiency, social-warmth and high scores in guilt proneness, individualism, sensitivity and tension of MAP(form-t). Subjects projecting symptoms 6+, 4-5, 1-2 and 0 were defined as affected, moderate, mild and normal respectively. SAS and MEII were administered on these groups.

Results

Table 1 : Mean, SD and F-values of affected, moderate, mild and normal adolescents on various dimensions of emotional intelligence.

Dimensions		*Affected*	*Moderate*	*Mild*	*Normal*	*F*
		N=15	*N=15*	*N=15*	*N=15*	
Intra-personal	Mean	15.34	20.06	65.66	72.83	31.25**
awareness	SD	21.38	16.37	23.80	20.78	
Inter-personal	Mean	19.12	31.76	70.26	82.03	40.47**
awareness	SD	17.99	24.51	15.05	13.86	
Intra-personal	Mean	20.87	29.16	54.33	77.27	22.46**
management	SD	24.97	21.16	19.14	17.52	
Inter-personal	Mean	18.30	29.63	62.06	77.90	25.13**
management	SD	16.27	26.74	21.65	19.67	
Total	Mean	11.61	21.37	68.11	83.89	70.48**
	SD	17.24	18.36	14.00	14.93	

$p<.01$**

Table 2: Summary mean differences for Duncan's post hoc test of affected, moderate, mild and normal groups for emotional intelligence

Dimensions	*Affected/ moderate*	*Affected/ Mild*	*Affected/ normal (mean differences)*	*Moderate/ mild*	*Moderate/ normal*	*mild normal*
Intra-personal awareness	4.27	50.32 **	57.49 **	45.60 **	52.77 **	7.17
Inter-personal awareness	12.64	51.14 **	62.91 **	38.50 **	50.27 **	11.77
Intra-personal management	8.29	33.46 **	56.40 **	25.17 **	48.11 **	22.94 **
Inter-personal management	11.33	43.76 **	59.60 **	32.43 **	48.27 **	15.84
Total emotional intelligence	9.76	56.50 **	72.28 **	46.74 **	62.52 **	15.78 **

**p <.01

Table 1 shows the mean scores and SDs of emotional intelligence of adolescents of each group. Highly significant F values reveal that means of emotional intelligence scores of the affected adolescents as well as moderate and mild adolescents are distinctly low in all the subscales such as intra-personal awareness (own emotions), inter-personal awareness (others emotions), intra-personal management (own emotions) and inter-personal management (others emotions), compared to their normal counterparts. The first hypothesis thus stands accepted. The mean scores ranging from M 11.66 to M 20.87 for the affected group are showing significantly low mean scores compared to moderate, mild and normal groups for all the dimensions of emotional intelligence. The moderate group shows significantly low emotional intelligence than mild and normal groups in all the dimensions (Table 2). The mild group however shows significantly low interpersonal management and total emotional intelligence than normal group.

Table 3: Mean, SD and F-values of affected, moderate, mild and normal adolescents on different dimensions of alienation.

Dimensions		*Affected*	*Moderate*	*Mild*	*Normal*	*F*
		N=15	N=15	N=15	N=15	
Powerlessness	Mean	74.31	70.30	37.36	22.51	19.35**
	SD	18.85	22.08	24.97	22.59	
Isolation	Mean	63.98	33.67	28.86	20.59	6.22**
	SD	35.75	26.28	29.18	25.25	
Self estrangement	Mean	76.50	57.20	31.30	19.85	19.52**
	SD	25.83	21.00	20.76	21.54	
Meaninglessness	Mean	43.50	21.79	13.18	14.13	8.37**
	SD	28.33	16.64	11.62	15.23	
Normlessness	Mean	41.61	31.65	13.44	11.41	7.80**
	SD	25.96	26.33	8.75	13.75	
Total	Mean	68.05	38.23	15.84	9.02	29.85**
	SD	26.23	22.45	14.21	6.30	

**p <.01

Table 2: Summary mean differences for Duncan's post hoc test of affected, moderate, mild and normal groups for emotional intelligence

Dimensions	*Affected/ moderate*	*Affected/ Mild*	*Affected/ normal (mean differences)*	*Moderate/ mild*	*Moderate/ normal*	*mild normal*
Powerlessness	4.01	36.95**	51.08**	32.94 **	47.79 **	14.85
Isolation	30.31 **	35.12**	43.39**	4.81	13.08	8.27
Self-estrangement	19.30	45.20**	56.65**	25.90 **	37.35 **	11.45
Meaninglessness	21.71 **	30.32**	29.37**	8.61	7.66	0.95
Normlessness	9.96	28.17**	30.20**	18.21	20.24	2.03
Total alienation	29.82 **	52.21**	59.03**	22.39 **	29.21 **	6.82

$p<.01$ **

Table 3 shows that affected, moderate and mild adolescents have reported higher mean scores in the areas of powerlessness, isolation, self-estrangement, meaning-lessness and normless-ness as well as total alienation scores indicating highly alienated behaviour as compared to their normal counterparts bringing corroboration to second hypothesis. The mean scores ranging from M 41.61 to M 74.31 for the affected group show significantly high alienation compared to moderate, mild and normal groups for all the sub-areas assessed. The moderate group however show significantly high powerlessness, self-estrangement and total alienation scores compared to mild and normal groups (Table 4). Adolescents with mild internalising symptoms however do not show significant difference between means in any of the alienation sub-areas measured by the scale.

Discussion

The results revealed that out of the clinically screened internalised adolescents, the affected and moderate groups have significantly low emotional intelligence and high alienation scores as compared to their normal counterparts. Mild group of internalised adolescents however are not significantly different from normals though Merrell (2001) suggests that the term "internalising" indicates that these problems are developed, maintained, experienced, and exhibited largely within the individual. It is frequently underreported mostly because they are often difficult to observe directly and as a result they have sometimes been described as a secret illness (Reynolds, 1992).

Very high alienation refers to the state of individual being non-involved and apathetic, feeling isolated, bewildered, and without hope. It is understood that outcome of alienated behaviour is so serious and harmful that it damages the personality of the individual. It has been observed that when scores on the ego identity scale increases a moderate decrease in alienation is reported simultaneously (Wilkerson et al., 1982). Studies have established that social anxiety and depression are related to social isolation (Nangle, Erdley, Newman, Mason, & Carpenter, 2003; Boivin, Hymel, & Bukowski, 1995). According to problem behaviour theory, adolescents who engage in problem behaviours, such as, substance use may tend towards psychosocial unconventionality and thus may be more likely to experience alienation and impaired social functioning (Jessor, 1991; Jessor & Jessor, 1977). Further, impaired social functioning may substantially worsen outcomes associated with psychiatric illness (Greene, Biederman, Faraone, Ouellette, Penn, & Griffine, 1996). The present investigation has reported that affected adolescents are significantly higher in powerlessness, isolation, self-estrangement, meaninglessness and normlessness as well as total alienation score than the normal adolescents. Studies indicate that an inability to cope with the curriculum for which the adolescent fails to achieve personal understanding leads to normlessness, which in turn leads to isolation in the classroom, a further lack of success, feelings of powerlessness and ultimately to alienation (Carlson, 1995). Feelings of powerlessness and hopelessness are again common indicators of depression.

Emotions influence the process of perception and reactions towards life which in turn determines how content and successful a person may be considered. Anyone can achieve emotional intelligence by attaining his goals and managing negative emotions. If unmanaged, negative emotions take control of life. Goleman (1995) suggests that concept of EI helps us to understand why people with high IQ's don't always do as well in life as those with more modest intellectual ability. Deficits in emotional intelligence can create serious problems in our relationship and influence our physical health. Similarly, if children misidentify their own feelings or those of others, they are likely to generate maladaptive solutions to a problem, regardless of their intellectual capabilities. With regard to emotional intelligence, in the area of inter-personal awareness and inter- personal awareness the affected adolescents were reported to be significantly lower than the normal adolescents. The same results were found in the area of intra-personal management and inter-personal management, where affected adolescents reported significantly lower capacity as compared to normal adolescents. The inability to manage negative emotions can lead to work and relationship difficulties and is associated with clinical problems such as anxiety and mood disorders (Gross, 1998). In support of the present result studies have indicated that children with emotional problems may manifest behaviour patterns like inability to build or maintain satisfactory interpersonal relation (Bower, 1992), psychosocial difficulties such as impaired personal relationships (Puig-Antich, Kaufman, Ryan, Williamson, Dahl, Lukens, Todak, Ambrosini, Rabinovich, & Nelson, 1993; Flament, Cohen, Choquet, Jeammet, & Ledoux, 2001), inability to identify emotional states (Zeman, Shipman, & Suveg, 2002), difficulty in interacting with peers or problems with expressing their wishes and needs to others (Achanbach, 1997).

Literature validates this finding. And also reveals that the level of alienation and emotional intelligence are the contributory factors for developing internalising symptoms. Concluding comments thus may be drawn that adolescents with internalising symptoms showing high alienated behaviour and low emotional intelligence are affected in their overall personality and their day-to-day functioning is also interfered.

It is very important to identify and recognise those who develop such symptoms at its initial stage and identify such characteristics which possibly trigger them and provide them appropriate help in the right direction. This attempt serves to handle or resolve the problems of such adolescents in an effort to find values and goals to guide their life. The study thus derives a conclusion that the children who have developed internalising symptoms are required to introduce psychological intervention for their depth in understanding, growth and overall health.

References

Achenbach, T.M. (1997), *Empirically based assessment of child and adolescent psychopathology,* Thousand Oaks, CA: Sage.

Boivin, M., Hymel, S., & Bukowski, W. (1995), The roles of social withdrawal, peer rejection, and victimisation by peers in predicting loneliness and depressed mood in childhood, *Development and Psychopathology, 7,* 765-785.

Bower, E.M. (1982), Defining emotional disturbance: Public policy and research, *Psychology in Schools, 19,* 55-60.

Carlson, T.B. (1995), We hate gym: Student alienation from physical education, *Journal of Teaching in Physical Education, 14,* 467-477.

Flament, M.F., Cohen, D., Choquet, M., Jeammet, P., & Ledoux, S. (2001). Phenomenology, psychosocial correlates, and treatment seeking in major depression and dysthymia of adolescence, *Journal of the American Academy of Child and Adolescent Psychiatry, 40,* 1070–1078.

Goleman, D. (1995), *Emotional intelligence,* New York: Bantan Books.

Greene, R., Biederman, J., Faraone, S., Ouellette, C., Penn, C., & Griffine, S. (1996), Toward a new psychometric definition of social disability in children with attention-deficit hyperactivity disorder, *Journal of the American Academy of Child and Adolescent Psychiatry, 35,* 571 –578.

Gross, J.J. (1998), The emerging field of emotion regulation: An integrative review, *Review of General Psychology, 2,* 271-299.

Hodges, E.V.E., Boivin, M., Vitaro, F., & Bukowski, W.M. (1999), The power of friendship: Protection against an escalating cycle of peer victimisation, *Developmental Psychology, 35,* 94-101.

Jessor, R. (1991), Risk behaviour in adolescence: A psychosocial framework for understanding and action, *Journal of Adolescent Health, 12,* 597–605.

Jessor, R., & Jessor, S. (1977), *Problem behaviour and psychosocial development: A longitudinal study of youth,* New York: Academic.

Kushner, M., Sher, K., & Beitman, B. (1990), Behaviour and emotional problems among Jamaican children and adolescents: An epidemiological survey of parent, teacher and self-reports for age 6-18 yrs, *International Journal of Intercultural Relations, 23,* 727-751.

Lewinson, P.M., Rohde, P., & Seeley, J.R. (1994), Psychosocial risk factors for future adolescent suicide attempts, *Journal of Consulting and Clinical Psychology, 62,* 297-305.

Mangal, S.K., & Mangal, S. (2004), *Manual for Mangal emotional intelligence inventory,* Agra: National Psychological Corporation.

Marchand, J.F., & Hock, E. (2003), Mother's and father's depressive symptoms and conflict-resolution strategies in the marriage and children's externalising and internalising behaviours, *Journal of Genetic Psychology, 164,* 227-239.

Mayer, J.D., Caruso, D., & Salovey, P. (2000), Emotional intelligence meets traditional standard for an intelligence, *Intelligence, 27,* 267-298.

Mayer, J.D., & Salovey, P. (1993), The intelligence of emotional intelligence, *Intelligence, 17,* 433-442.

Merrell, K.W. (2001), *Helping students overcome depression and anxiety: A practical guide,* New York: Guilford.

Muris, P., Merckelbach, H., Moulaert, V., & Gadet, B. (2000), Associations of symptoms of anxiety disorders and self-reported behaviour problems in normal children, *Psychological Reports, 86,* 157-162.

Nangle, D., Erdley, C., Newman, J., Mason, C., & Carpenter, E. (2003), Popularity, friendship quantity, and friendship quality: Interactive influences on children's loneliness and depression, *Journal of Clinical Child and Adolescent Psychology, 32,* 546-555.

PSY-COM Services (1996), *Handbook for multi-dimensional assessment of personality (form-t),* New Delhi: Psy-Com Services.

Puig-Antich, J., Kaufman, J., Ryan, N.D., Williamson, D.E., Dahl, R.E., Lukens, E., Todak, G., Ambrosini, P., Rabinovich, H., & Nelson, B. (1993), The psychosocial functioning and family environment of depressed adolescents, *Journal of the American Academy of Child and Adolescent Psychiatry, 32,* 244–253.

Reynolds, W.M. (Ed.) (1992), *Internalising disorders in children and adolescents.* New York: Wiley.

Scott, W.A., Scott, R., & McCobe, M. (1991), Family relationships and childrens personality: A cross cultural, cross source comparison, *British Journal of Social Psychology, 30,* 1-20.

Sharma, R.R. (1988), *Manual for student alienation scale,* Agra: National Psychological Corporation.

Wilkerson, J., Protinsky, H.O., Maxwell, J.W., & Lentner, M. (1982), Alienation and ego identity in adolescents, *Adolescence, 17,* 133-139.

Zeman, J., Shipman, K., & Suveg, C. (2002), Anger and sadness regulation: Predictions to internalising and externalising symptoms in children, *Journal of Clinical Child and Adolescent Psychology, 31,* 393-398.

13

Academic Stress and Adjustment among High School Students

—*Akbar Hussain, Ashutosh Kumar* and *Abid Husain*

Present study was undertaken to examine the level of academic stress and overall adjustment among Public and Government high school students and also to see relationship between the two variables (academic stress and adjustment). For that purpose 100 students of class IX were selected randomly from two different schools out of which 50 were taken from Public and the remaining 50 were taken from Government school Sinha and Sinha scale for measuring academic stress was used to see the magnitude of stress and Sinha and Singh Adjustment Inventory for school students was used to examine level of adjustment among the students. Results indicated that magnitude of academic stress was significantly higher among the Public school students where as Government school students were significantly better in terms of their level of adjustment. However, inverse but significant relationships between academic stress and adjustment were found for both the group of students and for each type of school.

Keywords: Academic Stress, Adjustment.

Stress and anxiety in children and teenagers are just as prevalent as in adults. Negligence of parents, high expectations in academic or other performances, abused childhood, growing up tensions and demand for familial responsibility, etc. are the main causes

This paper originally appears in the *Journal of the Indian Academy of Applied Psychology,* April 2008, Vol.34, Special Issue, pp. 70-73.

of childhood and teen stress. Parents who are not emotionally available for their children or lack positive coping mechanisms themselves, often spur stress in their offspring.

Stressed children show signs of emotional disabilities, aggressive behaviour, shyness, social phobia and often lack interest in otherwise enjoyable activities. In a study Dawood (1995) found that students stress affects their academic performance. He further showed that the most frequently mentioned stressor by students was school and fear-related stressors. Many teenagers tend to become non-conformist and fall prey to teenage depression in response to a variety of growing-up anxieties. However, stress-induced fears and anxiety in children adversely affects children's performances at various levels. Hodge (1996) investigated that prevalence of stress was found particularly among those students who were by their nature prone to anxiety.

Tung and Chahal (2005) examined relationship between stress and adjustment and found no significical causal relationship between stress and the adjustment. However the direction of the results implied that the level of adjustment influences the number of stressful events and the amount of stress experienced by them.

Each day we are faced with new situations that demand decisions, involve change in both our internal state and our external environment. The process of adjustment involves a person's attempt to cope with the master and transcend such challenges. This working definition provides a starting point for understanding adjustment. However, adjustments are not always definite. Neither is it right or wrong nor do they necessarily have clear starting points or endings. This combination of questions can make the concept of adjustment difficult to grasp. According to Aggrawal (2004) the adjustment of adolescent very much depends on the fulfilment of their significant specific needs that consist of physical needs, emotional needs, social needs, intellectual needs, moral needs and vocational needs. It may be helpful, therefore, to devote a little more space to two important qualities of adjustment.

First, it is a process that involves continuous changes and the second people develop consistent pattern of adjustment to these constant changes. Students make many transitions during their years of schooling: from home to school, middle to high school, and high school to college or work. These transitions are usually major events in the lives of students and parents. The stresses created by these transitions can be minimised when the new environment is responsive to each particular age group. This digest presents a brief overview of some of the issues involved in the transition from elementary to middle school and provide suggestions for transition programmes and activities. In a study Isakson et al (1999) employed a short-term longitudinal design to assess the adjustment of adolescents as they mode from junior high to high school and found that the adolescents did experience significant changes during the initial transition into high school that were related to sense of school membership, perceived support from parents was also related to adolescents adjustment to the transition.

Keeping in view the growing problem of academic stress among school students the study was undertaken to examine the level of academic stress among high school students and its probable impact on the overall adjustment among them. The hypotheses are as follows:

1. Level of academic stress among public school students will be significantly higher than the government school students.
2. Adjustment level of public school students will be significantly different from government school students.
3. There will be inverse relationship between academic stress and overall adjustment among high school students.

Method

Sample

Altogether 100 class IX male students were randomly selected from two different types of schools of Delhi. Out of 100 students, 50 were taken from public school and the remaining 50 were taken from government school.

Tools

For assessing academic stress of students a 30-item composite scale for assessing academic stress among students consisting of force choice type answer was used. The scale was developed by Sinha et al. (2003) and was published in the *Journal of Mental Health and Human Behaviour*. Similarly, for examining the level of adjustment of the subjects, a 60-item scale developed by Sinha and Singh (1971) was administered on the sample. The scale consist of items in three different areas, namely, emotional, social and educational with 20 items each. The answer is forced choice and higher score indicating poor adjustment.

Results and Discussion

Table 1: Mean, SD and t value of academic stress and adjustment scores of students of public (n=50) and private schools (n=50)

Group	*Mean*	*SD*	*t Value*
Public School	22.44	4.89	3.60 **
Govt. School	16.90	4.12	
Public School	26.74	4.89	2.97 **
Govt. School	78.08	4.12	

Table 2

Correlation between academic stress and adjustment scores for the students of two types of schools.

Group Students	*Public School School students*	*Govt.*
R between academic stress and adjustment	-.54**	-.49**

From the results given in Table 1, it appeared that the magnitude of academic stress among high school students was found to be high, particularly among the public school students as the mean scores were 22.44 and 16.90 respectively for public school and private school students. The difference in terms of academic stress between the two groups of students was also statistically tested by computing t ratio which was also found significant (t=3.61). Thus it can be said that the academic load and school environment of public school might be contributing towards enhancement of stress among students. Similar results were also obtained by

Bohannon (2000). He investigated the impact of school related stressors on public school students and found significant correlations among them. Hence it can be safely said that public school students suffer from higher level of stress related to their academics. Thus hypothesis presuming higher level of academic stress among public school students was found to be proved.

Results given in Table 2, indicating the level of overall adjustment among school students revealed that the overall adjustment of public school students was poorer than the government school students as the mean scores for adjustment were found to be 26.24 and 18.08 respectively for the public and private school students. The difference between the two groups of students with regard to their level of adjustment was also statistically tested and found significant (t=2.97). Isakson (1999) have also found that adolescents experienced significant changes during the initial transition into high school that were related to sense of school membership etc. and was also related to adolescents' adjustment to the transition. Hence adjustment among public school students was found to be poor probably because they suffer from high level of academic stress. Thus hypothesis of significant difference between the two groups of students with regard to their level of adjustment was also found to be proved.

It was apparent from the results presented in Table 2 that academic stress and overall adjustment of students were inversely related to each other for both public school as well as private school students as (r = -.54 and -.49 respectively). The association between the two variables was so strong that it was also found statistically significant for both the groups. On the basis of results it can be said that academic stress adversely affects overall adjustment of students. Hence the hypothesis presuming inverse relationship between academic stress and level of adjustment among school students was found to be proved as the two variables found to be affecting each other adversely.

Thus, it may be concluded that private school students by and large suffer from higher level of academic stress than their government school counterparts. Not only that, but their level of adjustment was also much poorer than the government school students. As far as relationship between the academic stress and adjustment is concerned inverse relationships between the two variables were found for each group of sample which that indicated the academic stress not only impedes academic performance but also adjustment to a greater extent.

References

Aggrawal, J.C. (2004), *Psychology of learning and Development,* Shipra Publication, Delhi.

Bohannon, A.P. (2000), The relationship of School related stressors to discipline referrals, attendance, grade point average and under achievement among high school students, *Dissertation Abstracts International,* 57, 1482.

Dawood, N. (1995), Stressors encountered by junior high school students and their relation to grade point average, sex and grade. Jordan, *Deanship of Academic Research,* 22, 3671-3706.

Hodge, Glenda Mae (1996), Adolescent Anxiety, distress and coping: A study of senior school students and higher school certificate examination stress, *Dissertation Abstract International, 57,* 01-14.

Isakson, K. (1999), The adjustment of adolescents during the transition into high school: A short-term longitudinal study, *Journal of Youth and Adolescence, 28,* 1-26.

Sinha, U.K. Sharma, V. and Nepal, M.K. (2003), Scale for assessing academic stress, *Journal of Mental Health and Human Behaviour,* 6, 35-42.

Sinha, A.K.P. and Singh, R.P. (1971), *Adjustment Inventory for school students,* National Psychological Corporation, Agra, India.

Tung, S. and Chahal, N. (2005), Relationship between Stress and Adjustment Adolescents females; A causal study, *Journal of Personality Study and Group Behaviour,* Amritsar, 25, 19-31.

14

Personality Patterns of Higher Secondary Boys across Different Demographic Groups

—*Manju Mehta, Prachi Maheshwari* and *V.Vineeth Kumar*

The *raison d'etre* of the study is to unravel and make a comparative study of the personality patterns of SC, ST and non–backward higher secondary boys. The prolonged social discrimination has produced an adverse impact on the development of the personality of these downtrodden, which is a severe stumbling block in providing 'social justice' and 'social equality' to the masses. By making a comparative study, the differences in personality patterns between backward and non-backward classes can be highlighted which will enable us to understand and eliminate not only the economical but also the educational, social and political backwardness of the society as a whole. For the study, on a sample of 600 rural and urban male students of XI standard from Jaipur district belonging to SC, ST & non-backward classes, the Cattell's High School Personality Questionnaire (HSPQ), Form A by Kapoor, Srivastava and Srivastava was administered. Results revealed significant differences in personality patterns among SC, ST and non-backward boys. These differences were more prominent in rural areas in comparison to urban areas.

Keywords: Personality patterns, Scheduled castes (SC), Scheduled tribes (ST), Non backward class boys.

It is well known that personality plays an important role in determining not only the behaviour of an individual but also his

This paper originally appears in the *Journal of the Indian Academy of Applied Psychology*, July 2008, Vol.34, No.2, pp.295-302.

overall success and prosperity in life. Allport (1937) has defined personality as "a dynamic organisation within the individual of those psychophysical systems that determines his unique adjustment to his environment." Interest in personality is as old as civilisation. Ancient philosophers and poets often speculated about why individuals were unique and why they differed from each other in so many ways. For ages person-situation interaction has played an important role in the development of an individual's personality. In this context not only the family environment but also the society and the culture in which the children are brought up becomes all too important.

In every culture and society children and adolescents are subjected to various kinds of pressures, both personal and social. These pressures exert great influence on the personality development of the children, which ultimately influences not only the all-round development of that particular society but also affects the future development of the country. In other words, the personality of the individual determines the nature of the society and the society in turn influences and nurtures the personality of an individual, thus, mutually reinforcing each other.

According to Cattell (1950) "the personality of an individual is that which enables us to predict what he will do in a given situation." Mischel and Shoda (1995) identified personal styles or strategies of individuals in dealing with the situations and found that these styles or strategies remain consistent over the years and they in turn, become a kind of behavioural signature of their personalities. These personality patterns or styles are determined largely by experiences of an individual, which develop within a socio-cultural world. The surroundings and the various interacting patterns that the child faces from the beginning of life determine the dynamics of personality.

Indian society and culture is unique, and has the credit of being one of the oldest civilisations of the world. It has developed a social system, which is unique in the world. The "Varna Vyavastha" of the Vedic times produced a caste division determined by birth and was an important aspect of Hindu Dharma. The divisions persisted through the ages, ossified and became rigid. With the passage of time, society as a whole not only started losing flexibility but also it obstructed the progress of the scheduled castes (SC) and scheduled tribes (ST) in innumerable ways.

In the medieval period the caste system became a tool of discrimination and oppression against the scheduled castes (SC) and scheduled tribes (ST). This tendency not only blocked the development of the society as a whole but also impeded the overall personality development of children belonging to scheduled castes (SC) and scheduled tribes (ST). Ultimately, it led to the evolution of various stereotypes pertaining to these classes, further reinforcing the prejudices about the personality characteristics of these scheduled castes (SC) and scheduled tribes (ST).

With the advent of independence many social, economical and political reforms were initiated for the upliftment of the downtrodden. A policy of 'protective discrimination' was initiated in the constitution to safeguard the interests of SCs and STs. The founders of the Indian democracy realised that without providing educational and occupational facilities, there could not be a 'dynamic democracy'. The ultimate goal of this 'protective discrimination' was to provide 'social justice' and 'social equality' to the masses so that all the factors hampering the personality development of children belonging to lower castes could be removed. But even today, it is argued that though there are regional variations, the caste system in fact represents a uniform and universal ideology when applied to an understanding of Indian society (Dirks, 2001). The socio-cultural and economic challenges that individuals of certain sections of society have and had to face over the years have made a deep impact on their personalities.

Due to this segregation from the mainstream society disadvantaged children have been found to possess negative self-image (Witty, 1967; Tannenbaum, 1969). Jiloha and Kishore (1998) found that SC and ST students are high on depressive tendency, emotional instability and low on social desirability traits. Similarly Agarwal (1975) found that SC students have more external locus of control (believing in systems, luck and chance for its accomplishments) than non-scheduled caste group. The effect of caste on intelligence has always remained a matter of controversy with studies conducted, both in support and against. Bhargava and Arora (1982) revealed that caste has significant influence on intelligence. On the other hand Sinha, Tripathi and Mishra (1982) revealed that there is no significant difference in basic intelligence of the two groups.

Vansteelandt and VanMechelen (1999) found that although personality factors play a significant role yet our behaviour in any given situation is a complex function of both our personality and situational factors in the world around us. This interactionist perspective is in vogue. Society and the culture, to which an individual belongs, always play a major role in shaping the personality. Adler (1934) postulated that human society is crucial not simply for the development of individual personality but also for the orientation of all behaviour and emotions in a person's life. He further observed that there is an urge in human nature to adopt oneself to the conditions of the social environment. Similarly, Erich Fromm (1955) also emphasized the role that society plays in structuring, shaping and limiting personality.

Deshpande (1984) found that tribal students were more emotionally stable than non-tribal students. Some other factors including parent and peer's relationship have also an impact on personality. Ara (1986) found that parent's personality was strongly associated with their adolescent children's personality. Aggressive and authoritarian parents had aggressive and authoritarian children. Similarly, neurotic parents had anxious children. Looking at all this, the present investigation was carried out to make a comparative study of personality pattern of scheduled caste (SC), scheduled tribe (ST) and non-backward boys to unravel the differences between these classes.

METHOD

Sample

The sample of 600 male students consisted of class XI. The sample was drawn from eight Hindi-medium Government Senior Secondary Schools of Jaipur District and representing both urban and rural areas. These schools were affiliated to the Board of Secondary Education, Rajasthan. Out of the 600 students, 150 were from SC category (75 urban and 75 rural), 150 were ST students (75 urban and 75 rural) and 300 from non-backward (150 urban and 150 rural) class category. The age of the students ranged between 15 and 17 years.

Tools

The personality pattern of the subjects was studied by using the Hindi version of "Cattell's High School Personality Questionnaire" (HSPQ), Form 'A', prepared by Kapoor, Srivastava and Srivastava (1980).

Procedure

The subjects were administered Cattell's High School Personality Questionnaire" (HSPQ), Form 'A', (Kapoor, Srivastava & Srivastava, 1980). in classroom setting. Further, the personality pattern or profile of subjects is seen by his scores on 14 traits of HSPQ. In order to get the raw score, the response obtained on HSPQ were scored as per manual, taking the help of stencil keys. Mean, SD and t-ratios of the scores obtained were calculated.

Results and Discussion

The results show that rural SC and rural non-backward boys differed on factors 'A', 'C' 'F', and 'H' (Tables 1 and 2) indicating that rural SC boys were more reserved, affected by feelings, sober and shy than rural non-backward boys who were more warmhearted, emotionally stable, enthusiastic, venturesome and socially bold. However urban SC and urban non-backward boys did not have much difference. They differed only on Factor 'J' (Tables 1 and 2) indicating that urban SC boys were more vigorous and zestful in their behaviour than urban non-backward boys, who were more obstructive and individualistic. When an overall comparison pertaining to SC boys is made, it is found that SC boys differed significantly from the non–backward boys on factors 'A', 'C' 'F' and 'J'. This shows that SC boys are generally more reserved, detached, affected by feelings, emotionally less stable, sober, serious, and zestful in comparison to non-backward boys, who are more outgoing, warmhearted, calm, emotionally stable, happy-go-lucky, enthusiastic and individualistic. The reason for this difference may be due to the fact that SC's are scattered and isolated, particularly in rural areas. Their condition has not improved much even after 55 years of constitutional benefits. It is presumed that constitutional safeguards like abolition of untouchability, provisions of reservation, scholarships, etc., have

Table 1 : Mean and SD of rural SC(n-75), urban SC(n-75), rural ST (n-75), urban ST(n-75), rural NBC(n-150) and urban NBC(n-150) boys on 14 factors of HSPQ

Factors	*Rural*		*Urban*		*Rural*		*Urban*		*Rural*		*Urban*	
	Mean	*SD*	*Mean*	*SD*	*Mean*	*SD*	*Mean*	*SD*	*Mean*	*SD*	*Mean*	*SD*
A (Reserved – Outgoing)	7.92	2.91	9.68	2.80	9.65	2.26	9.82	3.04	9.95	2.16	10.0	13.05
B (Less intelligent – Bright)	4.40	1.31	4.41	1.28	4.32	1.39	4.52	1.45	4.37	1.33	4.48	1.32
C (Easily upset – Emotionally Stable)	7.37	2.83	8.21	2.85	8.28	2.39	8.11	2.66	8.57	2.84	8.30	3.03
D (Phlegmatic- Excitable)	8.12	2.34	8.20	3.27	8.28	2.52	7.93	2.58	8.07	2.42	8.11	2.19
E (Obedient - Assertive)	6.77	2.99	6.93	3.14	6.24	2.78	6.84	3.04	7.15	2.78	7.13	2.83
F (Sober – Enthusiastic)	6.83	2.37	8.09	2.75	7.97	2.74	8,83	2.62	8.18	2.41	7.89	2.53
G (Expedient - Conscientious)	10.0	2.75	10.28	3.03	10.13	2.96	10.01	2.56	10.29	2.55	9.93	2.52
H (Shy - Venturesome)	6.41	2.74	8.39	3.40	7.16	3.00	7.76	2.79	7.98	2.96	7.91	2.63
I (Tough minded– Dependent)	7.36	2.96	7.29	2.61	6.96	2.59	7.33	2.89	7.43	2.62	4.47	2.62
J (Vigorous - Doubting)	7.15	2.96	6.27	2.45	7.24	2.42	7.04	2.77	7.64	2.68	7.05	2.41
Q1 (Placid - Apprehensive)	7.15	2.80	7.29	2.95	7.23	2.75	7.19	2.99	7.34	2.94	7.13	3.07
Q2 (Group Dependent Self Sufficient)	–7.27	2.46	7.17	2.78	6.52	2.61	6.71	2.65	7.23	2.14	7.09	2.22
Q3 (Undisciplined- Controlled)	10.21	2.53	10.24	2.94	10.28	3.07	9.81	2.83	10.05	2.79	10.34	2.46
Q4 (Relaxed - Tense)	7.80	2.86	6.87	2.89	7.57	2.62	7.19	2.73	7.21	2.82	6.88	2.83

SC=Scheduled caste ST= Scheduled tribe NBC=Non backward class not permeated to the rural areas *vis-à-vis* the urban areas. Resultantly, the personality of rural SC boys are still characterised by introvert tendencies and attitudes such as shyness, reserve nature, affected by feelings, etc., that makes them socially inhibited. Their inability to take initiative in dealing with the social environment causes a sense of low esteem and inferiority, which poses a serious threat to their path of upliftment.

Table 2: t ratio among rural SC, urban SC, rural ST, urban ST, rural NBC and urban NBC boys on 14 factors of HSPQ

Factors	*t-ratio*					
A (Reserved – Outgoing)	5.88**	0.78	0.94	0.42	4.07**	0.31
B (Less intelligent – Bright)	0.39	0.36	0.80	0.21	0.36	0.48
C (Easily upset–emotionally stable)	2.99**	0.21	0.77	0.47	2.12*	0.24
D (Phlegmatic- Excitable)	0.14	0.19	0.59	0.42	0.40	0.55
E (Obedient - Assertive)	0.94	0.47	2.32*	0.70	1.13	0.18
F (Sober – Enthusiastic)	3.98**	0.56	0.58	2.04*	2.74**	1.21
G (Expedient - Conscientious)	0.77	0.91	0.40	0.22	0.29	0.58
H (Shy - Venturesome)	3.83**	1.15	1.96*	0.40	1.59	1.23
I (Tough minded–Dependent)	0.17	0.49	1.26	0.37	0.88	0.09
J (Vigorous - Doubting)	1.26	2.28*	1.08	0.02	0.21	1.81
Q1 (Placid - Apprehensive)	0.47	0.39	0.28	0.14	0.18	0.22
Q2 (Group Dependent – Self Sufficient)	0.10	0.25	2.19*	1.13	1.80	1.05
Q3 (Undisciplined- Controlled)	0.63	0.27	0.42	1.44	0.14	0.92
Q4 (Relaxed - Tense)	1.48	0.03	0.94	0.78	0.51	0.70

*p<.05 **p<.001

Results further revealed that rural ST and rural non-backward boys differed on factors 'E', 'H' and 'Q2' (Tables 1 and 2) indicating that rural ST boys are more obedient, socially dependent, shy, restrained and timid than rural non-backward boys who are generally more dominant, self-sufficient, venturesome, socially bold and uninhibited, whereas, urban ST and non-backward boys differed only on factor 'F' (Tables 1 and 2) showing that urban ST boys were more enthusiastic, impulsive, lively and happy-go-lucky than urban non-backward boys who were rather sober, prudent and serious. However, no other significant difference in personality patterns was found between urban ST and urban non-backward boys. Overall, ST and non-backward boys differed significantly on factors 'E' and 'Q2'. Schedule tribe boys were found to be more obedient, mild, conforming, socially group-dependent and a sound follower than non-backward boys, who were rather more assertive, independent, aggressive, stubborn, self-sufficient and resourceful.

The existent differences in the rural areas may be accounted to the progressive social changes taking place within the rural community have not been able to break the rigid social structure of ancient times. But contrary to this, urban ST boys are at par with urban non-backward boys except for factor 'F'. It seems that urban SC boys have been able to gel well with the prevalent practices and learnt to strive against the odds by bearing an 'easy-going' personality. Mehta (1996) in her study on ST boys mainly 'Meenas', argued that they may have developed 'easy going personality' due to the new reservation policy in education and employment sector which may have made them perceive that they can achieve their goals without much hazard. Attainment of vocational goals seem easy to them, therefore they have developed 'easy going personalities' in comparison to non-backward boys who are rather very serious, particularly in urban areas.

The results of comparison between rural SC and rural ST boys revealed that, they differed on factors 'A', 'C' and 'F' (Tables 1 and 2) revealing that rural SC boys are more reserved, detached, sober, prudent, serious, affected by feelings, emotionally less stable and changeable than rural ST boys who were rather more outgoing, warmhearted, emotionally stable, calm, reality facing and enthusiastic. However, no significant difference was found between urban SC and urban ST boys (Tables 1 and 2) on any of the fourteen personality traits. Overall, SC and ST boys were found to have significant difference on factors 'A', 'F' and 'Q2' (Tables 3 and 4). SC boys were found to be more reserved, detached, cool, sober, prudent, serious, self-sufficient and resourceful in comparison to ST boys, who were found to be more outgoing, warmhearted, participating, lively, enthusiastic and socially group-dependent.

Table 3: Mean and SD of scheduled caste, scheduled tribe and non backward class on 14 factors of HSPQ

Factors	*SCn=150*		*STn=150*		*NBCn=300*	
	Mean	*SD*	*Mean*	*SD*	*Mean*	*SD*
A (Reserved – Outgoing)	8.80	2.98	9.74	2.67	9.98	2.64
B (Less intelligent – Bright)	4.40	1.30	4.42	1.42	4.48	1.32
C (Easily upset – Emotionally Stable)	7.79	2.86	8.19	2.52	8.43	2.94
D (Phlegmatic- Excitable)	8.16	2.83	8.11	2.55	8.09	2.83
E (Obedient - Assertive)	6.85	3.06	6.54	2.92	7.14	2.80
F (Sober – Enthusiastic)	7.46	2.64	8.30	2.69	8.03	2.47
G (Expedient - Conscientious)	10.14	2.89	10.07	2.76	10.11	2.54
H (Shy - Venturesome)	7.40	2.23	7.46	2.65	7.95	2.80
I (Tough minded –Dependent)	7.33	2.79	7.15	2.74	7.45	2.61
J (Vigorous - Doubting)	6.71	2.74	7.14	2.63	7.34	2.56
Q1 (Placid Apprehensive)	7.22	2.86	7.21	2.87	7.23	3.00
Q2 (Group Dependent – Self Sufficient)	7.22	2.85	6.61	2.63	7.16	2.18
Q3 (Undisciplined- Controlled)	10.23	2.73	10.05	2.95	10.40	2.63
Q4 (Relaxed - Tense)	7.33	2.90	7.38	2.67	7.04	2.82

SC=Scheduled caste ST= Scheduled tribe NBC=Non backward class

The comparison reveals that SC boys are more prone to depressive tendency and emotional instability which makes them low on social desirability and adaptability traits than the ST boys, particularly in the rural areas. This may be reflection of the arduous prejudices engraved in the hearts of the upper classes due to which they face a fear of rejection such that, they may be driven out of the village for their petty voices against the majority villagers. Coupled with it, they feel hesitant in standing up for their rights enshrined to them under the Indian constitution and are unable to get benefited by the special provisions provided to them. ST boys on the other hand may face lesser anxiety due to stronger group cohesion and greater social support within their nomadic community.

Table 4: t ratio among scheduled caste, scheduled tribe and non backward class on 14 factors of HSPQ

Factors	*t-ratio*		
	SC vs NBC	*ST vs NBC*	*SC vs ST*
A (Reserved – Outgoing)	4.26 **	0.89	2.88 **
B (Less intelligent – Bright)	0.53	0.42	2.08
C (Easily upset – Emotionally Stable)	2.21 *	0.87	1.28
D (Phlegmatic- Excitable)	0.24	0.05	0.17
E (Obedient - Assertive)	0.99	2.11 *	0.91
F (Sober – Enthusiastic)	2.27 *	1.05	2.73 **
G (Expedient - Conscientious)	0.11	0.14	0.20
H (Shy - Venturesome)	1.85	1.72	0.17
I (Tough minded –Dependent)	0.46	1.14	0.56
J Vigorous - Doubting)	2.43 *	0.79	1.40
Q1 (Placid - Apprehensive)	0.05	0.09	0.04
Q2 (Group Dependent – Self Sufficient)	0.26	2.34 *	2.01 *
Q3 (Undisciplined- Controlled)	0.64	1.28	0.55
Q4 (Relaxed - Tense)	1.02	1.21	0.14

* $p<0.05$ ** $p<0.01$

In urban areas there is not much difference between ST and SC because of the rapid pace of progressive social changes, which could be due to exposure to media, benefits of reservation policy or closed interaction between different communities, wheareas SC and ST boys in rural areas were found to be having more personality problems. This can be due to many socio-economic factors which are adversely affecting the psyche of socially disadvantaged backward caste boys, such as poverty (Jabbi & Rajyalaksmi, 2001), parental illiteracy (Dreze & Kingdon, 2001), social customs prevalent in villages (Sainath, 1996) on day-to-day basis. Due to these factors, they lack the inner resources needed to tolerate or reduce anxiety aroused by everyday life events. So they perceive themselves as inadequate and unworthy and develop a sense of helplessness and inferiority that in turn adversely affect the self-efficacy. However, in urban areas the differences among SC, ST and non-backward boys are lesser as compared to rural areas because of the fact that progressive social changes are not at such a rapid pace in rural areas as compared to urban areas.

It seems that in rural areas the caste system has its roots embedded deep inside the social structure, which prevents social changes. Hence, educational, occupational, political and other reforms initiated for the upliftment of the downtrodden should have more emphasis on rural areas taking into consideration the underlying psychological difference and needs of individual.

Conclusions

The findings indicate that differences in personality patterns are present among SC, ST and non-backward boys but they are more prominent in rural areas than in urban areas. So a concentrated effort needs to be taken for the overall development of SC and ST boys particularly in rural areas. Not only should the teachers in rural schools be trained to take care of each individual but also the curriculum should be designed in a manner that the leadership qualities in each individual can be nurtured so that the overall development of personality can take place.

References

Adler, A. (1956), *The individual psychology of Alfred Adler*, Eds. and Trans by John Linton. New York: G.P.Putnam.

Agarwal, Y.P. (1975), *A study of locus of control and general intelligence among Scheduled caste and Non- Scheduled castes students*, UGC Project. Kurukshetra University: Kurukshetra.

Allport, G.W. (1937), *The personality: A psychological interpretation*. New York: Holt

Ara, N. (1986), *Parent's personality, child-rearing attitudes and their children's personality - An interconnectional study*, Unpublished doctoral dissertation, Bhagalpur University: Bhagalpur.

Bhargava, M., & Arora, S. (1982), Personality traits as a function of prolonged deprivation, *Indian Journal of Clinical Psychology, 8*,161-171.

Cattell, R.B. (1950), *Personality: A systematic theoretical and factual study, New* York: McGraw Hill.

Deshpande, M.B. (1984), *An analytical study of cognitive, affective development and scholastic achievement of tribal secondary school students*, Unpublished doctoral dissertation, Nagpur University: Nagpur.

Dreze, J., & Kingdon, G.G. (2001), 'School participation in rural India', *Review of Development Economics, 5*, 1-24.

Dirks, N. B. (2001), *Castes of mind: Colonialism and the making of modern India*, NJ: Princeton University Press.

Fromm, E. (1955), *The sane society*, New York: Rhinehart.

Jabbi, M. K., & C. Rajyalakshmi (2001), 'Education of marginalised social groups in Bihar.' In: A. Vaidyanathan and P. R. Gopinathan Nair (eds.), *Elementary education in rural India: A grassroots view, strategy for human development in India – Volume 2*, New Delhi: Sage Publications, 395-410.

Jiloha, R.C. & Kishore, J. (1998), Socio-demography, personality profile and academic performance of various categories of medical students, *Indian Journal of Psychiatry, 40, 231-239.*

Kapoor, S.D., Srivastava, S.S., & Srivastava, G.N.P. (1980), *Junior senior high school personality questionnaire (Hindi edition)*, New Delhi, Psycho Centre.

Mehta, M. (1996), *Motivation, education and social environment*, Jaipur: Print Well.

Mischel, W., & Shoda, Y. (1995), A cognitive-affective system theory of personality: Reconceptualising situations, dispositions, dynamics and invariance in personality structure, *Psychological Review, 102,* 246-248.

Sainath, P. (1996), *Everybody loves a good drought: Stories from India's poorest districts*, New Delhi: Penguin.

Sinha, D., & Tripathi, R.C., & Mishra, G. (1982), *Deprivation: Its social roots and psychological consequences*, New Delhi: Concept.

Tannenbaum, A.J. (1969), Some non-intellectual concomitants of social deprivation. *Israel Annuals of Psychiatry and Retarded Disciplines, 7,* 9-31.

Vansteelandt, K., & VanMechelen, I. (1999), Individual differences in situation-behaviour profiles: A triple typology model, *Journal of Personality and Social Psychology, 75,* 751-765.

Witty, P.A. (1967), *The educational retarded and disadvantaged-In sixty six year of education (part-I)*, Chicago, Illinois: National Society for the Study of Education.

15

Relationship between Shyness and Guidancc Needs among Adolescents

—*Lancy D'Souza, Gururaj B Urs* and *Jayaraju R*

This study is an attempt to find out the extent of shyness and related guidance needs if any among adolescent students. A total of 260 high school students (131 male and 129 female) served as the subjects for the present study. To assess shyness, Crozier's shyness inventory and to assess guidance needs, inventory developed by Grewal on guidance needs inventory were employed. Results revealed that shyness had a direct relationship with two areas of guidance needs-social and educational, and total guidance needs and as the shyness levels increased, guidance needs were also increased. Shyness did not influence the guidance needs in the areas-physical, psychological, and in vocational areas. Male and female adolescents also did not differ significantly in their guidance needs. Treatment aspects of shyness have been delineated.

Keywords: Shyness, Guidance Needs, Adolescents, Educational and Vocational Needs.

Shyness is a form of excessive self-focus, a preoccupation with one's thoughts, feelings and physical reactions. Shyness may vary from mild social awkwardness to totally inhibiting social phobia. It may be chronic and dispositional, serving as a personality trait that is central in one's self-definition. Situational shyness involves

This paper originally appears in the *Journal of the Indian Academy of Applied Psychology*, July 2008, Vol.34, No.2, pp. 317-322.

experiencing the symptoms of shyness in specific social performance situations but not incorporating it into one's self-concept. The reactions for shyness can occur at any or all of the following levels: cognitive, affective, physiological and behavioural, and may be triggered by a wide variety of arousal cues. (Henderson & Zimbardo, 1996).

The percentage of adults in the United States reporting that they are chronically shy, such that it presents a problem in their lives, had been reported at 40 per cent ± 3 per cent, since the early 1970's. Recent research indicates that the percentage of self-reported shyness has escalated gradually in the last decade to nearly 50 per cent (48.7% ± 2%). The National Co-morbidity Survey in 1994 revealed a lifetime prevalence of social phobia of 13.3 per cent, making it the third most prevalent psychiatric disorder. The comparison of the two disparate results suggests that the proportion of the population suffering from chronic, even debilitating, shyness is not reflected in the numbers of people who visit anxiety disorders clinics. The recent estimate in Mysore and surrounding areas of south India was that 26.2 per cent of the children showed high levels of shyness, followed by 36.6% per cent moderate and remaining 37.3 per cent of the children showed low levels of shyness (Natesha & D'Souza, 2007). Most referrals to shyness clinics meet criteria for generalised social phobia, and many meet criteria for avoidant personality disorder. Chronically shy individuals frequently have obsessive and/ or paranoid tendencies.

Research in the United States typically indicates that shyness is the highest among Asian Americans and the lowest among Jewish Americans. This difference prompted efforts to assess shyness across diverse cultures. Using culturally sensitive adaptations of the Stanford Shyness Inventory, colleagues in eight countries administered the inventory to groups of 18- to 21- year olds, usually in college or work settings. The overall pattern of results indicates a universality of shyness since a large proportion of participants in all cultures reported experiencing shyness to a considerable degree- from a low of 31 per cent in Israel to a high of 57 per cent in Japan and 55 per cent in Taiwan. In Mexico,

Germany, India and New Foundland, shyness was more similar to the 40 per cent U.S. statistic (Henderson & Zimbardo, 1996).

A common observation in most of the shyness research is that the consequences of shyness are deeply troubling. Shyness leads to higher levels of anxiety (D'Souza, 2003), decreased levels of happiness (Sreeshakumar, D'Souza & Nagalakshmi, 2007), neurotic tendency and lower academic performance (D'Souza, Urs & James, 2000), lowered performance in physical education students (D'Souza, Singh, Basavarajappa, 1999), lowered self-esteem and decreased self concept (D'Souza, 2005; D'Souza, Urs & Ramaswamy, 2003), increased fear reactions (D'Souza, Gowda & Gowda, 2006) and social and emotional maladjustment (D'Souza & Urs, 2001). Some other studies revealed that young adults with high shyness may be at risk for Parkinson's disease later in life. A degree of shyness is normal whenever social expectations are new or ambiguous. Shyness begins to emerge as a problem if it becomes not merely situational but dispositional, so that the child is labelled as shy.

From the preceding discussion it is evident that high shyness leads to problems in various areas of life in adolescents and they definitely need guidance in various areas. In the present study an attempt is made to find out about the guidance needs of the adolescents, specially those with high shyness. It is hypothesized that adolescents with high shyness require specific guidance in certain areas.

Method

Sample

High school students studying in classes VIII, IX and X were selected for the present study. Of the total 260 students included in the study 131 were boys and remaining 129 were girls. They were studying in three high schools of Mysore city—Hardwicke High school, Cauvery High school and Maharaja's Pre-university college. Stratified Random sampling technique was used to select the sample. The sample involved students studying in both Kannada and English medium. Their age varied from 12 to 18 years. The sample involved students studying in both Kannada and English medium.

Instruments

Shyness questionnaire

It was developed by Crozier (1995) of University's College of Cardiff. It consists of 26 items and requires the subject to indicate his/her response by ticking "YES" "NO" OR "DON'T KNOW". The items of the questionnaire are based on situations or interactions like performing in front of the class, being made fun of, being told off, having one's photograph taken, and novel situations involving teachers, school-friends interaction and so on. Of the 26 items, shyness is indicated by a 'Yes' response for 21 items and a 'No' response for five items. The negative items are 9, 10, 15, 16 and 23. Item analysis of the scale using SPSS programme resulted in Cronbach's alpha coefficient of 0.817.

Guidance needs Inventory (GNI)

GNI is an instrument is developed by Grewal (1982), which can be used to identify the type and strength of guidance needs of an individual student in five areas, namely, physical, social, psychological, educational and vocational. This inventory consists of 65 items and requires the subject to answer, one of the options-highly true, mostly true, quite true, least true and not true. GNI requires about half an hour for answering 65 items. All the need items are in the form of positive statements. The test-retest reliability was estimated to be 0.82. Construct validity was established through method of selection and classification of items.

Results

Table 1 presents the mean guidance needs scores in areas, namely, physical, social, psychological, educational and vocational, of students with different levels of shyness and gender with the results of MANOVA.

Only in two areas as well as in total guidance needs, F values revealed significant differences among subjects having different shyness levels. In the case of social needs ($F=3.336$; $P<.037$), it was observed that as the shyness levels increased, guidance needs also

Table 1 : Mean scores of male and female students in different shyness levels for different guidance needs along with results of MANOVA

Shyness levels	Gender	Guidance needs											
		Physical		Social		Psychological		Educational		Vocational		Total	
		Mean	S.D	Mean	S.D	Mean	S.D	Mean	S.D	Mean	S.D	Mean	S.D
High	Male	8.09	3.88	15.09	8.70	12.00	7.38	15.06	9.56	7.73	6.14	57.97	26.07
	Female	9.91	4.68	16.78	6.84	13.34	6.79	13.47	8.34	5.81	4.28	59.31	22.69
	Total	8.98	4.35	15.92	7.83	12.66	7.07	14.28	8.95	6.78	5.35	58.63	24.29
Medium	Male	7.41	3.86	16.06	6.82	13.99	6.88	17.94	12.08	7.26	5.11	62.66	22.48
	Female	8.46	3.74	16.85	7.65	14.03	7.90	16.75	12.45	8.11	5.48	64.19	24.73
	Total	7.90	3.83	16.43	7.21	14.01	7.36	17.38	12.23	7.66	5.29	63.38	23.51
Low	Male	8.10	3.98	21.20	5.98	11.70	5.46	22.30	9.86	8.80	2.90	72.10	16.11
	Female	8.89	4.99	19.33	9.33	16.83	5.53	21.78	12.48	9.00	5.11	75.83	29.35
	Total	8.61	4.60	20.00	8.22	15.00	5.96	21.96	11.42	8.93	4.39	74.50	25.15
Overall	Male	7.63	3.86	16.21	7.38	13.31	6.93	17.55	11.41	7.50	5.25	62.20	23.14
	Female	8.88	4.18	17.18	7.70	14.25	7.38	16.64	11.76	7.67	5.24	64.60	25.23

(Contd...)

(Contd...)

Total	8.25	4.06	16.69	7.54	13.78	7.16	17.10	11.57	7.58	5.23	63.39	24.19
F (Shyness Levels)	F=1.689;		F=3.336;		F=0.909;		F=4.408;		F=1.643;		F=3.765;	
	P=.187(NS)		P=.037 (S)		P=.404 (NS)		P=.013 (S)		P=.195 (NS)		P=.024 (S)	
F (Gender)	F=3.412;		F=0.028;		F=3.454;		F=0.346;		F=0.113;		F=0.314;	
	P=.066 (NS)		P=.868 (NS)		P=.064 (NS)		P=.557 (NS)		P=.737 (NS)		P=.576 (NS)	
F [Interaction (Shyness levels x Gender)]	F=0.253;		F=0.520;		F=1.466;		F=0.021;		F=1.647;		F=0.026;	
	P=.777 (NS)		P=.595 (NS)		P=.233 (NS)		P=.980 (NS)		P=.195 (NS)		P=.974 (NS)	

Note: F-Fishers value: P-Probability: HS-Highly significant; S-Significant: NS-Non-significant increased linearly and significantly. Adolescents with high, medium and low levels of shyness had mean guidance needs scores of 15.92, 16.43 and 20.00 respectively. In educational guidance needs scores (F=4.408; P<.013), we find that as the shyness levels increased, guidance needs also increased linearly and significantly. The mean educational guidance needs scores for adolescents with high, medium and low levels of shyness are 14.28, 17.38 and 21.96 respectively. In total guidance needs also the same trend was observed, where, as the shyness levels increased, guidance needs also increased linearly and significantly (H=3.765; P<.024). The total guidance needs scores for adolescents with high, medium and low levels of shyness were 58.63, 63.38 and 74.50 respectively. In rest of the guidance needs like physical, psychological, and in vocational areas no significant differences were observed between adolescents with different levels of shyness.

Male and female adolescents did not differ significantly in all the areas of guidance needs as all the obtained F values were found to be non-significant. In other words male and female adolescents had equal guidance needs scores in physical, social, psychological, educational, vocational and total guidance needs.

All the interaction effects between shyness levels and gender were found to be non-significant, as all the obtained F values for interactions failed to reach significance level criterion. In other words, the pattern of guidance needs in all the areas and total guidance needs was the same for male and female adolescents irrespective of the shyness level they had.

Discussion

The main findings of the present study are:

1. Shyness had a direct relationship with two areas of guidance needs—social and educational and total guidance needs and as the shyness levels increased, guidance needs were also increased.
2. Shyness did not influence the guidance needs in the areas—physical, psychological, and in vocational areas.

3. Male and female adolescents also did not differ significantly in their guidance needs.

From the results it is evident that shy adolescents require guidance needs in social and educational areas and in total guidance. Shyness experts vary in their views about whether childhood shyness leads to mental health problems later. However, the practical and emotional problems caused by shyness are apparent. As a practical matter, shy children obtain less practice of social skills and develop fewer friends. They tend to avoid activities, such as sports, drama, and debate that would put them in the limelight. Shy children and adolescents tend to be perceived as shy, unfriendly and untalented, and they tend to feel lonely and have low self-esteem (Jones & Carpenter, 1986) and a higher than average level of gastrointestinal problems (Chung & Evans, 2000). Shy children tend to become anxious teens and shy adults tend to have smaller social networks and to feel less satisfied than others with their social support networks (Jones & Carpenter, 1986).

The use of video games, CD-ROM games, web surfing, and other computer-related marvels all interfere with the time required seeking out direct contact with others for fun and friendship. Increasingly, social time is being replaced with the anonymous exchange of information within an externally imposed medium that effectively promotes shyness in young people. While some shy children may benefit from using the anonymity and structural control features of cyberspace, the danger is that for many others virtual online reality may become a substitute for the reality of close human relationships. Many parents are concerned because their young children prefer "chat time" on their computers more than actually talking face to face with other children, so these children may not socialise as much in the homes of neighbours and friends.

One powerful source is the nature of the emotional bond parents forge with their children in the earliest years of life. According to psychologists, children whose parenting was such that it gave rise to an insecure attachment are more likely to end up shy. Children form attachments to their caregivers from the routine experiences of care, feeding and caressing. When caretaking is inconsistent and unreliable, parents fail to satisfy the child's need for security, affection and comfort, resulting in insecure bonds. As the first relationship, attachment becomes the blueprint for all later relationships. This may affect the academic career of subjects; further, they need guidance in educational field too.

Psychologists may apply procedures such as videotaping the child speaking at school (e.g., with only a parent present) and having the child/adolescent to view the tapes related to programmes overcoming shyness daily before going to school. Cognitive therapies aimed at treating shyness were found to be very effective than traditional therapies (Shariatnia & D'Souza, 2007). Some physicians will prescribe a selective serotonin reuptake inhibitor like Prozac for cases of severe shyness characterized as selective mutism or social anxiety disorder, but medication of children should be a last resort because of the unknowns about long-term side effects.

References

Chung, J. Y., & Evans, M. A. (2000), Shyness and symptoms of illness in young children, *Canadian Journal of Behavioural Science*, 32, 49-57.

Crozier, W.R. (1995), Shyness and Self esteem, *British Journal of Educational Psychology*, 65, 85-95.

D'Souza, L. (2003), Influence of Shyness on Anxiety and Academic achievement in High school students, *Pakistan Journal of Psychological Research*, 18, 3-4, 109-118.

D'Souza, L. (2005), Shyness/Social Phobia: Influence on self-concept and academic achievement in High school students. Suggested remedial measures, *Artha – a Journal of social sciences*. 4 (1), 23-29.

D'Souza, L., & Urs. G. .B. (2001). Effect of shyness on the adjustment of high school students, *Pakistan Journal of Psychological Research*, 16, 3-4, 85-94.

D'Souza, L., Singh, M. & Basavarajappa (1999). Influence of shyness on performance, personality and intelligence of students of physical education, *Psychological Studies*, 44, 92-94.

D'Souza, L., Urs, G.B., & James, M.S. (2000). Assessment of shyness: Its influence on the personality and academic achievement of High school students, *Indian Journal of Clinical Psychology*, 27, 286-289.

D'Souza, L., Urs. G. B., & Ramaswamy C. (2003), Relationship of self-esteem with shyness, personality and academic achievement in high-school students. *Artha- a Journal of social sciences*, 1, 228-234.

D'Souza, L., Gowda, H.M. R & Gowda, D.K.S. (2006), Relationship between shyness and fear among High school students. *Pakistan Journal of Psychological Research*, 21, 3-4, 53-60.

Grewal, J.S. (1982), *Questionnaire and manual for guidance needs inventory*. Agra: National Psychological Corporation.

Henderson, L & Sambaed, P. (1996), *Encyclopedia of mental Health*. San Diego: Academic Press

Jones, W. J., & Carpenter, B. N. (1986), Shyness, social behaviour, and relationships. In Jones, W; H., Cheek, J. M., & Briggs, S. R. (Eds.), *Shyness: perspectives on research and treatment* (pp. 227-238). New York: Plenum.

Natesha, N. & D'Souza, L. (2007), Prevalence of shyness among children: a developmental perspective of age and gender, *Asian Journal of Development Matters*, 1, 55-60

Shariatnia, K. & D'Souza, L. (2007), Effectiveness of Cognitive Behaviour Group therapy on shyness among Adolescent in Iran. *Psychological Studies*, 52, 372-376.

Sreeshakumar, H Y., D'Souza, L & Nagalakshmi, K, (2007), Relationship between shyness and happiness among high school students. *Psychological Studies*, 52, 120-122.

16

Creating Opportunities for Improving Problem- solving Skills in Infants with Developmental Delays

—M. Madhavi Latha

The study lays emphasis on improving problem solving skills in children with developmental delays by designing a model called as Problem solving Interactive model. The model was tested on 45 children with developmental delays. The efficacy of the Problem Solving Interactive Model (PSIM) was determined from Mental Age (MA), Mental Development Index (MDI) and Deviation Mental Quotient (DMeQ) derived from Bayleys Scale of Infant Development. The pre and post test differences on all the intervention outcome indicators were highly significant in experimental group MA (t=5.70), MDI (t=4.099), Dmeq (t=2.64) and Battery of Problem Solving Tasks (t=27.93), indicating the efficacy of the Problem Solving Interactive Model. The variations in intervention outcomes with respect to chronological age of infants and toddlers with developmental delays showed that children in age group of 24-33 months showed the highest rate of gain of 0.99 in experimental group and 0.76 in control group. Lowest rate of gain of 0.77 and 0.24 in experimental and control group was seen in children from 4-13 months chronological age. These variations in intervention outcomes indicate the need to plan and implement specialised early interventions targeting specific child characteristics.

The day-to-day activities of children involve finding strategies to solve the problems that they encounter. So, the basic requirements

This paper originally appears in the *Journal of the Indian Academy of Applied Psychology*, January 2008, Vol.34, No.1, pp. 101-106.

of problem solving – goals, obstacles, strategies for overcoming obstacles and evaluation of results – appear as early as infancy. Children's problem solving is marked by flexibility and opportunism from an early age, but their performances are limited by the strategies they have access to, resources available for problem solving, their ability to manage the process of solving problems, and the social contexts in which problems are presented and vanquished (DeLoache, Miller & Pierroutsakos, 1998). These problems involve people, as solution strategies and as obstacles for attaining a goal. The development of problem solving can be characterised as a process of overcoming cognitive limitations to make problem solving more reliable, systematic, and efficient ((DeLoache., et al., 1998). This leads to developmental changes in problem-solving skills in children. But children with cognitive delays engage in concrete strategic behaviour leading to poor performance. According to Vygotsky (1978), one of the reasons for concrete and rigid problem-solving nature of retarded children is that their environment is deficit in modelling effective strategies for a variety of problem solving situations.

The utility of Triarchic theory in understanding problem solving performance in mentally retarded has been attributed probably due to inferior use of all three information processing components (Sternberg, 1984). The inferior use of meta-components lead to three scenarios: the inadequate choice of which performance component and what knowledge acquisition component to use on a particular task, faulty coordination of controlled and automatic problem-solving strategies, and making corrections mid-stream.

Evidence from studies of children with cognitive delays or mental retardation report that they appear to be persistent on challenging tasks as other children with similar mental age during the infant and toddler period (Hauser-Cram, 2001; MacTurk., Vietze, McCarthy, McQuinston, & Yarrow, 1985; Ruskin, Mundy, Kasari, & Sigman, 1994). Robert White (1959) maintained that as children come to perceive their action as producing effects on the environment, they develop a sense of efficacy, accompanied by feeling of pleasure. He further proposed that this sense of efficacy leads to iterative series of transactions between the child and the environment that result in increasingly competent behaviour. Thus, the learning process is facilitated by the participation of young children with developmental delays, which helps in cognitive growth. Problem solving is an important "functional" cognitive skill that results in important achievement for infants and toddlers.

According to Shari & Siegler (1994), "It is not that social phenomena are being investigated that is new in the study of children's problem solving. What is new is the increasingly widespread realisation of how deeply the social world is implicated in the development of problem solving, a broadened vision of what the development of problem solving entails, and a growing commitment to explicating the mechanisms through which cognitive and social processes jointly contribute to children's developing ability to solve problems."

It is against this background that the present study lays emphasis on improving problem solving skills in children with developmental delays by designing and implementing the intervention model called Problem-solving Interactive model. Apart from determining the efficacy of the model the study will also focus on studying intervention outcomes with respect to chronological age of infants and toddlers. The interaction between the programme features and child characteristics provides a research framework for evaluating and understanding the mechanisms through which interventions operate (Guralnick, 2000). It is this issue of specificity that ultimately informs practice. Therefore, the intervention outcomes with respect to age of the child were also studied.

Objectives

1. To improve problem solving skills in children with developmental delays by designing a model called Problem-solving Interactive Model (PSIM).
2. To determine the efficacy of PSIM.
3. Assess the intervention outcomes with specific reference to chronological age of infants and toddlers.

Method

Sample

The sample comprised 45 children in experimental and 30 children in control group with developmental delays in the age range of four to 33 months. The children attending early intervention services at National Institute for the Mentally Handicapped, Secunderabad were selected for the purpose of the study. Only children with borderline to mild developmental delays for whom the severity of developmental delay was determined by administering the Developmental Screening Tool (DST) by Bharath Raj (1993) were included in the sample. The other criteria for inclusion in the sample was children showing variation with respect to chronological age, children of mothers with higher secondary education and children staying with their parents residing in twin cities of Hyderabad and Secunderabad.

Tools

Development Screening Tool (DST): As standardised by Bharath Raj (1993), the DST was administered by the psychologist to determine the level of developmental delay in the child.

Bayley's Scale of Infant Development (BSID)—As an outcome measure, the BSID was used to assess the intervention gains. The mental scale of the BSID was used for all the subjects. The research form of Bayley scale (1961) of Infant Development (BSID) as used in Baroda studies consisted of two sections: the motor development scales and the mental development scales. Both the scales are point scales and express the child's performance in terms of number of items passed by the child. These numbers are further expressed as motor age, mental age and DMoQs (deviation motor quotient) and DmeQs (deviation mental quotients). For the present study only mental development scale was taken. The mental scale consists of 163 items, covering different expressions of mental growth.

Battery of Problem Solving Tasks (BPST): The researcher developed and validated assessment-linked intervention, which has been designated as Battery of Problem Solving Tasks (BPST): It consists of 30 problem-solving tasks. The selected tasks on BPST address higher mental processes specifically for enhancing problem-solving skills. The tasks were constructed as familiar domains of content that are most commonly confronted by infants and toddlers in day-to-day activities. The tasks were constructed as per Piagets sensorimotor stages where purposeful problem-solving /means ends behaviour is an important functional cognitive skill. The process comprises testing, teaching and retesting. The change occurring between the initial testing and retesting reflects the individual's cognitive and structural modifiability. The theory of structural cognitive modifiability and mediated learning experience of Feureistein, Jensen, Kaniel, & Tzuriel (1987), as an approach to dynamic assessment formed the basis for the designing and validation of BPST.

Procedure

The study was undertaken in two stages. The first stage consisted of devising the problem-solving interactive model and then implementing the model. It may be noted here that children in control group received the general cognitive stimulation given as part of early intervention programme at NIMH while children in experimental group also received the PSIM.

Devising the problem solving interactive model

The intervention devised for the present study was problem solving interactive model which emphasizes both on psychological and environmental attributes which influences both, the child and the mother. The tridirectional influence of child on mother, mother on child and the influence of environment on both is an important aspect of this strategy. These aspects are essential for facilitating the process of learning. The problem-solving interactive model therefore comprised three components described below.

Components

Task analysis

For each of the targets which consisted of problem solving tasks a procedural manual entitled "Strategies to Enhance Problem solving skills—STEPSS" was prepared specifically for the purpose of intervention. This manual gives guidelines on task analysis, which consists of four-six steps for each of the problem-solving task.

Target-related interaction: The training for the mothers included teaching specified problem solving targets and modification of interactions and verbalisations to help child achieve the target. Therefore, training of mothers formed an essential facet of the present study.

Task specific instructional material: In the present study, instructional material has been exclusively prepared to suit the needs of mother and child. The task specific material enabled teaching of the problem solving task to the child. The problem-solving interactive model was implemented on each child by selecting four problem solving tasks.

Procedure for selection of target items for each subject

For each subject in the sample four target items consisting of problem-solving tasks were selected. The targets for each child were determined by administering the Battery of Problem-Solving Tasks (BPST) which was prepared and validated by the researcher. The item from where the child does not complete the task on BPST is taken as the first target and the following three tasks on BPST were the total four targets given for each subject. Therefore, the targets varied from subject to subject depending on the level of performance.

Implementation of the problem-solving tasks

One target was introduced for each subject at a time. No specific timeframe was allotted for achieving the task. The above mentioned components of problem-solving interactive model were used by the researcher to train the mothers in helping the child to learn the problem-solving task.

Results and Discussion

For determining the efficacy of the psycho-ecological intervention strategy the Bayleys Scale of infant development was administered to determine cognitive outcomes which give the Mental Age (MA) and Mental Development Index (MDI) and Deviation Mental Quotients (DMeq). The mean performance of child outcomes is given below in Tables 1 and 2.

As evident from Tables 1 and 2, the subjects in experimental group displayed more striking performance gains assessed in terms of mental age and mental development index than those of control group. The pre- to post-test differences of MA were 3.57 and 1.78 in experimental group and control group respectively. Corresponding mean differences of MDI were 5.08 and (–) 0.85

in experimental and control groups. The pre- to post-measures on MA (t=5.70) MDI (t=4.099), Dmeq (t=2.64) and BPST (t=27.93) were highly significant in experimental group while it was also significant only on MA (t= 8.9) and BPST (t=9.607) in control group. The significance on MA & BPST in control group could be attributed to the general cognitive stimulation given as part of NIMH early intervention programme.

Table 1. Mean performance of child outcome before and after Intervention in experimental group

Performance measure	*N*	*Pretest*		*Post test*		
		Mean	*SD*	*Mean*	*S.D*	*t-value*
Mental age	45	8.23	4.29	11.81	5.6	5.70**
MDI	45	54.88	14.36	59.91	16.29	4.09**
Dmeq	42	31.09	22.55	37.26	26.06	2.64**
BPST	45	6.63	4.47	11.20	4.77	27.93**

**p< .01

Table 2. Mean performance of child outcome before and after Intervention in control group

Performance measure	*N*	*Pretest*		*Post test*		
		Mean	*SD*	*Mean*	*S.D*	*t-value*
Mental age	30	6.99	3.89	8.77	4.42	8.92**
MDI	30	42.09	8.61	41.24	7.99	.69.00
Dmeq	28	14.65	10.56	13.05	7.48	1.04
BPST	30	3.47	3.05	4.90	3.5	9.60**

**p< .01

The substantial gains as seen from the mean differences of MA (3.57), MDI (5.03), DmeQ (6.17) and BPST (4.57) by experimental group when compared to control group MA (1.78), MDI (-0.85), DmeQ (-1.59) and BPST (1.43) is indicative of the efficacy of psycho-ecological interactive model. Reporting similar intervention gains from experimental groups, Sternberg (2002) pointed that the environment, training and motivation profoundly influenced the cognitive skills.

Table 3. Intervention outcomes with reference to age in experimental and control groups

Age (Months)	*Mental age (exp)*				*Mental age (control)*			
	Pre	*Post*	*Gain*	*Rate of gain*	*Pre*	*Post*	*Gain of gain*	*Rate*
4-13	05.16	07.92	2.76	0.77	3.84	4.82	0.98	0.24
14-23	10.56	13.63	3.06	0.94	7.33	9.43	2.09	0.51
24-33	13.82	16.97	3.15	0.99	14.42	17.23	2.81	0.76
Mean	8.33	11.33	2.97	0.87	7.00	8.78	1.78	0.44

The problem-solving tasks were the targets that formed the basis for planning activities where child's active engagement with the environment and emphasis on mother-child interactions helped the child to gain from intervention. In the present study, intervention targets, environmental arrangement coupled with following child's lead were considered important aspects of intervention. This further substantiates the efficacy of the problem solving interactive model. Intervention outcomes of PSIM with reference to chronological age.

In the experimental group, the children in the age group of 24-33 months had pre- and post-test MA of 13.82 and 16.97 and a higher rate of change of 0.99. The infants in the age range of 4-13 months exhibited lower performance outcomes on MA with a pre- to post-test difference of 2.76 and rate of difference of 0.77, which was the lowest. The infants in the age group of 14-23 months displayed a rate of change of 0.94 on MA. In control group the mean scores on MA in the age group of 24-33 months was notable with a pre- to post-test difference of 0.28 and rate of difference at 0.76. The lowest change on mean scores of MA was observed in four-13 months age group.

A comparison of experimental and control groups reveal similar trends where performance outcomes on mean scores of MA was higher in the 24-33 months (0.99 in experimental and 0.76 in control) and lowest in the four-13 months age (2.76 in experimental and 0.98 in control). The age was found to be a determining factor influencing MA. Intervention processes may be more likely to lead to differential outcomes. A plausible explanation could be mastery motivation. One aspect of mastery motivation relates to the children's attempts at object- related mastery. In early developmental stages, the children attempt to master problem-posing tasks. Studies (Jennings, Yarrow, & Martin, 1984) indicate that mastery motivation measured during infant and toddler period predict higher levels of cognitive performance. Different qualities of social and physical environment operate to support different aspects of development at different ages (Slade, 1987; Wachs & Gruen, 1982).

The Problem-Solving Interactive Model (PSIM) proved to be efficacious in promoting cognitive outcomes in children with developmental delays. This is clearly evident from the pre to post treatment differences, on mental age (3.57) mental development index (5.03) and deviation mental quotient (6.17) in the experimental group when compared to gains made on control group MA (1.78), MDI (-0.85), DmeQ (-1.59) and BPST (1.43) The pre- to post-test differences were highly significant on all performance indicators in experimental group MA (t=27.88) MDI (t=4.099), Dmeq (t=2.64) and BPST (t=27.93) while it also showed significance only on MA (t=8.9) and BPST (t=9.607) in control group. Comparative trends between experimental and control groups with regard to chronological age showed higher mean differences in 24-33 months (3.15 in experimental and 0.76 in control) and the lowest in four-13 months age (2.76 in experimental and 0.98 in control).

Conclusion

The PSIM model with its emphasis on tridirectional reciprocity, helped to improve the performance of children with developmental delays. Therefore awareness may be created on task analysis of problem-solving targets, task-related interactions and task-specific materials to mothers of children with developmental delays. The variations in intervention outcomes with respect to age of child indicated the need to plan and implement specialised interventions targeting these specific child characteristics. This also necessitates and calls for studying the interaction effects in further detail.

References

Bharath Raj, J. (1983), *DST Manual + Know your child's intelligence and how to improve it*. Sri Meera Printers: Mysore.

DeLoache, S.J., Miller, F.K., & Pierroutsakos, L.S. (1998). In Deanna Kuhn and Robert S. Siegler (Eds.), *Handbook of child psychology-cognition, perception and language,* (Vol. 2, 5th Ed.), (pp 801-850). New York: John Wiley & Sons.

Feurestein, R., and, Y., Jensen, M.R., Kaniel, S., & Tzuriel, D. (1987), Prerequisites for assessment of learning potential: The LPAD model, In C.S.Lidz (Ed.), *Dynamic Assessment,* (pp. 35-51), New York : Guilford.

Guralnick, M.J. (2000), *Second-generation research in the field of early intervention,* Baltimore: Paul Brooks publishing co.

Hauser-Cram, P., Warfield, M,E., Shonkoff, J. P., & Krauss, W.M. (2001). Children with disabilities. *Monographs of the Society for research in child development. (Serial* No.266, Vol. 66.).

Jennings, K.D., Yarrow, L.J., & Martin, P.D. (1984), Mastery motivation and cognitive development: A longitudinal study from infancy to 3 and 1/2 years of age, *International Journal of Behavioural Development, 7,* 441-461.

MacTurk, R.H., Vietze, P.M., & McCarthy, M.E., McQuinston, S., & Yarrow, L.J. (1985). The organisation of exploratory behaviour in Down syndrome and nondelayed infants. *Child Development, 56,* 573-581.

Ruskin, E.M., Mundy, P., Kasari, C.,& Sigman, M. (1994), Object mastery motivation of children with Down syndrome. *American Journal on Mental Retardation, 98,* 499-509.

Shari, E., & Siegler, R.S. (1994), Development of problem solving. In R.J.Sternberg (Ed.), *Thinking and problem solving,* New York: Academic press.

Slade, A. (1987), A longitudinal study of maternal involvement and symbolic play during the toddler period, *Child Development.* New York: Plenum.

Strenberg, R.J. (1984), Mechanisms of cognitive development: A componential approach. In R.J. Strenberg (Ed.), *Mechanisms of cognitive development.* New York: Freeman.

Sternberg, R.J. (2002), Individual differences in cognitive development. In Usha, Goswami (Ed.), Childhood cognitive development (pp. 515-536). Malden: Blackwell.

Vygotsky, L.S. (1978), *Mind in society: The development of higher psychological processes,* M. Cole, V. John-Steiner, S. Scribner, and E.Sarberman, (Ed.), Cambridge, MA: Harvard University Press.

Wachs, T.D., & Gruen, G.E. (1982), *Early experience and human development,* New York: Plenum.

White, K.R., Taylor, M.J., & Moss, V.D. (1992). Does research support claims about the benefits involving parents in early intervention programs? *Review of Educational Research, 52,* 91-125.

17

Assessing Validity of Web-based Computer Adaptive Training Modules

—*Debdulal Dutta Roy*

With rapid change in web technology, training method gradually shifts from manual to web based computer adaptive training. Here, each trainee is not exposed to same stimuli. Stimulus exposure depends upon individual differences in proficiency level accounted by the computer. Therefore, usual validity estimating statistical tools (ANOVA with repeated measurement) are not applicable. Aim of the current research is to examine the criterion related validity of one web based computer adaptive training program (Fast ForWord Language Gateway Edition Product). The program is based on the adaptive training techniques such as frequency, reward, intensity and motivation allowed for more rapid learning. It includes seven modules. All modules were classified into two as sound (Circus sequence, old McDonald flying farm, Phoneme identification) and Word (phonic match, phonic words, language comprehension builder and block commander) exercises. This internet based training program helps children in building oral language comprehension and in other critical skills necessary for learning to read or becoming a better reader. 25 randomly selected students of grades four and five were trained with Fast ForWord program for more than 20 days. Results of each individual trainee by treatments and by module in the form of percentage of success were downloaded from the computer.

This paper originally appears in the *Journal of the Indian Academy of Applied Psychology*, January 2008, Vol.34, No.1, pp. 127-136.

> In considering the typical data structure, Box whisker plot analysis was made to compare the results across treatments or trials. Several parameters of box plots (Outliers, box size, location of median in the box, location of upper and lower whisker, location of hinges, and fluctuation of box size after achieving the target) were identified as useful to estimate the validity of training modules. It provides insight about different psychological changes occurred during the different training programs. Box plot results suggest possible ability contamination in changing performance level. Therefore, in order to control contamination of ability on validity assessment, high and low ability groups were identified based on initial training performance. Learning graph profiles of both groups were compared finally. Results identified very poor validity in two modules out of seven. Finally role of box whisker plot analysis on validity assessment was discussed.

With the rapid change in computer network system, attention is gradually shifting from manual mode of training to web- based training exercises. Web-based training is useful as the programme can be imparted to large number of trainees at a time across different countries of the globe with minimum cost. It replicates manual operation on a scale which is beyond the capability of human organisation. Besides, it maintains vast storage facilities to record each operation of trainees which may be useful in cross-country comparison.

Web-based training focused on three things – (a) computer simulation technique (b) computer adaptive problem assignment and (c) computer adaptive feedback system.

Computer Simulation

Computer simulation, which have for years been used by the military and airlines, are increasingly finding their way into profession such as teaching, policing, sales and other fields that depend more on interpersonal skills than teaching proficiency. This provides trainees to enter into the virtual world spontaneously. In computer simulation, attention is paid to imitation of some real thing, state of affairs or process. It is the modeling of natural systems or human systems in order to gain insight into their functioning. Simulation can be used to show the eventual effects of alternative conditions and course of actions.

Computer Adaptive Problem Assignment

Computer adaptive methodologies have the potential to accommodate individual differences within required time limits to avoid instructional failures, ensure minimal proficiency outcome and the opportunity for maximising the outcome proficiency for each individual. Current advances in conceptual modeling and in artificial intelligence technologies may provide the basic components of machine-based instruction that adapts to and evolves with the individual. This instructional systems reduce training costs by avoiding unnecessary planning and management activities and by reducing elimination and setback rates. They can increase force readiness by producing more proficient practitioners and by returning subject matter expert instructional staff to operational positions.

Computer Adaptive Feedback

Computer systems can be programmed to provide performance feedback to the learner on a variety of reinforcement schedules. Feedback timing and frequency can be selected that is most appropriate to the training session. For example, immediate feedback is used for perceptual-motor tasks and at the early stages for other learning. However, as mastery is gained, immediate feedback can be disruptive and a longer interval is more appropriate. Computers can also be programmed to provide positive reinforcement which enhances learning, retention, and motivation. Control over the pace of learning can be provided for the trainee, as well as, infinite opportunities for material review and practice—until mastery.

To make training module more trustworthy, verification and validation are of crucial importance. In training, validity refers to what the training wants to achieve or the outcome. Usually validity of training is assessed by comparing pre- and during or post-training performance. But availability of same students in both pre- and post-training is difficult issue. Other technique is comparison among different success rates across trials. Purpose of the current study was to determine validity of one web-based computer adaptive training product.

Validity

Test validity concerns what the test measures and how well it does so. It tells us what can be inferred from test scores (Anastasi, 1990). Following the analogy of test validity, validity of training programme may be defined as what the training wants to develop and how well it develops. This definition indicates assessment of criterion-related validity. That is the level of difficulty and how well trainees improve their performance with successive treatments or trials.

METHOD

Participants

Participants in this study were 25 students of one English-medium school. Here English is the first language. Since, all the instructions of the exercises are in English, it was assumed that students could follow the instruction of the programme properly. School authorities agreed to fulfil the set of criteria for selection of school. The criteria were: (i) Arrangement of broadband system, (ii) Arrangement of continuous internet access to the 4 computers and the server, (iii) Arrangement of experimental lab, (iv) Providing four computers and server, (v) Providing infrastructure facilities and (vi) Arrangement of boys in the age group of 9-11 years for the training programme.

Random sampling was followed in selection of sample. Initially, the list of names of students for the age group of 10 to 11 years was prepared. Students of even number in the list were treated as samples for this study. Therefore, each student had equal chance to be selected for the training programme.

Training Module

Fast ForWord® is a CD-ROM and Internet-based training programme that helps children rapidly build oral language comprehension and other critical skills necessary for learning to read or becoming a better reader. Fast ForWord® evolved from the work of noted research scientists Michael Merzenich and Bill Jenkins from the University of California at San Francisco, and Paula Tallal and Steven Miller, experts on the neurological basis of language at Rutgers University. The product is based on the adaptive training techniques such as frequency, reward, intensity and motivation allow for more rapid learning. It includes seven modules. All modules were classified into two as sound (Circus sequence, old McDonald flying farm) and word (phonic match, phonic words, language comprehension builder and block commander) exercises (Table 1).

Table 1 Description of Exercises

Modules/Exercises	*Tasks*	*Benefits*
Sound Exercises Circus Sequence (CS)	Students hear a series of short, non-verbal tones. Each tone represents a different fragment of the frequency spectrum used in spoken language. Students are asked to differentiate between these tones.	It helps to improve listening accuracy.
Old MacDonald's Flying Farm (OM)	Students use the computer mouse to catch and hold a flying animal. The animal repeats a single syllable several times, and students must release the animal when they hear a change in the syllable.	It helps to improve phonological awareness, listening accuracy and working memory skills.
Phoneme Identification (PI)	First, students listen as one animal character utters a phoneme, and then two new animals utter similar phonemes. The students identify which of the latter two sounds was identical to the first phoneme.	It helps to improve phonological awareness skills, listening accuracy, and working memory.
Word Exercises Phonic Match (PM)	Students choose a square on a grid and hear a sound or word.	It helps to improve working memory, listening accuracy,

(Contd...)

	Each sound or word has a match somewhere within the grid. The goal is to find each square's match and clear the grid.	phonological awareness and auditory word recognition.
Phonic Words (PW)	Students see two pictures representing two similar words that differ only by initial or final consonant ("tack" versus "tag").	It helps to improve phonological awareness, listening accuracy, and auditory word recognition.

Procedure

After sample selection, parents meeting were made to establish rapport with the parents and the students. They were informed of the specific requirements of the product, i.e., nonstop participation into the programme for 40 days (5 days X 8 weeks) minimum. Each student will be allowed to attend at least three programmes per day. When the students arrived, trained teacher asked them to sit on the specific chair and turned on the computer. Figure 1 shows Computer network system used for collection of data.

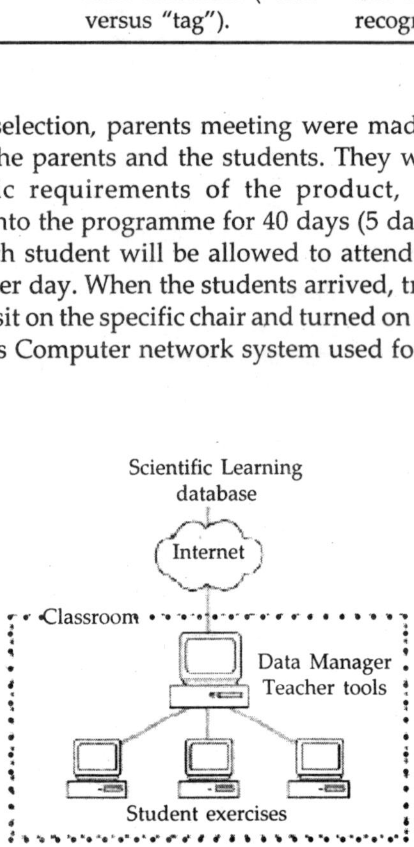

Figure 1 : Computer Network System

One black screen was placed around each computer in order to control attention to unwanted things. The room was airy, well illuminated and no one was allowed to make any sound. Each student was given instruction through the computer. They were asked to raise help stand when they needed. After completion of the training, the results were downloaded from the progress tracker. Progress tracker is an online service to download the results of each trainee. The total arrangement for collection of data was made by the trainers of the Step-one foundation in Kolkata.

Analysis of Data

Since the downloaded data were in percentage in stead of scores, box plot analysis was used to assess the validity of the training programme.

Box Whisker Plot

The boxplot was invented in 1977 by American statistician John Tuckey. A box plot or box and whiskers plot is a graphical way of representing the salient features of a distribution. It can be used with either Gaussian or non-Gaussian distributions. The box plot shows a rectangle stretching from the first to the third quartile of the distribution, these quartiles, the edges of the box, are called "hinges". The box displays in a pictoral fashion the variability in the data. A line inside the box shows the approximate position of the median. From the median, one can determine the central tendency or location. From the length of box, one can determine spread, or variability of observation. If the median is not in the middle of the box the distribution is skewed. The further the median is from the middle, the more skewed is the distribution. If the median is closer to the bottom of the box than to the top, the data are positively skewed. If the median is closer to the top of the box than to the bottom, the distribution is negatively skewed. Cases with values that are between 1.5 and 3 box lengths from the upper or lower edge of the box are called outliers and are designated with circle (Pyzdek, 1976).

Results

Results of the study were presented into two ways – box plot analysis and comparison of high and low ability groups in means and SDs across treatments.

BOX-PLOT Analysis

Outliers

No outliers were noted in any box plots (Figures 2-8), therefore, all data were accounted for analysis.

Box size reduction

Box sizes were systematically reduced across trials in case of CS (Figure 2), OM (Figure 3), and PM (Figure 5), LCB (Figure 7) suggesting gradual increase in proficiency level by trials in corresponding modules. In case of BC (Figure 8), box sizes were large and were similar for few trials after crossing reference point later on the sizes were reduced suggesting plateau stage in proficiency before achieving the target.

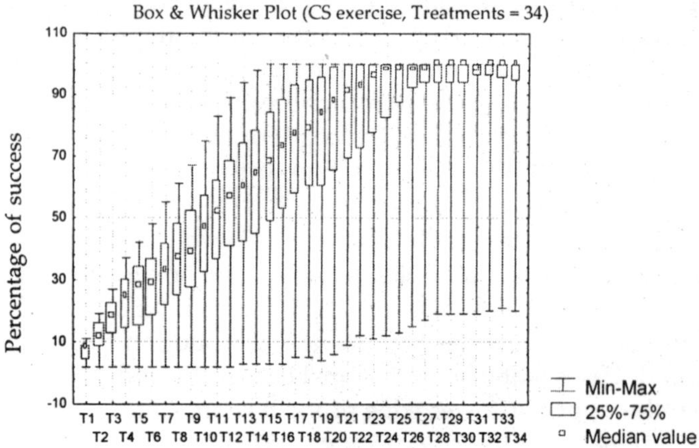

Figure 2: Box and Whisker Plot of CS Exercise

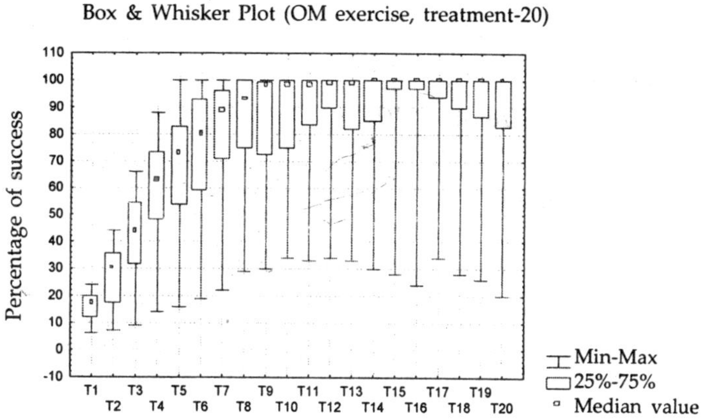

Figure 3: Box and Whisker Plot of OM Exercise

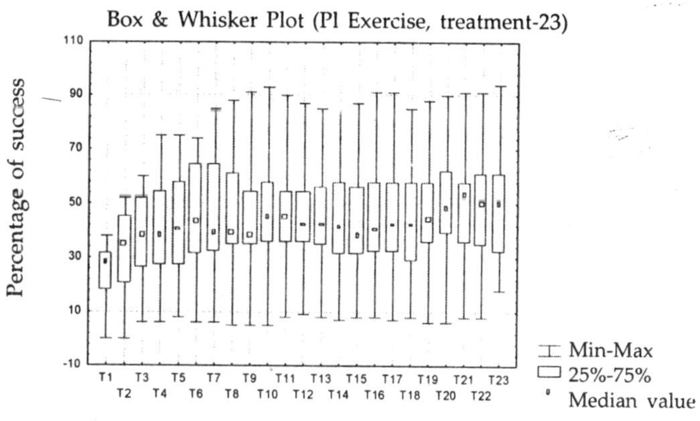

Figure 4: Box and Whisker Plot of PI Exercise

Location of Median

Good training provides systematic change in performance. It should not be too difficult or very easy. Out of seven modules, median always was below the 50 per cent efficiency level or reference point in case of PI (Figure 4) exercise. And in case of PW (Figure 6), median was above the reference point at the end of total trials. This suggests high difficulty experienced by the students in those two exercises. On the other hand, students experienced less difficulty in solving problems of three exercises, namely, BC(Figure 8), OM(Figure 3) and PM (Figure 5).

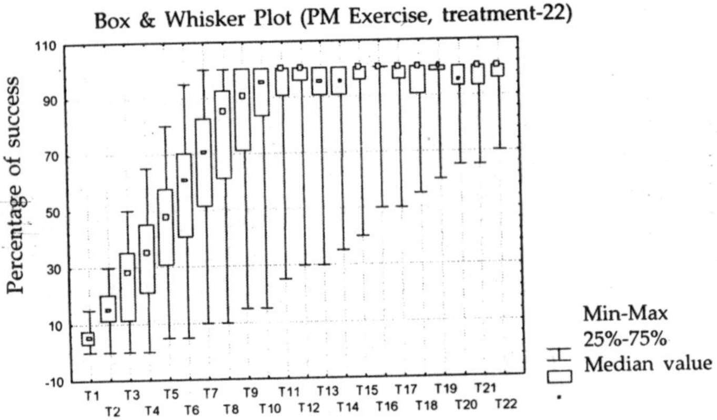

Figure 5 Box and Whisker Plot of PM Exercise

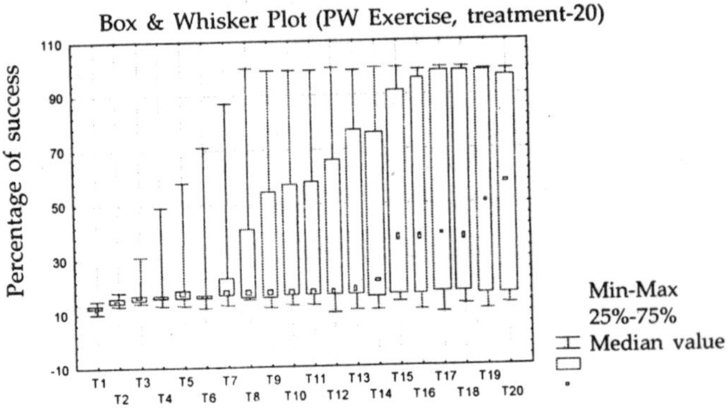

Figure 6 : Box and Whisker Plot of PW Exercise.

Length of Whisker

Length of whisker was large after the lower hinge of box in case of CS(Figure 2), OM (Figure 3),PM (Figure 5),LCB (Figure 7) suggesting failure of few students to show success in those exercises like most of the students. However, this was small in case of BC (Figure 8) exercise suggesting less difficulty experienced by all most all of the trainees. In case of PI (Figure 4), length of whisker above the upper hinge of the box was high suggesting better performance of few students in comparison with most of the students. But no one reached at the target as no whisker reached at the 100 per cent success level. Again, length of whisker below the lower hinge of box was high suggesting very poor performance of few students in comparison with most of the students in PI exercise. In case of PW(Figure 6), few whiskers above the upper hinge of box reached the target suggesting excellent performance of few students. Like, PI, whiskers below the lower hinge of box did not lie below the 10 per cent success level suggesting relatively less difficulty experienced by the few students in solving problems of PW module.

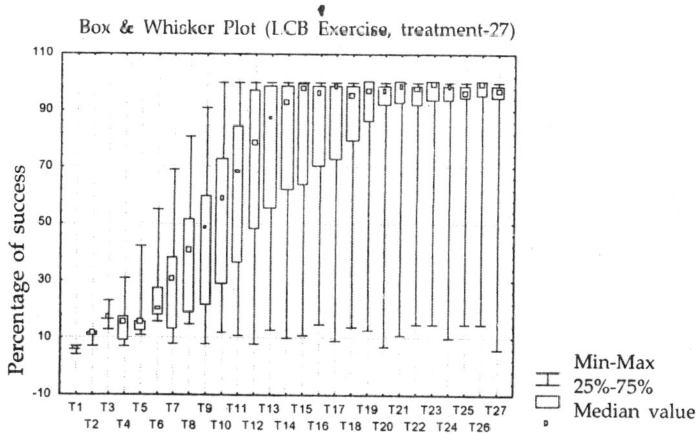

Figure 7: Box and Whisker Plot of LCB Exercise.

Fluctuation in Box Size

After achieving the target, sizes of the box varied suggesting possible concentration difficulty in solving problems of same module. This was noted in OM (Figure 3)and PM (Figure 5) exercises.

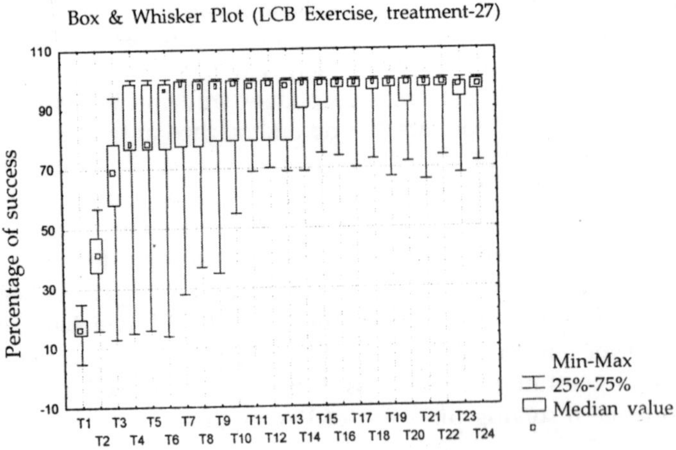

Figure 8 : Box and Whisker Plot of BC Exercise.

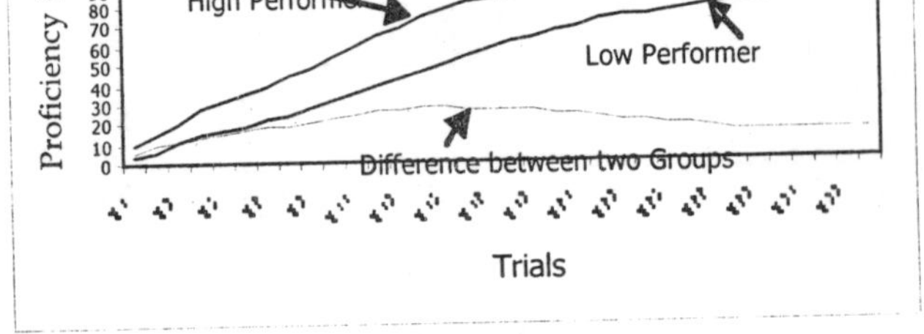

Figure 9: Mean Differences in Proficiency Across Trials for CS Exercise.

Differences between High and Low Ability Groups

Variation in different parameters of box plot analysis revealed possible within group variability in performance of the trainees under study. Therefore, it may be assumed that individual difference in ability plays critical role in changing responses from one level to another. This will lead to criteria contamination. In considering such limitation, high and low ability groups were compared using means and SD-wise differences.

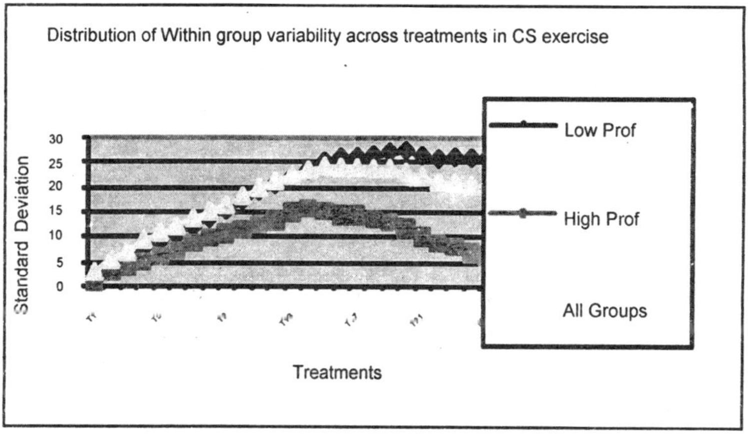

Figure 10 : Within group variability wise differences in proficiency across trials for CS exercise.

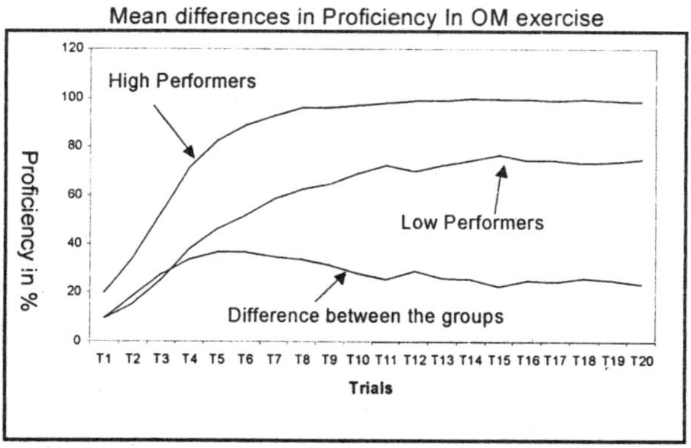

Figure 11 Mean differences in proficiency across trials for OM exercise.

Mean Differences

Individual difference in ability plays critical role in changing responses from one level to another. Box plot provides insight about distribution of data irrespective of ability wise differences. Figures 9, 11,13,15,17, 19, and 21 represent graphical distribution of average performance across trials by high and low ability groups.

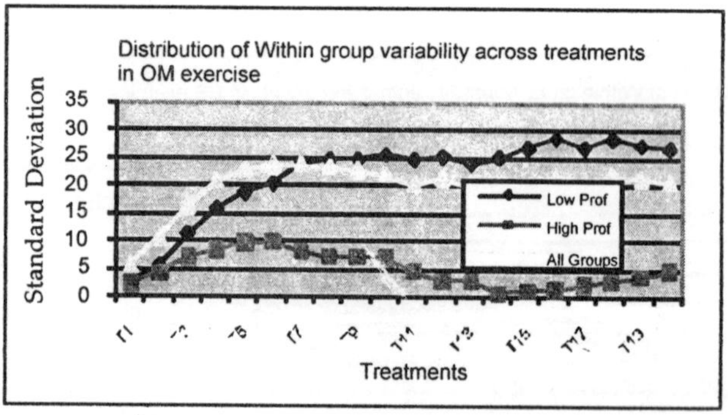

Figure 12: Within group variability wise differences in proficiency across trials for OM exercise.

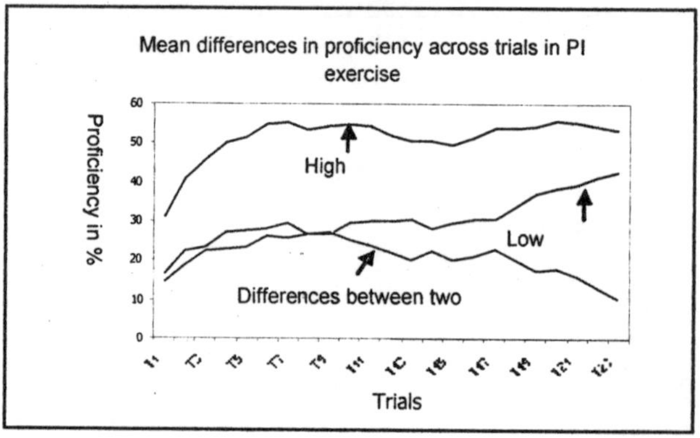

Figure 13: Mean differences in proficiency across trials for PI exercise

In all the exercises, the mean difference between the groups was noted suggesting appropriateness about the categorization. At the initial stage, the mean difference was high and gradually it was reduced. However, this reduction was high in case of PM exercise suggesting better proficiency among the low ability group with training. In case of PW exercise, the difference was high at the later treatment suggesting experience of difficulty by the students of low ability group in development of proficiency.

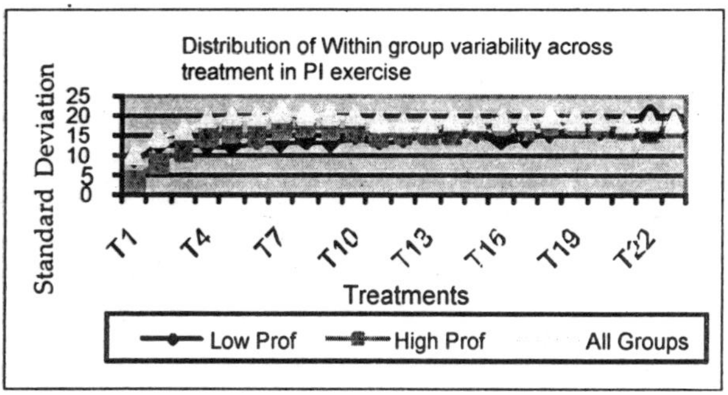

Figure 14: Within group variability wise differences in proficiency across trials for PI exercise.

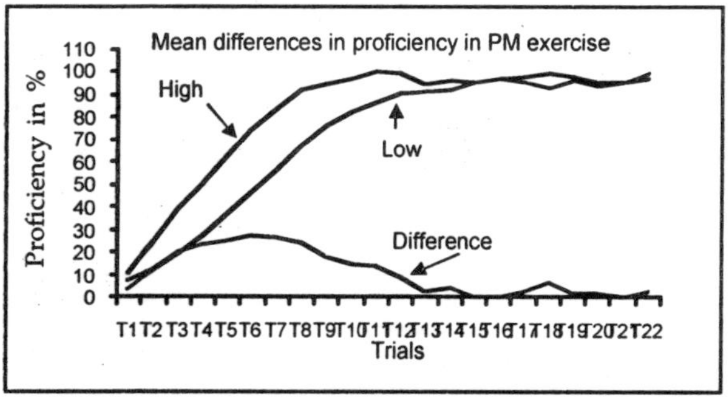

Figure 15: Mean differences in proficiency across trials for PM exercise

SD Wise Differences

Mean differences provide average distribution pattern but it fails to provide insight about pattern of errors committed by individuals. Figures 10, 12, 14, 16, 18, 20, 22 provide insight about within group variability or the pattern of errors experienced by each ability group across treatments.

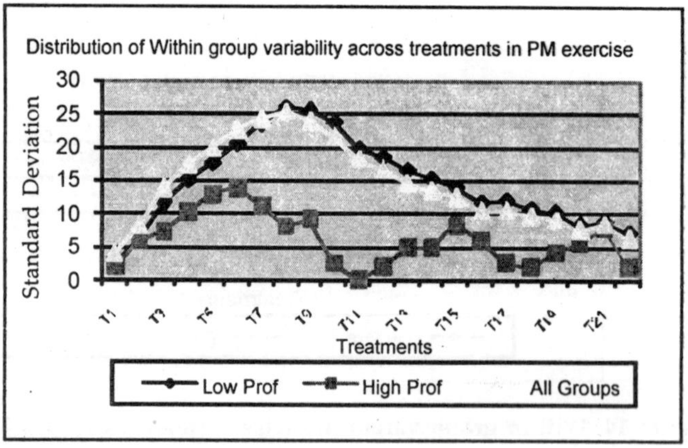

Figure 16 : Within group variability wise differences in proficiency across trials for PM exercise

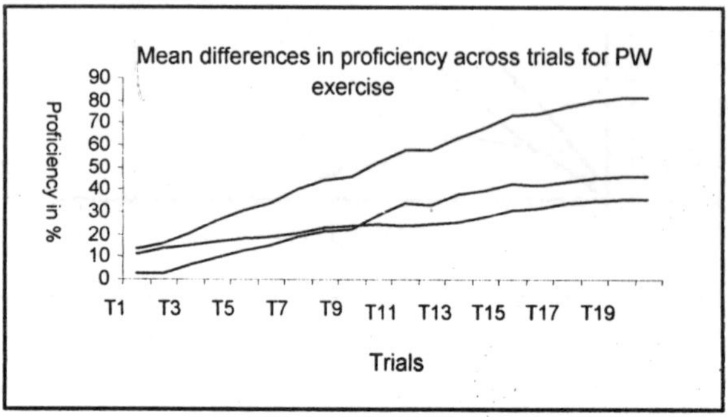

Figure 17: Mean differences in proficiency across trials for PW exercise

Figures 14 (PI) and 18(PW) show that SDs of both high and low ability group remained almost similar across trials suggesting more difficulty experienced by the students of two groups.

Discussion

Results noted that box plot analysis is useful in analysing various parameters of web-based computer adaptive training module. By using box plot current study explored pattern of increase in proficiency level, plateau stage in proficiency, level of difficulty, target or criteria achievement, possible concentration difficulty in different training modules. Out of seven modules, two modules were identified as least valid in achieving the criteria. These are PI and PW. Further, more different parameters of box plot analysis suggest possible within group variability across trials due to individual differences in initial ability level. Finally, mean and SD-wise line graphs were plotted for high and low ability groups and identified committing more errors by both high and low ability group in case of above two exercises.

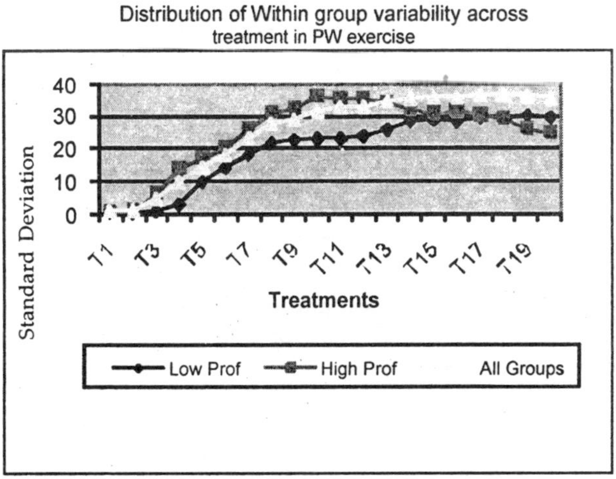

Figure 18: Within group variability wise differences in proficiency across trials for PW exercise.

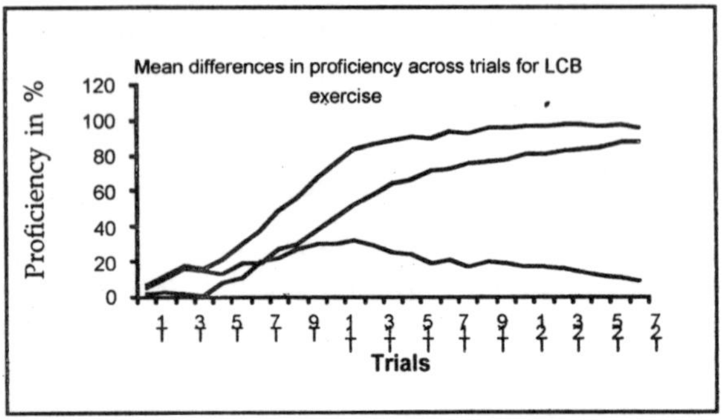

Figure 19: Mean differences in proficiency across trials for LCB exercise.

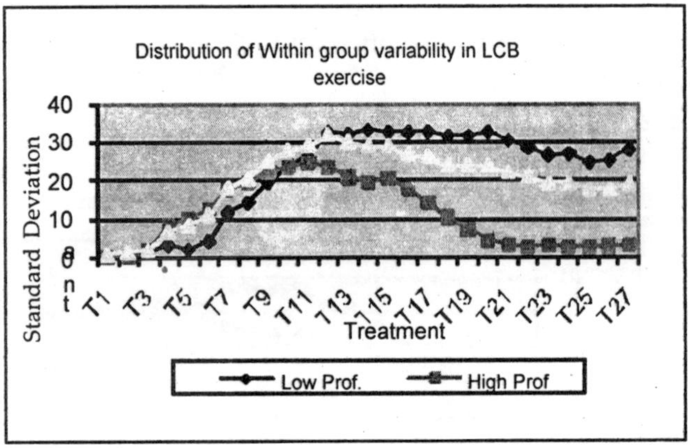

Figure 20: Within group variability wise differences in proficiency across trials for LCB exercise

By scrutinising the contents of these two modules, it was noted that both are meant for developing proficiency in western pronunciation and accent of English words. Though the participants of the study were English speaking but they could not follow the English accent used in the module as revealed in the results.

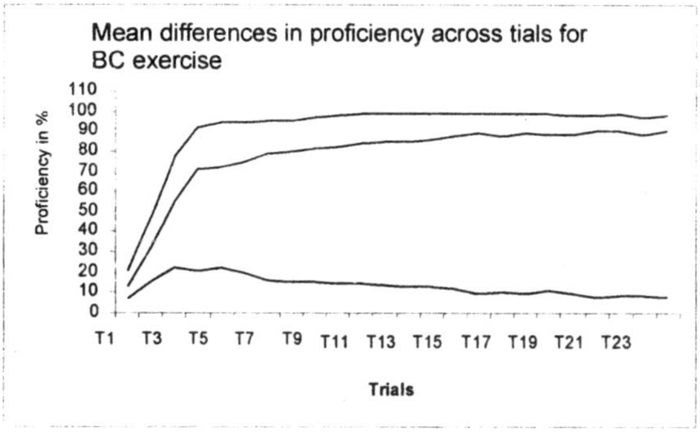

Figure 21: Mean differences in proficiency across trials for BC exercise.

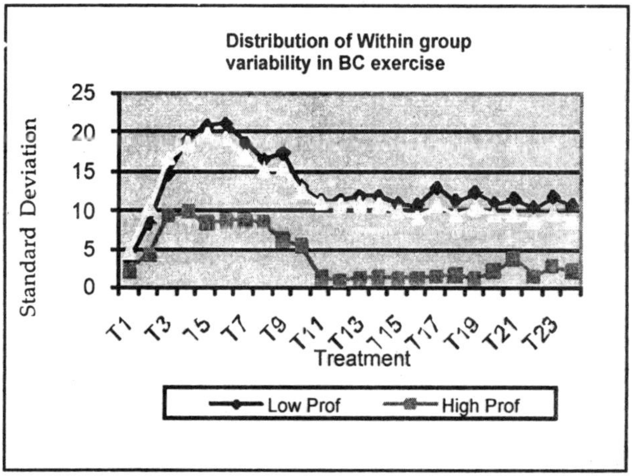

Figure 22 : Within group variability wise differences in proficiency across trials for BC exercise

To sum up, in considering typical data structure of the web- based computer adaptive training module current study explored role of box plot analysis in estimating validity.

References

Anastasi, A. (1990), *Psychological testing,* New York: Maxwell Macmillan International Editions.

Tukey, J.W. (1977), *Exploratory data analysis,* Addison-Wesley, Reading, MA.

Pyzdek, T. (1976), *The six sigma handbook,* New York: McGraw-Hill.

18

Parent-Child Interaction and Machiavellian Orientation

—*Hardeo Ojha*

The study aimed at exploring the relationship between perceived parental behaviours and children's Machiavellian orientation (MO) and also between parents' MO and children's MO. For this an unselected sample of 300 Plus-Two class male students aged 15-18 years were administered Personal Data Sheet, Parental Behaviour Inventory and Mach IV Scale. After data were obtained from them each subject was given two forms of Mach IV Scale, one-marked 'M' and another marked 'F' to be filled in by his mother and father respectively. The data analysed by product moment correlation coefficient revealed that loving and permissive behaviours of parents were negatively and significantly related with their sons' MO. It was also found that MO of parents and their sons were positively and significantly associated, providing support for modelling hypothesis.

Machiavellian orientation (MO) in interpersonal relation is defined by manipulation and exploitation of people for selfish ends with relative lack of affect and without any concern for conventional morality and ideological commitment (Christie & Geis, 1970). The Machiavellian, thus, stands for some one who views and manipulates others for his selfish ends. A Machiavellian has nothing to do with conventional morality and has low ideological commitment. He views human beings as objects to be manipulated and his views are more utilitarian than

This paper originally appears in the *Journal of the Indian Academy of Applied Psychology*, July 2007, Vol.33, No.2, pp. 283-288.

moral in interaction with others. The term has been coined after Niccolo Machiavelli, a great Italian political thinker of fifteenth century who wrote two books *The Prince* and *The Discourses*. The ideas expressed in the books were associated with use of guile, deceit and opportunism in interpersonal relation, and one who is found to agree with those ideas is termed as Machiavellian. The Machiavellian philosophy is that man is basically weak, fallible and gullible, and therefore a rational man should take advantage of this human weakness to maximise his own gain by manipulating people. Machiavellianism is found more or less in every individual but it is noted most obviously among politicians, administrator and heads of institutions

As regards personality characteristics, Machiavellians are distinguished by external locus of control orientation (Mudrack, 1990), dogmatism (Hunter et al., 1982), psychopathy (Skinner, 1982) moderate anxiety (Podrico, 1987), high risk-kaking (Rim, 1965), high ego strength and dominance and low friendliness and responsibility (Jha, 1995) and high leadership qualities (Bharathi & Sunitha, 1994). Their values are found to centre round power and utility (Ojha, 2007).

Machiavellianism has widespread use. Some have used it as an attitudinal factor (Bogart, 1971), while others have termed it a behavioural style (Geis & Moon, 1981, Tripathi & Sinha, 1981), but majority of social scientists have frequently used it as personality disposition (Christie & Geis, 1970; Kuo & Marshella, 1977; Pandey, 1981). As a personality disposition it is affected by several social and personal variables. One of the most crucial variables to influence this is parent-child interaction.

Every moment a child spends in contact with parents and family has some effect on his present behaviour and future potentialities (Sears et al., 1957). There are three aspects of childrearing which can be clearly distinguished. They are (1) childcare, i.e., feeding, weaning, toilet-training and bed-habit training, etc., (2) child discipline, which refers to the control of undesirable and antisocial behaviour; and (3) parental childrearing attitudes. The latter two are interrelated. While attitude is the cognitive aspect, discipline is the conative aspect. In fact parents' attitudes and their resulting behaviours towards children have been found to be of greater importance in the development of personality (Sears et al., 1957, Ojha & Parmanick,

1995). Parent's behaviours range from genuine affectionate acceptance to hostile rejection, extreme indulgence to carefree neglect, complete autonomy to licensed permissiveness (Piklinas & Albrecht, 1961, p. 115). Researches have discovered three relevant and important dimensions of parental attitudes, viz., love-rejection, autonomy-control and protection-neglect (de Boeck, 1976; Imperio & Chabot, 1980; Ojha, 1993; Schaefer, 1965; Sims & Paolucci, 1975).

Psychological literature is replete with studies regarding relationship between parental behaviours and personality traits. But Studies dealing specifically with Machiavellian orientation are few and far between. Therefore the present study was undertaken to explore the relationship of adolescents' Machiavellian orientation (MO) with perceived behaviours of parents and also the relationship between parents' and children's Machiavellian orientation.

Method

Sample

The sample constituted of 300 male students of Plus-Two classes selected incidently from the intermediate colleges of Bhagalpur and their 600 parents. The mean age of subjects was 17 years, the age range being 16-18 years. The mean age of parents was 45.25, the age range being 40-55 years.

Measures

Following tests were administrated to the subjects in small groups of 20-25.

Parental Behaviour Inventory (PBI)

The inventory developed and standardised by Ojha (1993) has two separate forms, one each for mother and the father. Each form consists of the same 48 items with the same serial order, the only difference being that in 'Mother Form' the items have been written in feminine gender in Hindi and in 'Father Form' the same have been stated in masculine gender. The inventory consists of three scales viz. restrictive-permissive, neglecting-protecting, and rejecting-loving. There are 16 items for each scale, half of the items being positive and remaining half negative. The items of the scales have been arranged cyclically. Each item has to be responded in four alternatives, viz., 'very true', 'true', 'untrue' and 'very untrue'. The subject is required to recollect the behaviours of his mother and father which they displayed towards him/her before 12 years of age and indicate how far each statement is true or untrue. The response categories for positive items are scored as 5,4, 2,1. For negative items scoring is reversed. A score of 3 is assigned to omission of an item invariably. The scores are summed up for each dimension for the mother and father form. A score on each scale ranges from 16 to 80. The combined score of three scales is named as overall behaviour score, the high score indicating positive and low score denoting negative behaviour. The average split half reliabilities for the mother and father form were 0.82 and 0.83 and the average test-retest rehabilitates for the same were 0.75 and 0.76. Two sample items of PBI are as follows: Used to keep stern eyes on me, and allowed me to go out with friends.

Mach IV scale

The scale is a measure of Machiavellian orientation in interpersonal situations, which is characterised by the use of guile, deceit, opportunism and manipulation of others in self-interest. It is a Hindi adaptation of Mach IV scale of Christie and Geis (1970) by Rai and Gupta (1987). It is a 20-item seven-point scale varying from 'strong agreement 'to' neither strong disagreement 'with' neither agreement nor disagreement' in the middle. It consists of three subscales: Views, Tactics and Morality. It consists of both positive and reverse items. For positive items a score of 1 is assigned to strong disagreement and 7 for strong agreement. For negative items scoring is reversed. The undecided response is invariably assigned a score of 4. Thus scores of subjects on the scale vary from 20 to 140. But to simplify the interpretation and to get 100 as midpoint, a constant of 20 is added in the score of each subject making highest possible score 160 (140+20) and lowest possible score 40 (20+20). The split-half and test-retest reliabilities of the scale for a sample of 100 Ss were found by the present author to be 0.712 and 0.658.

Two sample items of the scale are as follows: Most people forget more easily the death of father than the loss of property, and it is wise to flatter important people.

Results

In order to know the extent to which parental behaviours are associated with children's Machiavellian orientation (MO) the product moment correlations of coefficient were calculated between Mach IV scores and scores on each PBI scale. The correlations are mentioned in Table 1.

Table 1: Correlation coefficients (r) of Machiavellianism with parental behaviours (N=300).

Parental Behaviours	*Mother*	*Father*
Rest-Perm	–0.24	–0.22
Negl.-Protq	–0.08	–0.07
Rej.-Lov.	–0.35 *	–0.32 *
Overall	–0.21 *	–0.18 *

*p<.01

It may be observed from Table 1 that children's MO is associated negatively and significantly with permissive behaviour of mother (r (298) = -0.24, p< 0.01) and father (r (298) = 0.22, p< 0.01). Children's MO is found to be related negatively and significantly with loving behaviour of both mother (r (298) = 0.35, p<0.01) and father (r (298) = -0.32, p<0.01). However MO appears to be unassociated with protective behaviour of both mother (r (298)= -0.08, p>0.05) and father (r (298) –0.07, p> 0.05). The relationship of MO with overall behaviour, as expected, is also negative and significant either in case of mother (r (298) = 0.21, p<0.01) or in case father (r (298) = 0.18, p< 0.01). Thus it may be concluded that negative behaviour of parents like restriction and rejection foster Machiavellian orientation, while positive behaviours of parents like permissiveness and love hinder the growth of Machiavellian orientation among children.

In order to see the relationship between parents' and children's Machiavellian orientation product moment correlations of coefficient were computed between Mach IV scores of parents and their children. It was found that the value of correlations between MO of fathers and sons (r = 0.150, p<.01), mothers and sons (r = 0.245, p<.01) and parents (both parents taken together) and sons (r = 0.197, p<.01) were significant. Hence it may be inferred that children imitate their parents and parents serve as models for them.

Discussion

It has been noticed that the negative correlation coefficients of college students' Machiavellian orientation with parental permissiveness and love are higher in case of mother than in case of father. This may happen because there is close interaction of the child with mother than with father. Machiavellian orientation does not develop in children if they get loving attention of parents. According to Horney (1950) the quest for power arises from thwarted childhood needs of parental affection. This quest of power is in the root of Machiavellian orientation in interpersonal behaviour. Machiavellian orientation is associated with interpersonal insensitivity, while non-Machiavellian orientation is associated with interpersonal sensitivity. The child who does not receive unconditional love and affection develops feelings of anger and hostility which cannot be openly expressed for fear of further antagonising his/her parents. Thus the child is facing "double blind" of being angry and yet being afraid of being abandoned. When the child is unable to cope with this kind of conflict he/she experiences deep fears and anxieties and to be out of this vicious net he/she becomes exploitative.

Further it was found that the value of correlation coefficient between Machiavellian orientation of mothers and sons was greater than the value of correlation coefficient between fathers and sons. Hence it may be concluded that although parents in general get imitated by their sons with regard to Machiavellian orientation but mother's effect is greater than that of father. Here again the logic of closer interaction with mother applies.

Kraut and Lewis (1975) showed that parental modelling and parent child conflict could be the cause of Machiavellian orientation among children. One cannot refute the modelling hypothesis by demonstrating that children and parents disliked each other. Indeed in Machiavellian orientation, the reverse is likely to be true. Parents could best provide a model of emotional detachment for their children by being cold to them. In another extensive study Kraut and Price (1976) examined the development of Machiavellian orientation by examining the relationship between parent's and child's Machiavellian orientations, through a direct comparison of parents' and children's scores. It was found that Machiavellian orientations of fathers and mothers were positively related to their children's success at deceiving others but not at seeing through other's attempts at deception. In addition, father's Machiavellian orientation was positively related to their children's Machiavellian beliefs. These data support a modelling hypothesis towards the development of Machiavellian orientation. However, unexpectedly the children's own behaviours and beliefs were unrelated. This pattern of results suggests that a child's manipulative behaviours and beliefs are learned separately and only become consistent overtime. The findings of the present study are quite relevant and consistent in the context of the above-mentioned earlier findings.

However the present finding is not consistent with that of an earlier investigation carried in Japan by Dein (1974) who reported no support for "transmission" of Machiavellian orientation through modelling and teaching. Contrary to our results she found that low Mach parents were likely to have high Mach children because they were likely to fail in interactions involving interpersonal control with their children. This indicates that culture may act as intervening variable in modelling process.

References

Bharthi, G. & Sunitha, K. (1994), Machiavellianism among leaders and nonleaders, *Osmania Journal of Psychology, 17*, 43-47.

Bogart, K. (1971), Machiavellianism and individual difference in response to cognitive inconsistency, *Journal of Social Psychology, 85*,11-119.

Christie, R. & Geis, F.L. (1970), *Studies in Machiavellianism*, New York: Academic press.

de Boeck, P (1976), An alternative factor to the mother's form of the Parental Attitude Research Instrument and the relationship of PARI factors with social class, *Journal of Psychology, 94*, 79-86.

Dein, D.S. (1974), Parental Machiavellianism and children's cheating, *Journal of Cross-Cultural Psychology, 5*, 529-570.

Geis, F.L., & Moon, T.H. (1981), Machiavellianism and deception, *Journal of Personality and Social Psychology, 41*, 766-775.

Horney, K. (1950), *Neurosis and human growth*, New York: Norton.

Hunter, J.E., Gerbing, D.W. & Boster, F.J. (1982), Machiavellian beliefs and personality: Construct validity of the Machiavellianism dimension, *Journal of Personality and Social Psychology, 1*, 81-82.

Imperio, A.M., & Chabot, D.R. (1980), Male delinquent's perceptions of parents: A factor analysis, *Perceptual and Motor skills, 51*, 829-830.

Jha, P.K. (1995), Personality correlates of Machiavellians, *Indian Journal of Psychometry and Education, 26*, 65-70.

Kraut, R.E., & Lewis, S.H. (1975), Alternate model of family influences on student political ideology, *Journal of Personality and Social Psychology, 31*, 791-800.

Kraut, R.E., & Price J.D. (1976), Machiavellianism in parents and their children, *Journal of Personality and Social Psychology, 33*, 782-789.

Kuo, H.K.., & Marshella, A.J. (1977), The meaning and measurement of Machiavellianism in Chinese and American college students. *Journal of Social Psychology, 101*, 165-173.

Mudrack, P.E. (1990). Machiavellianism and locus of control: A meta analytical review, *Journal of Social Psychology, 130*, 125-130.

Ojha, H. (1993), A three dimentional inventory for assessing parental behaviour, *Psychological Studies, 38*, 31-32.

Ojha, H. (2007), A comparative study of needs and values of Machiavellian youth, *Praachi Journal of Psycho-Cultural Dimensions*, (Under publication).

Ojha, H., & Pramanick, M. (1995), Parental behaviour as related to some personality traits of adolescents, *Pscyhologia. 38*, 31-37.

Pandey J. (1981). Effects of Machiavellianism and degree of organisational formation on ingratiation, *Psychologia, 24*, 41-46.

Pilklinas, J., & Albrecht, E.J. (1961), *Psychology of human development*, New York: McGraw Hill Book Company.

Podrico, C. (1987), Machiavellianism and anxiety among Italian children, *Psychological Reports, 60*, 1041-1042.

Rai, S.N., & Gupta, M. (1987), *Mach IV scale*, Agra: Psychological Corporation.

Rim, Y. (1965), Machiavellianism and decisions involving risks, *British Journal of Social and Clinical Psychology, 5*, 50-56.

Schaefer, E.S. (1965), Children's report of parental behaviour; An inventory, *Child Development, 36*, 413-424.

Sears, R.R., Maccoby, E.E., & Levin, H. (1957), *Patterns of childrearing*, New York: Harper and Row.

Sims, L.S., & Paolucci, B. (1975), An empirical examination of the Parental Attitude Research Instrument (PARI), *Journal of the Marriage and the Family, 37*, 724-732.

Skinner, N.E. (1982), Personality correlates of Machiavellianism and psychopathology. *Social Behaviour and Personality, 9*, 155-157.

Triptathi R.C., & Sinha, Y. (1981), Social influences and development of Machiavellianism, *Psychological Studies, 26*, 58-61.

19

Meaning in Life and Psychological Well-being in Pre-adolescents and Adolescents

—Neerpal Rathi and Renu Rastogi

This study examined meaning in life and psychological well-being in male and female students of pre- adolescence and adolescence periods. A total of 104 students were randomly selected from various schools. Of these, 54 students were from class 12 and 50 students from class 9. Two questionnaires, one Personal Meaning Profile (PMP) by Wong and another Well-Being Manifestation Measure Scale (WBMMS) by Masse et al. were administered on the subjects. It was hypothesized that there will be significant differences in the perception of life as meaningful and psychological well-being of different groups of students. t-test was applied to analyse the data. Besides discussing the results, applied aspects of a meaningful life and psychological well-being are also discussed.

Keywords: Meaning in Life, Psychological Well-Being, and Adolescents.

Adolescence is a very critical and important stage in the development of human being. Most of the physiological, psychological, and social changes within the person take place during this period of life. The period of adolescence can be looked upon as a time of more struggle and turmoil than childhood. Adolescents have long been regarded as a group of people who

---

This paper originally appears in the *Journal of the Indian Academy of Applied Psychology*, January 2007, Vol.33, No.1, pp. 31-38.

are searching for themselves to find some form of identity and meaning in their lives (Erikson, 1968). They struggle to find a meaning of self. Having meaning or purpose in life can solve the identity crisis that a person normally faces during this period.

Meaning in life typically involves having a goal or a sense of unified purpose (Baumeister, 1991; Ryff, 1989). Recker, Peacock and Wong (1987) defined meaning as it "refers to making sense, order, or coherence out of one's existence and having a purpose and striving toward a goal or goals."

More recently Wong (1998) defined meaning as "an individually constructed, culturally based cognitive system that influences an individual's choice of activities and goals, and endows life with a sense of purpose, personal worth, and fulfilment." Thus the role of meaning in an adolescent's life can be a central point for a successful transition into adulthood. And an adolescent may derive meaning from a variety of sources. According to Wong's (1998) Personal Meaning Profile, these sources may be achievement, relationship, religion, self-transcendence, self-acceptance, intimacy and fair treatment.

Psychological well-being is a relatively complex notion with a variety of components that may contribute to it. Ryff (1989) extensively explored the meaning of psychological well-being and the definition closely parallelled with the Well-Being Manifestation Measure Scale (Masse, Poulin, Dassa, Lambert, Belair & Battaglini, 1998b) that was used in this study. The dimensions of well-being those were focused and operationalised are: autonomy, environmental mastery, personal growth, positive relations with others, purpose in life and self-acceptance. All of these factors can be considered as key components that make up the definition of psychological well-being. Therefore, adolescents who exhibit strength in each and every of these areas will be in a state of good psychological well-being, while adolescents who struggle in these areas will be in a state of low psychological well-being.

There are various factors that affect adolescents' level of psychological well-being. Several studies have shown that the quality of relationship within families, especially with parents is a major determining factor of psychological well-being in adolescents (Shek, 1997; Sastre & Ferriere 2000; Van Wel, Linssen & Abma 2000). Some other key factors that may contribute to a higher or lower level of psychological well-being in adolescents are stress (Siddique & D'Arcy, 1984) physical health (Mechanic & Hansell, 1987) and both popularity and intimacy in peer relationships (Townsend, McCracken & Wilton, 1988).

The importance of meaning in life and commitment to personal life satisfaction and psychological health has been well established (Erikson, 1982; Ledbetter, Smith & Vosler-Hunter 1991; Ryff, 1989; Stephen, Fraser & Marcia, 1992). Studies have shown that seeking meaning and fulfilment acts as a significant protector against emotional instability, and as a warrantor of psychological health and well-being (Lukas, 1991). Meaning in life has been found to be a strong and consistent predictor of psychological well-being (Zika & Chamberlain, 1987). Shek (1992) conducted a study on Chinese secondary students and found that students who scored highest in terms of quality of existence as well as purpose of existence also scored highest in psychological well-being.

Hypotheses

Based on the review of literature and past studies, the following hypotheses have been formulated for verification of this study through empirical investigation:

1. There is a significant difference between male and female students on the subscales of Personal Meaning Profile (PMP).
2. There is a significant difference between male and female students on the subscales of Well-Being Manifestation Measure Scale (WBMMS).
3. There is a significant difference between students of pre-adolescence and adolescence periods on the subscales of PMP.
4. There is a significant difference between students of pre-adolescence and adolescence periods on the subscales of WBMMS.

5. There is a significant difference between male and female students of adolescence period on the subscales of PMP.
6. There is a significant difference between male and female students of adolescence period on the subscales of WBMMS.
7. There is a significant difference between male and female students of pre-adolescence period on the subscales of PMP.
8. There is a significant difference between male and female students of pre-adolescence period on the subscales of WBMMS.

METHOD

Sample

The sample consists of total 104 students from various public schools. Out of these students, 34 boys and 20 girls were from adolescence period (class 12th) and 31 boys and 19 girls were from pre-adolescence (class 9th) period. Finally questionnaires were distributed to students and they were asked to give responses according to the instructions provided in the questionnaire. Mean age of pre-adolescents and adolescents was 13.9 years and 17 years respectively. The age range was 12-15 years for pre-adolescents and 16-18 years for adolescents.

Instruments

Following instruments have been used in this study:

Personal Meaning Profile (PMP): This scale was developed by Wong (1998) for the purpose of measuring meaning in life. This is a 57-item scale consisting of seven sub-scales; these are achievement, relationship, religion, self-transcendence, self-acceptance, intimacy, and fair treatment. The validity and reliability of the scale is quite high, with an overall Cronbach's alpha coefficient of 0.93 and 0.94 respectively.

Well-Being Manifestation Measure Scale (WBMMS): For measuring psychological well-being, WBMMS developed by Masse et al. (1998b) was used. The scale consists of 25-items with six factors. The six factors or subscales of the WBMMS are: control meaning in life and psychological well-being of self and events, happiness, social involvement, self-esteem, mental balance, and sociability. Masse, Poulin, Dassa, Lambert, Belair, & Battaglini (1998a) found an overall Crobach's alpha of 0.93 for the questionnaire, and a range of 0.71 to 0.85 on the subscales.

Results and Discussion

In order to test the postulated hypotheses, t-test was applied and t-values for different groups were obtained.

Hypothesis 1

While testing the hypothesis 1 it was found that males and females differ significantly on the subscales of relationship (t-value 4.05-significant at .01 level), self-acceptance (t-value 3.00-significant at .01 level), intimacy (t-value 2.63-significant at .01 level), and fair treatment (t-value 2.89-significant at .01 level).

Table 1: Mean, SD and t-values of males and females on the subscales of PMP and WBMMS.

N = Male 65; Female 39

Subscales of PMP		*Mean*	*SD*	*t-value*
Achievement	M	85.815	12.511	1.87
	F	90.128	9.119	
Relationship	M	46.569	7.875	4.05 **
	F	52.41	5.575	
Religion	M	46.83	7.612	1.67
	F	49.564	8.786	
Self-transcendence	M	41.646	6.692	1.52
	F	43.743	6.946	
Self-acceptance	M	29.932	5.5	3.00 **
	F	32.948	3.946	
Intimacy	M	24.969	5.536	2.63 **
	F	27.743	4.586	
Fair treatment	M	18.8	3.067	2.89 **
	F	20.794	3.894	

(Contd...)

(Contd...)

Subscales of WBMMS				
Control of self	M	13.6	3.086	0.67
and events	F	14	2.675	
Happiness	M	19.784	3.038	1.71
	F	20.769	2.432	
Social involvement	M	16.123	2.348	0.5
	F	16.384	2.843	
Self-esteem	M	14.2	2.469	2.65 **
	F	15.461	2.113	
Mental balance	M	14.507	2.845	2.24 *
	F	15.743	2.499	
SociabilityM	16.169	2.211	0.51	
	F	16.41	2.424	

**p< 0.01; * p< 0.05

PMP - Personal Meaning Profile,

WBMMS - Well-Being Manifestation Measure Scale

Results showed (Table 1) higher mean scores by females than males on all of the subscales of PMP. Results showed that females have higher tendency towards relationship, self-acceptance, fair treatment, and intimacy than that of males. No significant difference was found on the subscales of achievement, religion, and self-transcendence between males and females.

Hypothesis 2

In the second hypothesis results showed that female and male students differ significantly on self-esteem (t-value 2.65-significant at .01 level) and mental balance (t-value 2.24-significant at .05 level) subscales of WBMMS.

On the other hand no significant difference was found between males and females on other subscales of WBMMS. From the results (see Table 1) it is apparent that mean score of females (though very little in some cases) are higher than that of males. Femalesshowed a little higher score than male on subscales of mental health and self-esteem.

Table 2: Means, standard deviation, and t values of students of pre-adolescence and adolescence periods on the subscales of PMP and WBMMS. N = adolescence 54; pre-adolescence 50

Subscales of PMP		*Mean*	*SD*	*t-value*
Achievement	A	86.463	13.307	0.89
	PA	88.48	9.192	
Relationship	A	47.888	8.522	1.21
	PA	49.7	6.465	
Religion	A	47.388	8.666	0.6
	PA	48.36	7.585	
Self-transcendence	A	42.666	7.633	0.36
	PA	42.18	5.913	
Self-acceptance	A	30.222	5.193	1.7
	PA	31.96	5.038	
Intimacy	A	25.092	5.889	1.83
	PA	27	4.553	
Fair treatment	A	19.074	3.874	1.43
	PA	20.06	3.046	
Subscales of WBMMS				
Control of self	A	13.925	3.318	0.63
and events	PA	13.56	2.467	
Happiness	A	19.814	2.965	1.26
	PA	20.52	2.712	
Social involvement	A	16.148	2.558	0.3
	PA	16.3	2.533	
Self-esteem	A	14.574	2.559	0.43
	PA	14.78	2.261	
Mental balance	A	14.518	3.094	1.74
	PA	15.46	2.314	
SociabilityA	16.444	2.682	0.85	
	PA	16.06	1.766	

**p< 0.01; * p< 0.05
A = Adolescence, P.A. = Pre-Adolescence

Hypothesis 3

At the time of testing hypothesis 3, some differences were observed between students of pre-adolescence and adolescence periods on subscales of PMP (see Table 2). Though differences were there in the mean score of male and female students, but these differences were not found to be significant at any level of significance.

Table 3: Means, standard deviation and t-values of males and females of adolescence period on subscales of PMP and WBMMS. N = males 34; females 20

Subscales of PMP		*Mean*	*SD*	*t-value*
Achievement	M	85.205	14.735	0.9
	F	88.6	10.449	
Relationship	M	45.735	9.209	2.54 *
	F	51.55	5.735	
Religion	M	46.794	8.689	0.65
	F	48.4	8.756	
Self-transcendence	M	42.176	8.269	0.61
	F	43.5	6.525	
Self-acceptance	M	29.058	5.365	2.22 *
	F	32.2	4.323	
Intimacy	M	23.823	5.859	2.13 *
	F	27.25	5.418	
Fair treatment	M	17.941	3.567	3.00 **
		21	3.684	
Subscales of WBMMS				
Control of self and events	M	13.735	3.629	0.54
	F	14.25	2.769	
Happiness	M	19.47	3.202	1.11
	F	20.4	2.479	
Social involvement	M	16.294	2.316	0.54
	F	15.9	2.971	
Self-esteem	M	14.117	2.567	1.74
	F	15.35	2.412	
Mental balance	M	14	3.265	1.63
	F	15.4	2.623	
Sociability	M	16.294	2.668	0.53
	F	16.7	2.754	

**p< 0.01; * p< 0.05

Hypothesis 4

Here also no significant difference was found between students of pre-adolescence and adolescence periods on any subscale of WBMMS (see Table 2). An analysis of mean scores showed higher mean score (though very small in number) by adolescents than those of pre-adolescents on the subscales of control of self and events, mental balance and sociability. While on the subscales of happiness, social involvement, and self-esteem pre-adolescents score higher on means than adolescents.

Hypothesis 5

By analysing the results of males and females of adolescence period, we found that mean scores of females are higher than that of males on all subscales of PMP (see Table 3). The difference is significant on the subscales of relationship (t-value 2.54-significant at .05 level), self-acceptance (t-value 2.22-significant at .05 level), intimacy (t-value 2.13-significantat .05 level) and fair treatment (t-value 3.00-significant at .01 level) while on other subscales no significant difference was found at all.

Hypothesis 6

In testing sixth hypothesis we found that male and female students of adolescence period do not differ significantly in their mean scores on any of the subscales of WBMMS (see Table 3). Between females and males no significant difference was found at all. On this scale the mean scores of females were higher than that of males on all subscales except the social involvement subscale.

Hypothesis 7

Between males and females of pre-adolescence period a significant difference was found on the subscales of achievement (t-value 2.02-significant at .05 level), relationship (t-value 3.41-significant at .01 level) and self-acceptance (t-value 2.01-significant at .05 level) of PMP scale (see Table 4). On rest of the subscales no significant difference at any level was found. The mean scores on all subscales of PMP are higher among female students than that of male students.

Table 4: Means, standard deviation, and t-values of males and females of pre-adolescence period on the subscales of PMP and WBMMS. N = male 31; female 19

Subscales of PMP		*Mean*	*SD*	*t-value*
Achievement	M	86.483	9.705	2.02 *
	F	91.736	7.415	
Relationship	M	47.483	6.114	3.41 **
	F	53.315	5.406	
Religion	M	46.871	6.37	1.81
	F	50.789	8.885	
Self-transcendence	M	41.064	4.434	1.73
	F	44	7.535	
Self-acceptance	M	30.871	5.578	2.01 *
	F	33.736	3.445	
Intimacy	M	26.225	4.951	1.55
	F	28.263	3.587	
Fair treatment	M	19.741	2.081	0.94
	F	20.578	4.194	
Subscales of WBMMS				
Control of self and events	M	13.451	2.406	0.39
	F	13.736	2.621	
Happiness	M	20.129	2.86	1.31
	F	21.157	2.386	
Social involvement	M	15.935	2.407	1.3
	F	16.894	2.685	
Self-esteem	M	14.29	2.397	2.01 *
	F	15.578	1.804	
Mental balance	M	15.064	2.22	1.56
	F	16.105	2.378	
Sociability	M	16.032	1.601	0.14
	F	16.105	2.051	

**$p < 0.01$; * $p < 0.05$

Hypothesis 8

Finally, results of males and females of pre-adolescence period were analysed on WBMM scale. Results of both groups showed that on self-esteem (t-value 2.01-significant at .05 level) subscale of WBMMS males and females differ significantly (see Table 4). While on other subscales no significant difference was found with reference to these two sexes. By having a look on mean scores of males and females on subscales of WBMMS it was found that the mean scores of females were higher than that of males on all subscales.

Table 5: Correlation among the subscales of main scales: subscales of well-being manifestation measure scale

Subscales of personal meaning profile	*Control of self and events*	*Happiness*	*Social involve-ment*	*Self-esteem*	*Mental balance*	*Soci-ability*
Achievement	.499**	.368**	.232**	.599**	.328**	.182
Relationship	.426**	.547**	.284**	.583**	.412**	.467**
Religion	.229*	.413**	.177	.166	.068	.178
Self-tran-scendence	.423**	.357**	.244*	.438**	.336**	.124
Self-acceptance	.282**	.368**	.163	.287**	.351**	.304**
Intimacy	.210*	.382**	.110	.290**	.271**	.263**
Fair treatment	.254**	.244**	.187	.438**	.205*	.096

The aim of the present study was to have a look on meaning in life and psychological well-being of different groups of students especially with reference to gender and grade of students. In our study it was found that meaning in life is highly correlated with psychological well-being (see Table 5). This shows that if a person perceives his or her life to be meaningful then he or she will feel more psychologically well off than those who do not perceive their life to be meaningful. Some studies also show the similar results while evaluating the relationship between meaning in life and psychological well-being (Debats, Drost & Prartho, 1995; Shek, 1992; Zika & Chamberlain, 1987; Recker, Peacock & Wong

1987). In the present study it was found that adolescents did not score significantly higher than pre-adolescents on subscales of PMP and WBMMS. Similar results were also found by Weber (1996). In his study scores of grade twelve students were not significantly higher than grade nine students on psychological well-being. A reason for the good psychological well-being of pre-adolescents may be that they have not started to take things very seriously and also that they do not have high pressure for their career formation.

On the subscales of PMP females scored higher than that of males. In some other studies similar findings were observed. For example, Anderson (1999) found that the quality of salient parent-child and peer relationships significantly predicted adolescent relationship identity for girls but not for boys. Also, Beutel and Marini (1995) found that adolescent females were more likely than males to indicate that finding purpose and meaning in life is extremely important.

Thus it can be said that there can be various factors such as developmental level of person, family and social environment and relationships, schooling, career orientation, grade and gender that influences meaning in life and psychological well-being of persons.

Limitations

It is felt that there are two main limitations of the study. First limitation is concerned with the sample size of the study. A sample of 104 students is not sufficient for any generalization on all students of similar age groups. Further the sample was drawn from a particular locality, it would be more acceptable and representative if the samples are taken from diverse localities with students of diverse backgrounds.

Second limitation is related with the age group of students taken in the study. Age difference between two groups is not large enough to show a clear difference on the dimensions studied. Results are expected to be more diverse if the intake of boys and girls is of wider age range, from 11-12 years to 20-21 years.

Conclusion

This study has provided an insight of the meaning in life and psychological well-being of students of early and late adolescence period. It has been well established by prior studies in this field, that a meaningful and purposeful life enhances the psychological well-being of persons. With a better understanding of meaning and psychological well-being within adolescents, various counselling or educational implications can be derived for assisting adolescents to develop holistically in terms of body, mind and spirit as they venture into the world of adulthood.

References

Anderson, F. (1999), The prediction and correlates of adolescent relationship Identity (Doctoral dissertation, University of Minnesota, 1999), *Dissertation Abstracts International: Section B: The Sciences and Engineering, 60,* 2382.

Baumeister, R. F. (1991), *Meanings of life,* New York: Guilford.

Beutel, A., & Marini, M. (1995), Gender and values, *American Sociological Review, 60,* 436-448.

Debats, D., Drost, J., & Prartho, P. (1995), Experiences of meaning in life: a combined qualitative and quantitative approach, *British Journal of Psychology, 86,* 359-375.

Erikson, E. (1968), *Identity, youth and crisis,* New York: Norton.

Erikson, E. (1982), *The life cycle completed,* New York: Norton.

Ledbetter, M.F., Smith, L.A., & Vosler-Hunter, W.L. (1991), An evaluation of the research and clinical usefulness of the spiritual well-being scale, *Journal of Psychology and Theology, 19,* 49-55.

Lukas, E. (1991), Meaning-centered family therapy, *The International Forum for Logotherapy, 14,* 67-74.

Masse, R., Poulin, C., Dasa, C., Lambert, J., Belair, S., & Battaglini, A. (1998a), Elaboration et validation d'un outil de mesure du bien-etre psychologique : L'emmbep. *Canadian Journal of Public Health, 89,* 352-357.

Masse, R., Poulin, C., Dassa, C., Lambert, J., Belair, S., & Battaglini, A. (1998b), The structure of mental health higher-order confirmatory factor analyses of psychological distress and well-being measures, *Social Indicators Research, 45,* 475-504.

Mechanic, D., & Hansell, S. (1987), Adolescent competence, psychological well-being, and self-assessed physical health, *Journal of Health and Social Behaviour, 28,*364-374.

Recker, G., Peacock, E., & Wong, P. (1987), Meaning and purpose in life and well-being: A life-span perspective, *Journal of Gerontology, 42,* 44-49.

Ryff, C. D. (1989), Happiness is every thing, or is it? Explorations on the meaning of psychological well-being, *Journal of Personality and Social Psychology, 57,* 1069-1081.

Sastre, M., & Ferriere, G. (2000), Family decline and the subjective well-being of adolescents, *Social Indicators Research, 49,* 69-82.

Shek, D. (1992), Meaning in life and psychological well-being: an empirical study using the Chinese version of the purpose in life questionnaire, *Journal of Genetic Psychology, 153,* 185-190.

Shek, D. (1997), The relation of family functioning to adolescent psychological well-being, school adjustment, and problem behaviour, *The Journal of Genetic Psychology, 158,* 467-479.

Siddique, C., & D'Arcy, C. (1984), Adolescents, stress and psychological well-being, *Journal of Youth and Adolescence, 13,* 459-473.

Stephen, J., Fraser, E., & Marcia, J.E. (1992), Moratorium-achievement (MAMA) cycles in life span identity development: Value orientations and reasoning system correlates, *Journal of Adolescence, 15,* 283-300.

Townsend, M., McCracken, H., & Wilton, K. (1988), Popularity and intimacy as determinants of psychological well-being in adolescent friendships, *Journal of Early Adolescence, 8,* 421-436.

VanWel, F., Linssen, H., & Abma, R. (2000), The parental bond and the well-being of adolescents and young adults, *Journal of Youth and Adolescence, 29,* 307-318.

Weber, J. (1996), Meaning in life and psychological well-being among high school freshmen and seniors (Doctoral dissertation, Northern Arizona University, 1996).

Dissertation Abstracts International: Section B: The Sciences and Engineering, 57, 2912.

Wong, P. (1998), Implicit Theories of Meaningful Life and the Development of the Personal Meaning Profile. In P. Wong & P. Fry (Eds.) (1998). *The human quest for meaning: a handbook of psychological research and clinical applications,* Mahwah, NJ: Erlbaum.

Zika, S., & Chamberlain, K. (1987), Relation of hassles and personality to subjective well-being, *Journal of Personality and Social Psychology, 53,* 155-162.

20

Adjustment Problems among School Students

—*M.V.R. Raju and T. Khaja Rahamtulla*

The present study is intended to examine the adjustment problems of school students from urban and rural schools of Visakhapatnam district. Adjustment is a process by which a living organism maintains, a balance between the needs and the circumstances. The variables included for the study apart from adjustment (family, social, academic, financial and emotional) are age, gender, class, type of school etc. The study was conducted on a sample of 461 students (197 boys, 264 girls) randomly selected from the various government and private schools from urban and rural areas of Visakhapatnam district, Andhra Pradesh. A standardised questionnaire developed by Jain (1972) was adopted for this study. The data was analysed to examine the influence of individual factors on adjustment variables. The major findings of the study have shown that adjustment of school children is primarily dependent on the school variables like the class in which they are studying, the medium of instruction present in the school, and the type of management of the school. Parental education and occupation of the school children also significantly influenced adjustment.

The term 'adjustment' is often used as a synonym for accommodation and adaptation. Strictly speaking, the term denotes the results of equilibrium, which may be affect by either of these processes (Monroe, 1990). It is used to emphasize the individual's struggle to along or survive in his or her social and physical environment.

This paper originally appears in the *Journal of the Indian Academy of Applied Psychology*, January 2007, Vol.33, No.1, pp.73-80.

Good (1959) sates that adjustment is the process of finding and adopting modes of behaviour suitable to the environment or the changes in the environment. Shafer (1961) emphasized that adjustment is the process by which a living organism maintains a balance between its needs and the circumstances that influence the satisfaction of these needs. Kulshrestha (1979) explained that the adjustment process is a way in which the individual attempts to deal with stress, tensions, conflicts etc., and meet his or her needs. In this process, the individual also makes efforts to maintain harmonious relationships with the environment.

In adjustment, the two crucial factors are the individual and the environment. In the study of the individual, the considerations are the heredity and biological factors, the psychological factors, and the quality of socialisation given to him or her whereas, the environment includes all the social factors.

Every individual from the time he or she steps out of the family and goes to school makes to a long series of adjustments between the whole unique personality and the environment. The ardent desire of each boy and girl to become an individual person having a healthy physique, a growing intellectual ability, a greater degree of emotional poise, and increased participation in social groups, such characteristics enhance one's personality. Even parents, teachers and other significant members of the society to which person belongs will encourage this desire.

The school is the major socialisation institution for any child. It is the child's first contract with the world outside the house. For nearly 12 years a child spends five to seven hours a day in the school. School is one the most important foundation pillars on which the child's personality develops. Children learn proficiencies in various abilities like, learning process and home work, social communications, handling emotion, and the management of day-to-day interactions at home and school. In reality, the growing child is dependent on the immediate environment, i.e., the house and the school to meet his growth needs. The concern, therefore" extends to how the school facilities can be enhanced and improved to meet the growth needs of the children.

Several studies have been reported in the area of social, educational, health and emotional adjustment of school students of both sexes. Some studies try to relate adjustment with variables like intelligence, achievement, age, sex, socio-economic status, needs, anxiety, and security. Student's reaction to frustration has also been studied. A few studies focused on the nature, causes, and extent of indiscipline among students. The relation between indiscipline and variables like achievement, participation in co-curricular activities, etc., were also examined.

A review of the studies carried out in the field of adjustment as reported in the three surveys of educational research edited by Buch (1991) reveals that no systematic attempt has yet been made to develop a tool for the assessment of adjustment problems of school students.

Objectives

To examine the adjustment problem's among school children from different schools.

To examine the influence of demographic variables like age, gender, class, medium of instruction, types of schools, parents' education, parents' occupation, on the adjustment problems of school children.

Method

Sample

The sample consists of 461 students from sixth to tenth class, 197 boys and 264 girls. The sample boys included 132 from Telugu-medium schools and 65 from English-medium schools. Out of 264 girls, 211 were studying in Telugu-medium schools and 53 in English-medium schools. The mean age is 13.88 years, boys = 14.20 and girls = 13.77 years.

Tools

An adjustment scale developed by Jain (1972) was adopted for this study. It consists of the 50 items, which measure adjustment in five different areas: family adjustment, social adjustment, academic adjustment, financial adjustment and emotional adjustment. The students had to indicate if they experienced a particular described situation. The scoring of this scale involves counting the number of answers marked below the column 'YES' in all the areas of adjustment excepting Emotional Adjustment. Only statements that are marked in column 'YES' were counted

Table 1: Age, gender, class and medium of instruction and its impact on adjustment

		Age			*Gender*			*Class*			*Medium of instruction*		
		<13yrs	*>13yrs*	*t*	*Boys*	*Girls*	*t*	*upp.pri*	*Sec*	*t*	*EM*	*TM*	*t*
Dimension	M	n=180	n=280			n=180	n=280	n=180	n=280		n=118	n=342	
Family	M	7.60	7.54	.30	7.51	76.0	0.54	7.75	7.42	1.90*	7.59	7.59	.17
Adjustment	SD	2.50	1.74	1.81	1.91	1.92	1.82	1.94	1.84				
SocialM	7.97	8.21	1.44	7.94	8.25	1.86	8.07	8.15	.49	8.07	8.14	.34	
Adjustment	SD	1.96	1.59	1.71	1.76	1.80	1.70	1.75	1.74				
Academic	M	8.05	8.24	2.08	8.11	8.21	0.56	8.13	8.19	.36	8.08	8.19	.56
Adjustment	SD	1.96	1.84	1.82	1.94	1.89	1.89	1.77	1.93				
Financial	M	7.49	7.64	.70	7.31	7.78	2.23*	7.59	7.57	.70	7.64	7.56	.33
Adjustment	SD	2.24	2.18	2.20	2.19	1.14	2.25	2.34	2.16				
Emotional	M	6.08	5.86	1.01	5.70	6.13	1.97*	5.96	5.94	.65	5.56	6.08	2.09
Adjustment	SD	2.42	2.25	2.38	2.26	2.33	2.31	2.63	2.19				

* *p*<. 05 ** *p*<. 01

to obtain score on the particular dimension. For the Emotional Adjustment, the number of items marked 'NO' was counted to obtain a score. In this case, high a score indicated lesser emotional adjustment. A total adjustment score can be calculated by summing the scores on the first four dimensions and subtracting from this total score on Emotional Adjustment.

Results and Discussion

Table 1 provides results regarding the influence of age on adjustment. It can be noted from the table that age does not have a significant influences on adjustment. There are no significant differences between the two groups on any of the adjustment factors.

It also provides the findings with regard to gender and adjustment of the students. The results indicated a significant influence of gender on adjustment. Significant difference is observed between boys and girls on the financial and emotional factors of adjustment. On the financial adjustment dimension, girls have higher mean scores than the boys indicating that they have better financial adjustment. An examination of the individual items of the financial adjustment factor indicated that girl students as compared to boy students' feel their parents' fulfil their needs easily. This could be because parents of girl students tend to give more importance to the needs of their daughters.

The emotional adjustment factor, as mentioned in the methodology chapter, is reverse scored, with a higher score indicating lesser adjustment. Thus, it can be observed that boys are significantly better adjusted than girls. The analysis of the individual items of the emotional adjustment dimensions indicated that boys as compared to girls have not expressed any fear to go out alone in night, see a dead body or control their anger whenever things are not happening according to their wish. Similar findings are reported by Kasinath (1990) and Pradhan (1993).

Table 1 also proves the results with regard to class and adjustment. The sample of students has been categorised into groups of the basis of the class in which, they are studying. The group labelled us Upper Primary group includes students studying between 5th and 7th standards while the group named Secondary includes students studying between 8th and 10th class.

The table shows that the class has a significant influence on family adjustment. The students studying Upper Primary have better family adjustment than their counterparts in Secondary classes. An analysis of the individual items shows that the former feel proud that their parents are educated, their family member take positive criticism in their future planned, feel that their parents, instead of accepting old familial traditions are modern and they do not hesitate to invite their friends to home.

The findings indicate that pre-adolescent students are more influenced by their parents as they form the main role models for them. It is only when they enter into adolescence that they would experience peer pressure and associated specific opinions and attitudes about themselves and their family. It also provides results regarding the influence of median of instruction on adjustment. The medium of instruction has been categorized into two categories on the basis of the language in which instruction is provided to the students. Category 1 includes English medium while Category 2 includes Telugu medium. It can be observed from the table that the medium of instruction has a significant influence on emotional adjustment. English-medium students have better adjustment than Telugu-medium students on this dimension. An examination of the individual items indicates that students from the English medium schools are not afraid to talk with others, do not feel jealous when somebody supercedes them, go out alone in the night or get angry when things do not go according to their wishes.

It is a common practice in English-medium schools to provide training to their children to make oral presentations, face competition and control their negative emotions. Consequently, they are more likely to exhibit better emotional adjustment.

Table 2 shows the results regarding the type of school and adjustment. The sample of schools of school has been categorised into four groups on the basis of type of management of the school. Group 1 includes private un-aided English- medium schools, while group 2 includes municipal school, group 3 includes zilla parishad schools and group 4 includes private aided schools. Significant differences are observed among four schools on the academic and emotional factors of adjustment. On academic dimensions, zilla parishad school children have higher mean scores than the children of other schools. Observation of the individual items of the academic adjusted compared to children of other schools. These students feel they easily get cooperation from co-students, they usually think that they will complete their studies adequately, their teachers never try to downgrade them and their parents insist on study instead of joining service.

In emotional adjustment dimension private unaided English-medium school students are better adjusted than other schools students. An examination of individual items of the emotional adjustment dimension indicated that the private un-aided English-medium school students display the following qualities: they are not afraid of talking to others, they do not have tears in their eyes seeing anybody in trouble or distress, they do not feel jealous whenever anybody supercedes them and do not get angry nor like to beat others if they joke at them.

Table 2 Type of school and adjustment

		Type of schools				
Dimensions		*S1(n=100)*	*S2 (n=116)*	*S3 (n=87)*	*S4 (n=157)*	*F value*
Family	Mean	7.59	7.56	7.35	7.67	547
adjustment	S.D	2.05	1.68	1.99	1.81	
Social Mean	7.89	8.05	8.32	8.21	1.184	
adjustment	S.D	1.94	1.60	1.72	1.72	
Academic	Mean	7.85	7.59	8.43	8.41	3.158*
adjustment	S.D	1.99	1.86	1.76	1.86	
Financial	Mean	7.45	7.61	7.43	7.73	0.493
adjustment	S.D	3.45	1.92	2.59	2.08	
Emotional	Mean	5.33	6.11	6.17	6.10	3.106*
adjustment	S.D	2.40	2.02	2.44	2.36	

* p<. 05 ** p<. 01

S1 = private English-medium school (urban). S3= zilla parishad Telugu-medium school (Rural)

S2= municipal Telugu-medium school(urban). S4= aided Telugu-medium school (urban).

As mentioned earlier, students from English-medium school tend to exhibit better emotional adjustment while their counterparts from rural schools display relatively better educational adjustment as they do experience stress from their teachers and parents regarding their academic performance.

Studies by Sharma and Gakkar (1991) and Pradhan (1992) have obtained similar results.

Table 3: Parents' education and adjustment

Parents education		*Below inter (n= 297)*	*Above inter (n=63)*	*'t' value*
Family adjustment	Mean	7.44	8.14	2.630 **
	SD	1.97	1.60	
Social adjustment	Mean	8.05	8.52	1.890 *
	S.D	1.88	1.26	
Academic adjustment	Mean	8.13	8.04	780
	S.D	2.03	1.48	
Financial adjustment	Mean	7.38	8.23	2.690 **
	SD	2.32	2.04	
Emotional adjustment	Mean	5.90	5.77	390
	SD	2.37	2.49	

Table 3 provides results regarding the influence of parents' education on adjustment. The sample of parents' education has been categorised into two groups on the basis of their education. Group 1 includes students whose parents have an intermediate or less education while group 2 includes students whose parents have an inter medium. It can be noted from the table that parents' education has a significant influence on adjustment. Significant differences are observed between group I and group II in family, social and financial factors of adjustment. On the three dimensions, students of group II have higher mean scores then group I. An examination of the individual items of the family adjustment factor indicates the former get love and affection in the family and they get pleasure from the family members. In social adjustment, they get pleasure in respecting the aged people of the society. And available in their home, they do not suffer in their life due to poverty and they do not select friends on the basis of financial status. A study by Mishra and Singh (1998) showed that parental education had a significant influence on the aspiration levels of their children.

Table 4 indicated that the influence of parents occupation on adjustment. The sample of parents occupation divided into three categories on the basis of their profession. Category I include labour while category II includes clerical and category iii includes executives. Significant differences are observed among clerical, labour and executives in the family factors of adjustment. In this dimension, children of executives have higher mean scores than the labour and clerical.

Table 4: Parents' occupation and adjustment

Parents occupation Dimensions		*Labour (n= 199)*	*Clerical (n= 122)*	*Executive (n- 58)*	*"F value*
Family adjustment	Mean	7.34	7.62	8.08	3.600 *
	S.D		1.92	1.91	1.63
Social adjustment	Mean	8.02	8.09	8.54	1.881
	S.D		1.84	1.81	1.48
Academic Adjustment	Mean	8.15	8.19	8.43	463
	S.D		1.99	1.96	1.56
Financial Adjustment	Mean	7.43	7.45	8.20	2.804
	S.D		2.24	2.51	1.88
Emotional Adjustment	Mean	6.15	5.86	5.34	2.738
	S.D		2.11	2.58	2.62

* p<. 05 ** p<. 01

An examination of the individual items of the family adjustment factor indicated that children of executives are better adjusted compared to children whose parents are doing labour and clerical jobs. These children feel that their family members take active criticism in their future plans, because their parents have status in the society and generally parents take care of the welfare of their children. Executive parents by virtue of their better educational back group may offer a more conducive atmosphere at home thereby facilitating better family adjustment among their children.

Conclusion

The adjustment of school children is determined by their gender, the class in which they are studying, the medium of instruction adopted in their school, the type of management of the school and their parents education and occupation. Differences across the children with regard to their adjustment are noted mainly with regard to the school in which they are studying. While family adjustment is more higher classes, academic adjustment, is better among children from schools that are founded by the government, and emotional adjustment is higher for students from English and privately managed schools. Further parental education and occupation significantly influenced the emotional adjustment of the school children.

References

Bell, HM (1962) Manual, Bell adjustment inventory (revised student form (P.3), California.

Buch, M.B. (Ed) (1991), *Survey of research in education,* New Delhi: NCERT.

Good, C.V. (1959), *Dictionary of education,* (P: 6), New York: McGraw - Hill Book Company.

Jain P., (1972), Agra psychological Association Cell, New Delhi.

Kasinath, H.M. (1990), Adjustment between migrated Hindi and non-Hindi speaking students studying in Jawahar Navodaya Vidyalayas, *The Progress of Education, 9,* 8-10.

Kulshrestha, S.P. (1979), *Educational psychology,* Meerut, India: Loyal Book Depot.

Mishra, S.K., & Singh, RD. (1998), Personality adjustment of graduates with reference to their socioeconomic status, *Praaachi Journal of Psycho Cultural Dimensions, 14,* 43-44.

Monroe, P. (ed.) (1990), *International encyclopedia of education,* New Delhi: Cosmo Publications.

Pradhan, G.C. (1992), Values pattern of school students as a function of types of schools and levels of intelligence, *The Educational Review, XCII,* 133-136.

Pradhan, G.C. (1993), Major judgment of secondary school students as a function of types of school and sex, *The Educational Review, XCIX, 64,* 65,67.

Sharma. N., & Gakkar, S.C. (1991), Adjustment of students of denominational schools a comparative study, *The Educational Review, 105,* 136-138.

21

Self-concept, Emotional Maturity and Achievement Motivation of the Adolescent Children of Employed Mothers and Homemakers

—*Suneetha Hangal and Vijayalaxmi A. Aminabhavi*

The present study assessed the impact of maternal employment on the self-concept, emotional maturity and achievement motivation of adolescents. The sample consisted of 75 adolescents of employed mothers and 75 adolescents of homemakers, studying in 8th and 9th standards in Hubli-Dharwad cities of North Karnataka. Children's Self-concept Scale by Ahluwalia, Emotional Maturity Scale by Singh and Bhargava and Deo-Mohan Achievement Motivation Scales were used to collect the data. The data were analysed by 't' test and ANOVA. The results revealed that the adolescent children of homemakers have significantly higher self-concept. It was also noticed that children of employed mothers have high emotional maturity and female children of employed mothers are highly achievement oriented.

According to Samuel Ullman, "Youth is not only a time of life, it is also a state of mind and a matter of will...." The future of any nation depends on the quality of its youth. Long ago, the great Indian philosopher, Swami Vivekananda, aptly had said, "Youths are not useless but are used less." Hence, proper guidance at this crucial phase of life is all the more important for enhancing their

This paper originally appears in the *Journal of the Indian Academy of Applied Psychology*, January 2007, Vol.33, No.1, pp. 103-110.

positive self-concept, enriching their knowledge and skills in decision making, conflict resolution and management of emotions.

Adolescence is one of the important periods of life. It is characterised by innumerable and unique problems. With the demands of globalisation, the nature and number of challenges have become still more compared to the yesteryear. Family, which plays an important role in the personality development of adolescents, is undergoing structural, emotional and interactional transformations. The contributions of mothers in shaping the personality of their children cannot be ignored. But an unprecedented number of women, especially mothers, are entering the labour force either due to economic necessity or in search of identity. This has led to radical shift in the traditional role of mother as a 'caretaker' to a 'bread earner' and has altered child-rearing goals and practices.

Quite a large number of empirical studies have yielded conflicting evidences regarding the impact of maternal employment on their children. Based on these research works, especially two theories regarding the impact of maternal employment have emerged: the guilt-over protection theory and the neglected theory. According to the first theory, the employed mother feels guilty about leaving her children and tries to compensate with smothered love and overprotection. The second theory presumes that the dual role creates 'role strain' and leads to child neglect.

Roy (1963) found that adolescent sons of working mothers had lower school grades. Rees and Palmer (1970) from their longitudinal study on children aged 6-15 years belonging to higher socio-economic strata, also found that in general, maternal employment was related to high IQ in girls and low IQ in boys, whereas Kurien (1982) reported that children of employed mothers do better in schools. So also Scarr (1984) noticed that school achievement of children of employed mothers was good compared to children of non-employed mothers But Gottfried and Bathurst (1988), in contrast, found that the number of hours the mothers work was negatively correlated with school achievement.

Mody and Murthy (1988) reported low intelligence scores in children of employed mothers at the early age of 12 years. They also found children of employed mothers to be careless and slightly emotionally unstable in the early years but independent during later years as compared to children of non-employed mothers.

Nanda and Monochas (1971) revealed that employment of mothers had a negative influence on their children and they became less cooperative, less sympathetic and exhibited indifferent social behaviour. However, Muni (1995) observed that adolescents of employed mothers had a positive physical, intellectual and educational self-concept and were better adjusted than the children of housewives.

Mittal (1997) compared the self-concept and scholastic achievement of the daughters of employed and non-employed mothers, and observed that there was no significant difference in any of the areas of self-concept and scholastic achievement. Deka and Kakkar (1998) also supported the same, that maternal employment had no impact on the self-concept of adolescents. Muni and Panigrahi (1997) concluded that maternal employment is not a liability, rather an asset for their children, as it helps in grooming better adjusted children.

In the background of such varied results, an attempt has been made by the investigators to study the impact of maternal employment on their adolescent children. The above-reviewed literature reveals that there is dearth of information related to the effect of maternal employment on some psychological variables such as self-concept, emotional maturity and achievement motivation of their adolescent children. The study by Pastey and Aminabhavi (2006) has revealed that the adolescents with high emotional maturity may have significantly high stress ($t=10.44$, $p<0.001$) and self-confidence ($t= -2.92$, $p<0.001$) when compared to those with low emotional maturity.

OBJECTIVES

i) To investigate the impact of employed mothers on the self-concept, emotional maturity and achievement motivation of their children.

ii) To study the sex differences in children of employed mothers and children of homemakers in relation to self-concept, emotional maturity and achievement motivation.

iii) To determine the differential impact of mothers employed in high, middle and lower level occupations on the variables under study.

METHOD

Sample

For this study, 150 adolescents (75 children of employed mothers and 75 children of home makers) studying in 8th and 9th standards in the age range of 13 to 16 years were randomly selected from the following four schools of the twin-cities, Hubli-Dharwad, in Karnataka State: (i) N.K.Takkar's High School, Hubli, (ii) K.H.Kattimani High School, Hubli, (iii) St.Joseph's High School, Dharwad and (iv) Sri.Shivananda High School, Dharwad.

Tools

In addition to bio-data sheet, the following psychological tests were used to collect the data and study the impact of maternal employment on their adolescent children:

i) *Children's Self-concept Scale (Ahluwalia, 2002):* This test contains 80 items with 'yes' or 'no' responses. It also includes 16 lie items. This scale consists of six subscales: Behaviour, Intellectual and school status, Physical appearance and attributes, Anxiety, Popularity, Happiness and satisfaction. It has a high test-retest reliability and the concurrent validity range from 0.397 to 0.621.

ii) *Emotional Maturity Scale (EMS) (Singh & Bhargava, 1991):* This scale has 48 questions related to the following five categories: Emotional Instability, Emotional Regression, Social Maladjustment, Personality Disintegration and Lack of Independence. The test-retest reliability has been estimated at 0.75 and validity against the Adjustment Inventory by Singh and Bhargava (1980) at 0.46.

iii) *Deo-Mohan Achievement Motivation Scale (Deo & Mohan, 2002):* This scale consists of 50 items, out of which 13 are negative and 37 are positive items. The responses are made on a five-point scale. The test-retest reliability of the scale is 0.69 and the validity against Aberdeen Academic Achievement Inventory is 0.75.

Table 1: Means, SDs and 't' values for the scores of Self-concept, Emotional Maturity and Achievement Motivation of adolescent children of employed mothers and homemakers (N=75 in each group)

Variables	*Groups*	*Mean*	*SD*	*Mean Difference*	*SEM*	*t value*
Self–concept behavior	CEM	51.05	5.00	–0.45	0.6	–0.75
	CHM	51.50	0.70			
Intellectual & school status	CEM	52.20	7.65	–3.3	1.03	–3.20 **
	CHM	55.50	4.50			
Physical appearance	CEM	54.00	6.00	3.00	0.9	3.33 **
& Attributes	CHM	51.00	4.80			
Anxiety	CEM	52.4	6.70	–4.1	0.99	–4.14 **
	CHM	56.50	5.50			
Popularity	CEM	53.00	5.00	1.00	0.84	1.2
	CHM	52.00	5.25			
Happiness & satisfaction	CEM	52.80	6.24	–3.7	0.94	–3.94 **
	CHM	56.50	5.00			
Total	CEM	53.00	3.2	–3.00	0.62	-4.84 **
	CHM	56.00	4.35			
Emotional maturity	CEM	68.17	11.70	–4.33	1.53	-2.8
Emotional instability	CHM	72.50	6.10			

(Contd...)

(Contd...)

Emotional regression	CEM	69.55	6.00	20.05	1.64	12.22***
	CHM	89.60	12.70			
Social maladjustment	CEM	84.10	7.20	12.60	1.14	11.1**
	CHM	71.50	6.70			
Personality disorganization	CEM	70.55	6.00	6.00	0.9	4.94**
	CHM	75.00	4.70			
Lack of independence	CEM	78.50	7.50	12.50	1.11	11.3**
	CHM	66.00	6.00			
Total	CEM	69.50	6.00	–5.50	1.10	–5.0**
	CHM	75.00	6.70			
Achievement motivation	CEM	52.50	9.27	–3.30	1.2	–2.8**
	CHM	55.45	4.15			

** $p < 0.01$ *** $p < 0.001$ CEM=Children of Employed Mothers, CHM= Children Home Makers

Collection of data: The investigator visited the randomly selected schools and also the respondents. The scales were administered separately in two sessions.

Analysis of the data: For a descriptive analysis of the data, the means and SDs of the adolescents on self-concept, emotional maturity and achievement motivation scales were calculated for the two groups of employed mothers and homemakers. The first and second objectives were tested using 't' test and the one-way analysis of variance (ANOVA) was carried out to test the third objective.

Results and Discussion

Table 1 shows that there is significant difference between the children of employed mothers and that of homemakers in relation to the variables studied, self concept (t=-4.84, p<0.01) emotional maturity (t=-5, p<0.01), and achievement motivation (t= -2.8, p<0.01). In other words, adolescent children of homemakers have significantly higher self-concept and higher achievement motivation than the children of employed mothers. However, a close perusal of the same table reveals that there is highly significant difference between the two groups with regard to the sub-components of the self-concept like intellectual and school status (t= -3.20, p<0.01), physical appearance and attributes (t= 3.33, p <0.01), anxiety (t= -4.14, p <0.01), happiness and satisfaction (t=-3.94, p<0.01).

Though the adolescent children of homemakers are more anxious than their counterparts, they have higher intellectual and school status and are happier and satisfied. This may be due to the feelings of security they enjoy in the constant company of their mothers and the higher level of anxiety in the children of homemakers can be attributed to the greater demands and expectations from their mothers to excel in curricular aspects. The same table also shows that adolescent children of employed mothers have higher self-concept with regard to physical appearance and attributes. This may be due to their awareness of the importance of the role of physical appearance and attributes in social acceptance and success as they are exposed to a wider world apart from home and school because of maternal employment

Table 2: Means, SDs and 't' values for the scores of self-concept, emotional maturity and achievement motivation of male and female adolescent children of employed mothers and homemakers (Within the group comparison)

Variables	*Status of Mother*	*Sex of the adolescents*	*N*	*Mean*	*SD*	*t -value*
Self-concept	Employed	Male	42	52.75	4.50	–1.14
		Female	33	54.18	5.99	
Homemakers		Male	43	56.85	5.03	–0.96
		Female	32	57.80	3.55	
Emotional maturity	Employed	Male	42	67.00	9.4	–0.43
		Female	33	67.75	5067	
Homemakers		Male	43	70.90	7.03	7.48 ***
		Female	32	58.91	4.76	
Achievement motivation	employed	Male	42	52.71	8.0	–5.99 ***
		Female	33	62.12	5.65	
Homemakers		Male	43	52.19	6.37	–1.05
		Female	32	53.90	7.4	

*** $p < 0.001$ CEM=Children of Employed Mothers, CHM=Children of Home Makers

Table 1 further shows that the children of employed mothers and children of homemakers differ significantly in their emotional maturity (t= -5, p <0.01). The results also reveal that children of employed mothers are emotionally more mature than their counterparts. A highly significant difference was noticed between the two groups in the areas of emotional instability (t= -2.8, p <0.01) and personality disorganisation (t= -4.94, p<0.01). The two groups differed to very great extent in areas of emotional regression (t= -12.22 p < 0.001), social maladjustment (t=11.1,p<0.001) and lack of independence (t=11.3,p<0.001).

Table 3: Means, SDs and 't' values for the scores of self-concept, emotional maturity and achievement motivation of male and female children of employed mothers and homemakers (between the groups comparison)

Variables	*Sex of the children*	*Status of mothers*	*Mean*	*SD*	*t value*
Self-concept	Male	Employed	52.75	4.50	–3.97 **
		Homemakers	56.90	5.03	
	Female	Employed	54.18	5.99	–2.97 *
		Homemakers	57.80	3.60	
Emotional Maturity	Male	Employed	67.00	9.40	-2.20 *
		Homemakers	70.90	7.03	
	Female	Employed	67.75	5.64	6.80 ***
		Homemakers	58.91	4.76	
Achievement Motivation	Male	Employed	52.71	80.00	0.35
		Homemakers	52.19	6.37	
	Female	Employed	62.12	5.65	5.01 ***
		Homemakers	53.9	7.40	

*p < 0.05 ** p < 0.01 *** p <0.001 CEM=Children of Employed Mothers, CHM=Children of Home Makers

Table 3 shows that there is a highly significant difference between the male children of employed mothers and that of homemakers with regard to self-concept (t= -3.97, p<0.01) and this difference in self-concept is greater than that of female children of employed mothers and homemakers (t= -2.97, p<0.05). One of the reasons for this may be that though our society is progressive and advanced, still there is a tendency to hold the sons at a higher level compared to daughters, and this positive regard from the family, especially mothers, contributes for the enhanced self-concept in male children. So also there are very highly significant differences between the female children of employed mothers and that of homemakers with regard to emotional maturity (t= 6.8, p <0.001) and achievement motivation (t= 5, p<0.001). Table 3 reveals those female children of homemakers are more emotionally mature than the female children of employed mothers, and so also from the male children of both employed mothers and homemakers. This may be due to their constant contact of a matured adult (mother) to emulate the balanced way of managing their emotions. At the same time, it is observed from the table that female children of employed mothers are highly achievement motivated than the male children of the employed mothers and homemakers as well as the female children of homemakers.

The differential impact of socio-economic status of maternal employment on their children was also studied. The ANOVA results showed that there is class difference in relation to emotional maturity among children of employed mothers (F= -5.41;p<0.01). It was found that children of the employed mothers at the middle class occupational status are more emotionally mature compared co the children of mothers from the upper and lower levels of occupation. This can be attributed to the challenges and responsibilities placed on them because of maternal employment.

Conclusions

The children of homemakers have significantly higher self-concept in various dimensions of self-concept such as intellectual and school status, anxiety, happiness and satisfaction, as well as in overall self-concept compared to children of employed mothers. Children of employed mothers have significantly higher self-concept in the area of physical appearance and attributes in comparison to their counterparts. Children of employed mothers have significantly high emotional maturity compared to their counterparts. Children of homemakers have significantly higher emotional instability, emotional regression and personality disorganisation compared to children of employed mothers. The children of employed mothers are more socially maladjusted and lacked independence to a very highly significant level compared to the children of homemakers. Female children of homemakers have significantly higher emotional maturity compared to male children. Female children of employed mothers have significantly higher achievement motivation compared to the male children of employed mothers. The children of employed mothers working at the upper, middle and lower levels of occupations do differ significantly among themselves with regard to their emotional maturity.

It is revealed from the results that both the groups, though they differ significantly from each other in most of the dimensions of the variables, their scores of self-concept, emotional maturity and achievement motivation are not very pronounced (they are just above the average). Hence there is a felt need to counsel these children to enhance their positive self-concept, emotional maturity and achievement motivation. There is a need for training in management of emotions, increasing the degree of happiness and satisfaction among adolescents, and lessen anxiety. It is revealed by the *American Psychologists* (2006) that "happy nations" are likely to be more prosperous than miserable (Harkin, 2006). Mothers are also in need of guidance and counselling as far as bringing up their male and female children effectively with the egalitarian attitude.

References

Ahluwalia, S.P. (2002), *Manual for Children's Self-Concept Scale,* Agra: National Psychological Corporation.

Deo, P., & Mohan, A. (2002), *Manual for Deo-Mohan Achievement Motivation Scale,* Agra: National Psychological Corporation.

Deka, N., & Kakkar, A. (1998), The impact of maternal employment on perceived behaviour and self-concept of Indian adolescents, *Journal of Indian Academy of Applied Psychology, 24,* 93-98.

Gottfried & Bathrust (1988), In Venkatalashmi, T.R. (1991). Perception of adolescents towards mother's employment. Unpublished M.Sc.Thesis, University of Agricultural Sciences, Dharwad.

Harkin, J. (2006), Happiness is an idea too. Panorama, *Deccan Herald,* 4th January, Wednesday, Page 9.

Kurien, P. (1982). *How working mothers manage,* Cliffton House.

Mody, S.N., & Murthy, V.N. (1988), The Study of mental health of children of working mothers, *Journal of Personality and Clinical Studies,* 4,161- 164.

Mittal, S. (1997), Self-concept and scholastic achievement of children of working mothers and non-working mothers, *Journal of Community Guidance and Research, 14,* 47-52.

Muni, A.K. (1995), Effect of maternal employment on adolescents' self-concept and adjustment, *International Journal of Behavioural Sciences,* 13.

Muni, A.K, & Panigrahi, B. (1997), Effect of maternal employment on school children' adjustment problems, *Journal of Community Guidance and Research, 14,* 209-216.

Nanda, P. & Monachs, M.K. (1977), Comparative study of the social behaviour of nine year old children of working and non-working mothers, *Indian Journal of Home Sciences, 11,* 50-53.

Paste, G., & Aminabhavi, V. (2006), Impact of emotional maturity on stress and Self-confidence of adolescents, *Journal of Indian Academy of Applied Psychology, 32,* 69-75.

Rees, A.N., & Palmer, F.H. (1970), Factors related to change in mental test performance, *Developmental Psychology Monograph,* 3.

Roy, P. (1963). Adolescent roles: Rural urban differentials. In F.I. Nye and L.W. Hoffman (Eds.), *The employed mothers in America,* pp 165-181. Chicago: Rand McNally.

Scarr (1984), *Mother care-other care.* New York: Basic Books.

Singh, Y., & Bhargava, M. (1990), *Manual for Emotional Maturity Scale,* Agra: National Psychological Corporation.

22

Styles of Learning and Thinking

—*Kalpana Vengopal* and *K. Mridula*

The present study is aimed at examining the hemispheric preferences for information processing and styles of learning and thinking in children. A sample of 250 students of class VIII which included both boys and girls from five English medium schools were selected. The tool Styles of Learning and Thinking was administered. Results revealed that there was significant difference in the right and left (brain) hemisphere preference for information processing among children and that boys were more right hemispheric oriented and girls were more left hemispheric oriented in information processing. Significant difference in the styles of learning and thinking and concept preference among right hemisphere and left hemisphere dominant children was also observed with respect to both genders.

What happens to us in life depends on not just 'how we' think, but 'how well' we think and learn. Of all the factors that influence an individual, his styles of learning and thinking play a major role. Parents and teachers are able to perceive children and their natural tendencies of how they think, act and learn in different ways and in different situations. For example, one child may welcome structure in learning while another may welcome new ways of doing things. One child may perform tasks in an orderly and systematic pattern and another may perform tasks in an

This paper originally appears in the *Journal of the Indian Academy of Applied Psychology*, January 2007, Vol.33, No.1, pp. 111-118.

unsystematic pattern. This is due to individual differences in their style of learning and thinking.

In academic institutions, learning and teaching processes are mismatched. Teaching and thinking styles of the teachers and learning and thinking styles of students differ because learning differences are not tied up to the understanding and thinking abilities of students. Many educators are still perplexed about the styles of students in learning and thinking process; what effect these styles have on children's performance in schools and why attention should be given to children's performance to assess their levels of ability.

Styles depend upon cerebral dominance of an individual in retaining and processing different modes of information in his/her own style of learning and thinking. Style indicates the hemisphericity functions of the brain and students' learning strategy and information processing are based on the preferences of the brain area (Venkataraman, 1994).

Hemisphericity is the cerebral dominance of an individual in retaining and processing modes of information on his/her own style of learning and thinking. (Raina, 1984). Researches conducted during the last two decades have shown that the human left cerebral hemisphere is to be specialised for primarily verbal, analytical, abstract, temporal and digital operations (Bogen, 1989; Gazzaniga, 1990; Fitzerald & Hattie, 1993). The same investigations revealed that the right cerebral hemisphere is to be specialised for primarily non-verbal holistic, concrete, creative, analogic and aesthetic functions. The differences in preference of the two hemispheres for information processing have been referred to as styles of learning and thinking (SOLAT) by Torrance.

Styles are propensities rather than abilities. They are the ways of directing the intellect which an individual finds comfortable. The styles of learning and thinking are as important as levels of ability and we ignore to identify and develop then in students at an early and appropriate stage. Torrance and others have developed the SOLAT tool based on the hemisphericity functions of the brain. It identifies hemisphericity dominance by way of studying the hemisphere functions. It indicates a student's learning strategy and brain hemisphere preference in problem-solving.

Objectives

i. To measure right hemisphere and left (brain) hemisphere preferences for information processing in children.

ii. To find the differences in the right hemisphere and left hemisphere preferences for information processing in boys and girls.

iii. To measure styles of learning and thinking in right hemisphere and left hemisphere dominant children.

iv. To find the difference in the styles of learning and thinking in right hemisphere and left hemisphere dominant boys and girls.

Method

Sample

The sample consists of 250 students of Class VIII which included both boys and girls from five English-medium schools.

Tools

SOLAT (Styles of Learning and Thinking) developed by Venkataraman (1994) is used in the present study. It is a modified version of the tool developed by Torrance. It identifies hemisphericity dominance by way of studying the hemisphere functions. It indicates the learning and thinking styles and brain hemisphere preference.

Results and Discussion

Right and Left (brain) Hemisphere Preference for Information Processing in Children

Table 1 shows the number of children who preferred the right brain (R), the left brain (L) and whole brain (W) irrespective of gender. It indicates that the calculated χ^2 value 166.016 with degree of freedom 2 is highly significant at 0.000 level. Thus there is a significant difference in the right hemisphere and the left (brain) hemisphere preference for information processing among children.

Table 1

Chi-square table for the hemisphericity preference for information processing in children

Brain	*Observed N*	*Expected N*	*Residual*	*Hemisphere*
Right hemisphere	178	83.3	94.7	Chi-square 166.016
Left hemisphere	50	83.3	–33.3	df(2)
Whole hemisphere	22	83.3	–33.3	P .000
Total	250			

Right and Left (brain) Hemisphere Preference for Information Processing in Boys and Girls

Table 2 shows gender-wise hemisphere preference. From the values calculated through gender hemisphere cross-tabulation, it is clear that overall the right hemisphere dominates among children for information processing. The table indicates that boys are more right-hemisphere oriented and girls are more left-hemisphere oriented in information processing.

Table 2. Gender hemisphere cross tabulation to find the hemisphere preference for information processing in boys and girls

Gender	*Hemisphere Preference*			*Total*
	Right	*Left*	*Whole*	
Boys (100%)	102 (77.9%)	21 (16.0%)	8 (6.1%)	131
Girls (100%)	76 (62.9%)	29 (24.4%)	14 (11.8%)	119
Total (100%)	178 (71.2%)	50 (20%)	22 (8.8%)	250

Table 3: Preference of Styles of Learning and Thinking among Children

	Right Hemisphere									Left Hemisphere									
	Learning Style				*Thinking Style*						*Learning Style*				*Thinking Style*				
	Content preference	Class preference	Learning preference	Imagination	Logical fractional	Convergent/ Divergent	Creative	Problem solving	Imagination	Verbal	Conduct preference	Class preference	Learning preference	Imagination	Logical fractional	Convergent/ Divergent	Creative	Problem solving	Imagination
Boys Total	523	411	486	191	419	425	910	473	376	154	95	131	144	102	93	193	166	93	113
Girls Total	2.94	2.31	2.73	2.76	2.30	2.39	2.31	2.89	2.11	3.08	1.9	2.02	2.81	2.04	1.88	2.71	2.12	1.88	2.70

Styles of Learning and Thinking among Right Hemisphere and Left Hemisphere Dominant Children

Table 3 shows the hemispheric preference and styles of learning and thinking accordingly.

It is indicated that the χ^2 value 6.449 with df 1 is significant at 0.0000 level. So there is a significant difference in the style of learning and thinking among the right hemisphere and the left hemisphere dominant children.

Styles of Learning and Thinking and Hemispheric Preference among Boys and Girls

Table 4 shows the preferences of styles of learning and thinking in the left and right hemisphere dominant boys and girls.

It is indicated that the χ^2 value 256.0117 with df 1 is highly significant at 0.0000 level. So there is a significant difference between the right hemisphere learning and thinking styles and the left hemisphere learning and thinking styles for information processing in boys and girls.

It is indicated that in learning style χ^2 value 82.33 with df 1 at 0.000 level is highly significant. So there is a significant difference in the right hemisphere and the left hemisphere learning style for information processing in boys and girls. In thinking style χ^2 value 42.229 with df 1 at 0.0000 level is highly significant. So there is a significant difference in the right and the left hemisphere thinking style for information processing in boys and girls.

Table 5 shows the preference for learning and thinking of concepts among the hemispheric dominance in boys and girls.

Learning style: The concept 'Verbal' shows, χ^2 value 8.45 with df 1 which is highly significant at 0.00036 level; the concept 'Content Preference', the χ^2 value 6.28 with df 1 at 0.0122 level is significant; the concept 'Class Preference' shows χ^2 value 7.57 with df 1 which is significant at 0.0059 level; the concept 'Learning Preference' shows χ^2 value 22.25 with df 1 at 0.000 level which is highly significant; the concept 'Interest' shows χ^2 value 42.19 with

Table 4: Preference of Styles of Learning and Thinking in Right and Left Hemisphere Dominant Boys and Gilrs

	Right Hemisphere										*Left Hemisphere*									
	Learning Style					*Thinking Style*					*Learning Style*					*Thinking Style*				
	Verbal	Content preference	Class preference	Learning preference	Imagination	Logical fractional	Convergent/ Divergent	Creative	Problem solving	Imagination	Verbal	Conduct preference	Class preference	Learning preference	Imagination	Logical fractional	Convergent/ Divergent	Creative	Problem solving	Imagination
Boys Total	126	315	240	284	303	240	246	282	284	219	60	44	56	52	27	43	57	44	39	47
Mean	1.23	3.09	2.22	2.78	2.97	2.35	2.41	2.76	2.78	2.15	2.86	2.10	2.67	2.48	1.29	5.05	2.71	2.10	1.86	2.24
Girls Total	107	209	185	202	189	170	180	213	195	156	94	51	75	92	75	50	79	62	54	66
Mean	1.41	2.75	2.43	2.66	2.49	2.24	2.37	2.87	2.57	2.05	3.24	1.76	2.50	3.17	2.59	1.72	2.72	2.14	1.86	2.34

Table 5: Difference in the Preference for Learning and Thinking Concepts among Right and Left Hemisphere Dominance in Boys and Gilrs

	Learning Style														
	Verbal			*Content Preference*			*Class Preference*			*Learning Preference*			*Interest*		
	R*	L*		R	L		R	L		R	L		R	L	
Boys	126	60	χ^2 =	315	44	χ^2 =	240	86	χ^2 =	284	52	χ^2 =	303	27	χ^2 =
Girls	107	94	8.45	209	51	6.28	185	75	7.57	202	92	22.25	189	75	42.19
			df =1			df =1			df =1			df =1			df =1
			P=0.0003			P=0.0122			P=0.0122			P=0.0000			P=0.0000

	Learning Style														
	Logical/Fraction			*Convergent/ Divergent*			*Creative*			*Problem Solving*			*Imagination*		
	R	L		R	L		R	L		R	L		R	L	
Boys	240	43	χ^2 =	246	57	χ^2 =	282	44	χ^2 =	284	39	χ^2 =	219 .	47	χ^2 =
Girls	170	50	4.66	180	79	10.4	218	62	7.801	195	54	9.54	156	66	9.89
			df =1			df =1			df =1			df =1			df =1
			P=0.0309			P=0.0013			P=0.0052			P=0.0020			P=.0017

df 1 and is significant at 0.0000 level. This shows that there is a significant difference in the preference for concepts of learning styles among the right hemisphere and the left hemisphere dominant boys and girls.

Thinking style: The concept 'Logical / Fractional' shows χ^2 value 4.66 with df 1 at 0.0309 level and is significant; the concept 'Convergent /Divergent Thinking' shows χ^2 value 10.40 with df 1 at 0.0013 level and is significant; the concept 'Creative Thinking' shows χ^2 value 7.801 with df 1 at 0.0052 level and is significant; the concept 'Problem Solving' shows χ^2 value 9.54 with df 1 at 0.0020 which is significant; the concept 'Imagination' shows χ^2 value 9.89 with df 1 at 0.0017 level and is significant. This shows that there is a significant difference in the preference for concepts of thinking styles among the right hemisphere and the left hemisphere dominant boys and girls.

In the light of the above χ^2 values it is concluded that there is a significant difference in the preference for learning and thinking styles of concepts among the right hemisphere and the left hemisphere dominant boys and girls. Thus it is concluded that there is a significant difference in the styles of learning and thinking among the right hemisphere and the left hemisphere dominant boys and girls.

Out of the 250 children taken for the present study 178 (71.2%) children preferred the right hemisphere, 50 (20%) children preferred the left hemisphere and 22 (8.8%) preferred whole brain for information processing. Psychological and split-brain researches show that the two hemispheres have specialised complementary functions. The left hemisphere apparently specialises in sequential logical, verbal, symbolic, convergent production and logic functioning (Raina, 1984; Rubenzer, 1998). The studies of Hunter (1996) and Sperry (1998) concludes that the right hemisphere has a great neuronal capacity to deal with informational complexity. The right hemisphere has a greater ability to process many modes of information with a single cognitive task, while the left hemisphere is superior in tasks which require fixation upon a single mode of representation or execution.

Interpretation of complex visual patterns analysis of voice intonation, face processing, awareness of body position, spatial orientation and the perception of fine and gross motor activities, dreaming, imagery, creativity and music come under the realm of right hemisphere (Venkataraman, 1994). Samples in this study are more right-hemisphere oriented and they tend to exhibit these qualities. The left hemisphere specialises in sequential logical, verbal, symbolic, convergent production and logic functioning (Venkataraman, 1994). Those who were left-hemisphere oriented tend to exhibit these qualities. But in no way the one hemisphere is superior over the other. Differences in brain functions is what causes individual differences in learning and thinking styles (Torrance and Reynolds, 1980).

Results indicate that gender plays a role in hemisphere preference for information processing. In the right hemisphere preference, boys dominated while in left the hemisphere preference, girls dominated. This has been observed by Jangaiah (1998) on a study on learning and cognitive styles for the same age-group. In total, the right hemisphere dominated in hemisphericity preference among children.

There is a difference in the styles of learning and thinking among children. Children who preferred the right hemisphere for information processing were more "content preferred" in learning style and "creative" in thinking style. Those children who preferred the left hemisphere for information processing were more "verbal" in their learning style and "convergent and divergent" in their thinking style. The right hemisphere preference for the concepts of learning style is in the following order: Content Preference, Interest, Learning Preference, Class Preference and Verbal. The preference for the concepts of learning style in the left hemisphere is in the following order: Verbal, Learning Preference, Class Preference, Interest and Content Preference. In the right hemisphere the preference for the concepts of thinking style are the following: Creative Thinking, Problem Solving, Convergent/ Divergent Thinking, Logical/Fractional and Imagination. In the left hemisphere, it is Convergent/Divergent Thinking, Creative, Imagination, Problem Solving and Logical/

Fractional. Reynolds and Torrance (1978) concluded that teacher-directed learning tends to favour students with a left the hemisphere style of learning, while self-directed learning favours right hemispheric learners. Such a conclusion may not be possible here, but the probability of such a case may exist since the components of each hemisphere styles are so.

Results indicate that there are gender differences with respect to the styles of learning and thinking; the right brain learning and thinking style and the left brain learning and thinking style; the right and left hemisphere learning style and the right and left hemisphere thinking style; and the preference for each concept under learning and thinking styles for right and left hemisphere.

The boys who are more right-hemisphere oriented preferred learning styles of concepts in the order of Content Preference followed by Interest, Learning Preference, Class Preference and Verbal. The boys who are left-hemisphere oriented preferred learning styles of concepts in the order of Verbal, Class Preference, Learning Preference, Content Preference and Interest. Under thinking styles, those boys with the right hemisphere preference showed preference for concepts in the order of Problem Solving, Creativity, Convergent/Divergent, Logical/ Fractional and Imagination respectively. The boys who were left-hemisphere oriented in their preference of concepts of thinking styles showed the order of preference as Convergent/ Divergent, Imagination, Creativity, Logical, Fractional and Problem Solving respectively. The preference of conceptualisation bears close resemblance to the description given by Springer and Deutsch (1989).

Among the girls who preferred the right hemisphere for information processing in learning style, they preferred the concept Content Preference followed by Learning Preference, Interest, Class Preference and Verbal. Among the girls, who preferred the right hemisphere for information processing, in learning style of concepts the order of preference is Verbal, Learning Preference, Class Preference, Interest and Content Preference respectively. Pask (1986) too found that females (similar age group) of the right hemisphere dominance showed greater preference for learning styles of concepts that are more verbal followed by other concepts. In the concepts of thinking style the girls who preferred the left hemisphere for information processing showed the order as Convergent and Divergent Thinking, Imagination, Creativity, Problem Solving and Logical/Fractional respectively. Those who showed the right hemisphere preference in thinking style among girls showed preference for Creative Thinking followed by Problem Solving, Convergent/Divergent Thinking, Logical/Fractional and Imagination. The right and left hemispheres have their own peculiarities and significance. But for an individual to function better, an integrated function of both the hemispheres is necessary (Kane & Kaane, 1999).

The two hemispheric functions may be activated thereby influencing the styles of learning and thinking. Researches done by Reynolds and Torrance (1978), Pask (1986) and Gazzaniga (1989) indicate that it is possible to modify a person's preferred style of learning and thinking over relatively brief period (six to ten weeks). It is also possible to control the general direction of the changes in the styles of learning and thinking with the knowledge of styles of learning and thinking mechanism. It may also be possible to train individuals to modify their information processing procedures to best fit their demands of the cognitive tasks (Jangaiah, 1998).

Conclusion

To conclude it is essential to identify the styles of learning and thinking of children in order to facilitate the process of learning and teaching. Since the focus is on child-centred pedagogy giving primacy to the child's experiences, voices, thoughts and participation in learning which the National Curriculum Framework (2005) reiterates in its chapter on 'Learning and Knowledge', it becomes necessary to change our approach to teaching. In fact, knowledge of the child's information processing styles would enhance teaching and make the exercise fruitful. The teaching techniques in the schools can be undertaken in consonance with the students' style of learning and thinking.

Further it would enable the teacher to organise the teaching and learning procedures in such a way that they tone up and activate the hemisphere functions of the brain in students. Different teaching techniques and methodologies can be adopted to activate and influence the hemisphere functions of the brain (Samples, 1978; Raina, 1984).

References

Bogen, J.E. (1989), The other side of the brain-II, an appositional mind. *Bulletin of the Los Angeles Neurological Society, 49,* 135-162.

Fitzgerald, D. & Hattie, J.A. (1993), An evaluation of your style of learning and thinking inventory, *British Journal of Educational Psychology, 63,* 336-346.

Gazzaniga, M.S. (1989), Hemispheric lateralisation of the human brain, *UNCLA Educato, 22,* 9-12.

Gazzaniga, M.S. (1990), The bisected brain, New York: Applenton-Century Crofts.

Hunter, M. (1996), Right brained kids in left brained schools, *Journal of Today's Education, 38,* 45-68.

Jangaiah, C. (1998), *Learning styles,* Hyderabad: Booklinks Corporation.

Kane, N. & Kaane, M. (1999), Comparison of right and left hemisphere function, *The Gifted Child Quarterly, 46,* 157-67.

National Curriculum Framework (2005), New Delhi: National Council of Educational Research and Training.

Pask, G. (1986), Styles and strategies of learning, *British Journal of Educational Psychology,* 56, 128-148.

Raina, M.K. (1984), *Education of the left and right hemispheres: implications of hemispheric specialisation,* Madras: Allied Publishers.

Reynolds, C.R. & Torrance, E.P. (1978), Perceived changes in styles of learning and thinking (hemisphericity) through direct and indirect training, *Journal of Creative Behaviour, 12,* 245-52.

Rubenzer, R. (1998), *The left and right hemisphere model for information processing: possible implications for education,* New York: Columbia University Press.

Samples, R.E. (1978), Are you teaching only one side of the brain? *Learning*, 23, 24-30.

Sperry, R.W. (1998), Left brain-right brain. *Saturday Review*, February 1998, pp.18-20.

Springer, S.P. & Deutsch, G. (1989), *Left brain – right brain*, San Francisco: WH Free Man and Co.

Torrance, E.P. & Reynolds, C.R. (1980), *Technical manual for your style of learning and thinking*, form C Athens, Georgia: University of Georgia Press.

23

State Self-esteem and Causal Attribution in Reattribution Training among Self-worth Protective Students

—*S.P. Sinha* and *Sandhya Gupta*

This study examined self-worth protective subjects who intentionally withdraw effort from situations reflecting low ability. On occasions, when failure is unavoidable, self-worth protective subjects attribute their failures to internal attributions. This learned helplessness leads to low self-esteem, low self-concept, hopelessness and worthlessness. Self-worth protection scale was administered to identify self-worth protective subjects. The sample of the study consisted of 100 subjects of eleventh standard. Pre and post-test design was used. To test the effect of individual counseling, high self-worth protective subjects were selected. Counseling was given in order to modify the distorted perceptions of self-worth protective subjects. Results showed significant increase in self-esteem and external attributions and significant decrease in internal attributions of high self-worth protective subjects, following reattribution training

Keywords: Self-worth protection, Reattribution Training.

A self-worth theory of achievement motivation (Beery,1975; Covington,1984a, 1984b; Covington & Omelich, 1991) holds that in certain situations students stand to gain by not trying, by deliberately withholding effort, thereby protecting their self-worth. Thus, self-worth protection is a defensive technique

This paper originally appears in the *Journal of the Indian Academy of Applied Psychology*, 2006, Vol.32, No.1-3, pp. 145-152.

which students adopt to refrain themselves from situations reflecting their low ability. When poor performance increases the plausibility of reflecting low ability, a situation of high evaluative threat is created. In such situations, these students perform poorly. On the contrary, where a mitigating excuse allows poor performance to be attributed to a factor, unrelated to ability, a situation of low evaluative threat is generated.

In the short-term withdrawing effort spares the individual from conclusions of inability and diminished self-worth. On the other hand, in the longer term the effects of self-worth protection are evident in perpetual resort to avoidance strategies in situations that involve threat to self-worth, compounding suspicions of personal incompetence to such a degree that, eventually, conclusions of low ability are inescapable. Covington (1984a) observes that the defensive and self-defeating tactics of failure-avoidance progressively cut students off from classroom rewards. Ultimately, self-worth protective students have no recourse but to attribute failure to low ability. As a consequence, the avoidance strategies of these students ultimately backfire. The end result is internalisation of failure, diminished expectancies for success and low achievement (Thompson, 1996, 1999).

A variety of self-handicapping strategies have been described as pecųliar symptoms of self-worth protection (Beery, 1975; Covington & Beery, 1976; Covington, 1984b; Thompson, 1994). These include lack of confidence, low self-esteem, withdrawal of effort, procrastination, low goal-setting and last-minute study.

According to Elliott and Dweck(1988), self-worth protective children develop learned helplessness, attribute their failures, not their successes, to ability. And on occasions in which they do succeed, they are likely to conclude that external factors, such as, luck are responsible. Furthermore, such children have come to believe that ability is a fixed characteristic of the self that cannot be changed. They do not think competence can be improved by trying hard. So, when a task is difficult, these children experience an anxious loss of control. They quickly give up, saying, "I can't do this", before they have really tried.

Attributional styles affect the goals children pursue in learning situations. Self-worth protective students focus on less challenging tasks or courses and even less demanding careers. Self-worth protection prevents children from pursuing tasks that they are capable of mastering and from realising their potential. Experiential research confirms the potent impact of adult feedback on children's attributional styles (Thompson, 1996).

So, this study endeavoured to investigate the effect of intervention program on high self-worth protective subjects.

Hypotheses

1. After receiving insolvable line drawing task, high self-worth protective subjects would make more internal and less external attributions, state self-esteem as compared to low self-worth protective subjects.
2. After intervention program, there would be an increase in state self-esteem and external attributions and decrease in internal attributions of high self-worth protective subjects.

Method

Sample

Self-worth protection scale was administered on 100 students of eleventh standard of Gayatri Public School and Army School, Agra. On the basis of quartile deviation, 10 subjects scoring above Q3 (Q3=212) were considered high self-worth protective subjects and 10 subjects scoring below Q1 (Q1=180) were considered as low self-worth protective subjects. So, the total sample comprised 20 subjects.

Measures

Self-worth protection scale. This scale was developed by Thompson and Dinnel (2003) to measure students' tendencies who intentionally withdraw effort in order to avoid negative implications of poor performance in terms of damage to self-worth. It is a 33- item scale. Respondents rate each item on a 7-point scale ranging from "not very true of me" to "very true of me".

Post experimental questionnaire: The items were pooled from Srivastava's (1992) questionnaire and Palenzuela's (1988) Multidimensional Academic Locus of Control scale for measuring internal and external attributions and state self-esteem. The questionnaire consisted of 15 items rated on a 5 point scale indicating the extent to which the subjects evaluate their state self-esteem and causal attributions for performance on the test.

Line drawing task: The line drawing task was taken from Glass and Singer (1961). It consists of two insolvable line drawings. The maximum time for each line drawing task was two minutes.

Procedure

First of all, subjects were given insolvable line drawing task. In the line drawing task, subjects were not allowed to lift the pencil till they finished each line drawing task. Also, they were not permitted to revert back to the lines they had already drawn in each line drawing task. After completion of task, subjects were asked to fill the post-experimental questionnaire. Thereafter, high self-worth protective subjects were selected for an intervention programme. After completion of a counselling procedure, these subjects were, again, given insolvable line drawing task and then, post-experimental questionnaire was filled by them.

Intervention Programme

An intervention plan was contrived to ameliorate the distorted perceptions of high self-worth protective subjects. A brief cognitive-behaviour therapy (CBT) was individually adhibited.

Stage 1: Interview and Alliance Building (Session 1): In this session, both parents and the subject were interviewed. It inquired about subject's functioning with particular reference to parent-child relationships and inter-parental relationships.

Stage 2: Counselling Procedure : It is a family-based approach. It helps family members communicate clearly and openly about problems and related issues. It encourages joint problem-solving with respect to the subject's difficulties and optimises family support for the subject. The entire counselling procedure is divided into the following sessions:

Reattribution Training (Session 2) : A particular failure situation that has led to negative thoughts reflects an internal and stable attribution. The subject was trained to reinterpret the threatening situations in a less pessimistic way.

Communication Skills (Session 3): When parents have difficulty in listening to their children and children have difficulties in clearly articulating their views to their parents, communication training is appropriate.

Problem Solving (Session 4): In this session, the subjects were given one problem at a time and were asked to give as many solutions as they could. Therefore, they were asked to explore the pros and cons of each and every solution of a problem. In the end, they were asked to choose the best possible solution for the problem.

Supportive Play (Session 5): In this session, parents were trained to provide their children with support. The subject was asked to decide what he/she wanted to do. The parents were required to actively participate in the activity, praising the child regularly and avoiding teachings and commands.

Disputation (Sessions 6-9): It is one of the general ways to change the habitual beliefs that follow adversity. It consists of ABCDE (Adversity-Belief-Consequence-Disputation-Energisation) model given by Seligman (1991).

Session 6 : First of all, the ABC model was explained to the subject. It was made clear to the subject what he/she thought when things went badly actually change how he/she felt. As a result, a thought always triggered the feeling. If he/she could learn to find that thought, he/she could change it. The subject was given three examples to work with. Once the subjects, grasped the ABCs concept, they were asked to find ABCs in their daily life.

Session 7: This session started by reviewing the Adversity-Belief-Consequence link. During this session, each ABC of the subject was discussed and emphasized how sadness, fear and giving-up are all produced by his/her beliefs and hinted broadly that these were not unchangeable. When the subject had found his/her five ABCs, the session came to an end.

Session 8: In this session, Disputation-Energisation link was explained to the subject. The counsellor gave three examples to work with and explained the subject that the thought he/she possessed did not mean that the thoughts were true. They could be disputed. When the subject said negatives to himself/herself were disputed, he/she would stop believing them and would become cheerful and able to do more.

Session 9: This session began by reviewing the link between disputation and energisation. The subject was asked to turn back to his/her own ABC record and take each of the five instances and get him/her to dispute the beliefs. After the end of each session, the subjects were asked how they felt after discussion.

Results

Results depicted in Table 1 show the mean scores of internal attributions of high and low self-worth protective subjects. The value of "t" is 4.67 with 9 df is significant at 0.01 level of significance. This indicates that the internal attributions of high self-worth protective subjects are more as compared to low self-worth protective subjects. Similarly, the value of "t" ratio (Table 1) is 8.02 with 9 df is significant at 0.01 level of significance, indicating that the external attributions of high self-worth protective subjects are less as compared to their counterparts. Table 1 shows that the mean scores of self-esteem of high and low self-worth protective subjects. The value of "t" ratio is 17.03 with 9 df is significant at 0.01 level of significance. This concludes that the self-esteem of high self-worth protective subjects is less in comparison to low self-worth protective subjects.

Table 1: Mean scores of internal attributions, external attributions and self-esteem of high and low self-worth protective subjects before intervention. (N = 10 in each group), df = 9

	Internal Attributions			*External Attributions*			*Self-esteem*		
Group	*Mean*	*SD*	*t*	*Mean*	*SD*	*t*	*Mean*	*SD*	*t*
High	18.3	3.33	4.67*	10.05	11.10	8.02*	15.4	3.65	17.03*
Low	11.0				17.11			22.10	

*p< .01

Table 2: Comparison of mean scores of internal attributions, external attributions and self-esteem of high self-worth protective subjects before and after intervention. (N = 10 in each group), df = 9

	Internal Attributions			*External Attributions*			*Self-esteem*		
Group	*Mean*	*SD*	*t*	*Mean*	*SD*	*t*	*Mean*	*SD*	*t*
interve.	18.3	3.33	10.05	11.1	4.99	15.4	3.65	1.64	
After									
interve.	11.2	3.33	0.58	12.1 *	18.2	3.16	0.56	14.23*	
20.01	1.17	0.34	4.71 *						

*p< .01

Table 2 reveals the mean scores of internal attributions of high self-worth protective subjects before and after interventions. The value of "t" is 12.07, which is significant at 0.01 level of significance. This significant value clearly shows reduction in internal attributions of high self-worth protective subjects. On the contrary, the value of "t" ratio in Table 2 is 14.23 significant at 0.01 level, indicating increase in external attributions of high self-worth protective subjects. Perusal of Table 2, shows mean scores of self-esteem of high self-worth protective subjects. The value of "t" ratio at 9 df is 4.71, significant at 0.01 level of significance. Thus, it may be concluded that there is an increase in self-esteem of high self-worth protective subjects, following interventions.

So, it can be stipulated that the intervention programme was helpful in modifying the distorted perceptions of high self-worth protective subjects. Thus, both the hypotheses have been accepted.

Discussion

The relevance of attributional style to behavioural problems may be related to the development of self-concept. The most critical demand is to succeed. Failing to meet this demand may result in negative evaluations that pose difficulties in developing a meaningful self-concept and further reinforce the young person's low status (Tony, 2003). Internal attributions for failure and external attributions for success have been found to serve as a means of maintaining an individual's low self-concept (Kukla, 1972; Weiner & Kukla, 1970; Weiner & Potepan, 1970; Wortman & Brehm, 1975).

The helpless reformulation predicts that a pessimistic attributional style is associated with loss of self-esteem. This prediction is supported by empirical evidence (Brewin & Shapiro, 1984; Devins, 1982; Girodo, Dotzenroth & Stein, 1981; McFarland & Ross, 1982; Rothwell & Williams, 1983; Weiner, 1979).

In the second part of the study, there is a considerable reduction in the internal attributions and increase in external attributions and self-esteem of high self-worth protective subjects (before and after interventions). On the basis of feedback given by subjects after each session, it was concluded that high self-worth protective subjects found themselves occupied with negative thoughts, lack of confidence and feeling helpless. Their attitude was very pessimistic. So, in this session counselor trained these subjects to interpret the negative mood-state in a less pessimistic way. After reattribution training, subjects felt relaxed and started to think on a positive note.

A joint communicating session between parents and the subject was convened. As a result, they were able to articulate their views to each other and helped them to convince each other more frequently. Before the problem-solving session, these subjects were finding difficulty in solving their problems and consequently feeling helpless. During this session, problem-solving skills were developed in these subjects which enabled them to find solutions of their problems and felt much more confident.

Parents were convinced to give a positive feedback to their child in the form of praise, encouragement and appreciation. This attitude of parents helped the subjects to buildup their confidence. After receiving a positive feedback from their parents, the subjects were feeling confident and had the feeling that they could also do something.

Generally, a negative thought always triggers the feelings of sadness and helplessness. During these sessions (6-9), the counsellor trained the subjects how to identify these negative beliefs, which has caused the negative mood-state. And trained how to overcome these negative thoughts through disputation. As a result, subjects became more optimistic and started to believe in their potential and were much more confident than before.

This clearly revealed that failure in any task tend to increase the repertoire of internal attributions of high self-worth protective subjects. At the same time, their external attributions decreases. This will have a deleterious effect on the self-esteem of such individuals. But the distorted perceptions of such people can be improved by effective counseling.

References

Beery, R. (1975), Fear of failure in the student experience, *Personnel and Guidance Journal, 54,* 191-203.

Brewin, C.R., & Shapiro, D.A. (1984), Beyond locus of control : Attribution of responsibility for positive and negative outcomes, *British Journal of Psychology, 75,* 43-49.

Covington, M.V. (1984a), Motivation for self-worth. In R. Ames & C. Ames (Eds.), *Learning and Motivation in the Classroom* (pp. 139-164), Hillsdale, NJ: Lawrence Erlbaum Associates.

Covington, M.V. (1984b), The self-worth theory of achievement motivation. Findings and implications. *Research on Motivation in Education* (pp. 77-113). New York: Academic Press.

Covington, M.V., & Beery, R. (1976), *Self-worth and school learning,* New York: Holt, Rinehart & Winston.

Covington, M.V., & Omelich, C.E. (1991), Need achievement revisited: Verification of Atkinson's original 2x2 model. In C. D. Speilberger, I.G. Sarason, Z. Kulesar & G.L. Heek (Eds.), *Stress and emotion: anxiety, anger, curiosity* (Vol. 14, pp. 85-105), New York: Hemisphere.

Devins, G.M. (1982), Perceived self-efficacy, outcome expectancies and negative mood states in end-renal disease, *Journal of Abnormal Psychology, 91,* 241-244.

Elliott, E.S., & Dweck, C.S. (1988), Goals: An approach to motivation and achievement, *Journal of Personality and Social Psychology, 54,* 5-12.

Girodo, M., Dotzenroth, S.E., & Stein, S.J. (1981), Causal attribution bias in shy males: Implications for self-esteem and self-confidence, *Cognitive Therapy and Research, 5,* 325-338.

Glass, D.C., & Singer, J.E. (1961), *Urban stress,* New York: Academic Press.

Kukla, A. (1972), Attributional determinants of achievement-related behavior, *Journal of Personality and Social Psychology, 21,* 166-174.

McFarland, C., & Ross, M. (1982), Impact of causal attributions on affective reactions to stress and failure, *Journal of Personality and Social Psychology, 43,* 937-946.

Palenzuela, D.L. (1988), Refining the theory and measurement of expectancy of internal vs external control of reinforcement,*Personality and Individual Differences, 9,* 607-629.

Rothwell, N., & Williams, J.M.G. (1983), Attributional style and life events, *British Journal of Clinical Psychology,* 22, 139-140.

Seligman, M. (1991). The optimistic life, *Learned Optimism* (pp. 207-234), New York: A. A. Knopf.

Srivastava, H. (1992), Learned resourcefulness and learned helplessness: Effect on puzzle solving performance and attributions. Dissertation submitted to Dayalbagh Educational Institute, Agra

Thompson, T. (1994), Self-worth protection: Review and implications for the classroom, *Educational Review,* 46(3), 259-274.

Thompson, T. (1996), Self-worth protection in achievement behavior: A review and implications for counseling, *Australian Psychologist, 31,* 41-51.

Thompson,T. (1999), Underachieving to protect self-worth: *Theory, research and interventions,* Aldershot: Avebury Press.

Thompson, T., & Dinnel, D.L. (2003), Construction and initial validation of the self-worth protection scale, *British Journal of Educational Psychology, 73,* 89-97.

Tony, T.S.K. (2003), Locus of control, attributional style and discipline problems in secondary schools. *Early Child Development and Care, 173*(5), 455-466.

Weiner, B. (1979), A theory of motivation for some classroom experiences, *Journal of Educational Psychology, 71,* 3-25.

Weiner, B., & Kukla, A. (1970), An attributional analysis of achievement motivation, *Journal of Personality and Social Psychology, 15,* 1-20.

Weiner, B., & Potepan, P.A. (1970), Personality characteristics and affective reactions toward exams of superior and failing college students, *Journal of Educational Psychology, 61,* 144-151.

Wortman, C.B., & Brehm, J.W. (1975), Responses to uncontrolled outcomes: An integration of reactance theory and the learned helplessness model. In L. Berkowitz (Ed.), *Advances in Experimental Social Psychology* (Vol. 8). New York: Academic Press.

24

Performance among High and Low Self-efficacious Students

—*Roshan Lal Zinta*

The purpose of the present study is to investigate the impact of rural and urban background on performance among the high and low self-efficacious students studying in various senior secondary schools of Shimla District of Himachal Pradesh in India. The data were collected on a sample of 416 (208 rural and 208 urban) self-efficacious subjects (mean age of 16.5 years) by following the criterion of selection M ± 1 SD. The students were divided into eight groups, four from rural (males and females) and four from urban (males and females) with high and low in self-efficacy comprises of n = 52 subjects in each group. The subjects from both the backgrounds (rural and urban) were given problem solving task (anagram solution) to perform. The task comprises of several English letters words selected from adjectives placed in a jumbled up manner. The subjects have to solve these jumbled up words in a meaningful way within stipulated time. For recording the performance multifarious comparison were made by applying the appropriate statistical procedure in order to detect performance within rural and urban as well as between rural and urban conditions of both the gender with high and low in self-efficacy. The result revealed that there was a non-significant difference ($p > 0.05$) in the performance of boys and girls with high and low in self-efficacy within rural and urban settings but highly significant ($p<0.01$) differences in performance

This paper originally appears in the Journal of the Indian Academy of Applied Psychology, 2006, Vol.32, No.1-3, pp. 255-266.

> were found between rural and urban setting with the males and females high and low in self-efficacy. The urban students high as well as low in self-efficacy significantly ($p < 0.01$) outperformed the rural students in problem solving task. Urban high self-efficacious females significantly ($p<0.01$) outperformed both rural males and females with high and low in self-efficacy as well as urban females with high and low in self-efficacy and urban females with low in self-efficacy. Overall the urban self-efficacious students significantly outperformed rural self-efficacious students and the females of rural and urban backgrounds competed equally well with males in problem solving task.

In India more than 76 per cent of the country's population resides in about six lacks villages and 72 per cent rural population is engaged in agriculture and allied occupations. The same is the position of Himachal Pradesh, a Hill State, where more than 90 per cent population resides in rural areas or in villages (Census, 2001). There is general misgiving among the scientists that the urban students are more intelligent and superior in cognitive and social abilities as compared to their counterparts. But the situation can be vice versa where rural students can equally perform well by showing all types of abilities, provided that they are given an opportunity to reside in an enriched environment. The figure as stated above compels us to think that can such huge rural population be really inferior in all types of abilities as compared to the lot? This is a question of great concern that requires microanalysis to record the change (Bandura, 1977). There have been few researches in the area and their generalisation seems to be stereotyped to some extent. The psychology essentially seems to be an urban discipline, which originated from the database of urban middle class population from colleges and universities. Following independence there emerged a great trend by undertaking insightful researches in the topic in India (Sinha, 2002), which was not trustworthy and satisfactory before independence.

The rural and urban setting among the scientists is always a question of, and has led to, several researches in the area. A study conducted by Sharma (2005) on rural and urban background civil servant and engineers, concluded that the civil services personnel without experience belonging to urban area have maximum creativity as compared to the engineering personnel without experience belonging to the rural area. The study pointed out that the subjects belonging to the urban area are more creative. Further a fresher is more creative than experienced personnel.

Another study, as conducted by Faroqi (1981) on communication and influence processes among rural and urban areas, reported that rural people avails less information from media yet interact very well and perform equally better than the urban one. Agrawal and Misra (2002) also found differences among rural and urban samples in terms of their achievement. In their findings the rural sample held a distinct conception of achievement goals in which the individuals personal and societal concerns were undifferentiated while the urban sample construed the goals distinctly at the three levels, individual, family and group. The factors, like approval and life satisfaction, independence, learning and knowledge and personal success, noted in the urban group denoted a different set of value orientation and lifestyle. In contrast, the rural sample was not able to project a picture of individualistic goal structure.

Bandura (1967, 2001, 2004) explained that social cognitive of human functioning is rooted in social systems, the personal agency operates within a broad network of socio-structural influences. There is triadic reciprocal causal relationship between internal, personal factors, behavioural patterns and environmental influences. Bandura distinguishes between imposed, selected and constructed environment that can play an important role in the performance accomplishment. Cultural factors and the power structure also play an equally important role in developing sense of self-efficacy and consequently resilience to the stressors. The social cognitive theory assumes that socio-structural factors operate through psychological mechanisms of the self-system to produce behavioural effect. The core belief in Bandura's social cognitive theory can help the person in dealing with the situation effectively. The social cognitive theory specifies four core features of human agency: internationality, forethought, self-reactiveness, and self-reflectiveness. The basic tenet of this theory is that a human being is an agent, who can intentionally make things happen by his actions. The agents are not only the planner and fore-thinker, but also self-regulators as well (Bandura, 2004).

The self-efficacy has also been linked to the expectancy theory (Vroom, 1964) by suggesting that expectation can influence the thought patterns, emotional reactions, and the orchestration of performance through the adroit use of sub-skills, ingenuity, resourcefulness and so forth. The self-efficacy expectancies predict behaviour in varieties of contexts, one such being in decision making (Cervone, Jiwani & Wood, 1991), task performance (Bandura, 1982, 1999; Bandura, Adams, & Beyers, 1977; Bandura, Adams, Hardy & Howells, 1980, Feltz, 1982), and problem-solving task. In a study self-efficacy and problem-solving (anagram solution) task, Sanna, (1977) found that the people with high in self-efficacy reported high capability of coming up with solutions and experience in performing the task successfully as compared to the students low in self-efficacy. Some studies have not found differences in high and low level of self-efficacy groups in the measure of performance (Bandalos, Yates & Thorndike, 1995; Vancouver, Thompson, Tischner & Putka, 2002).

The human differentiation on the basis of gender is a fundamental phenomenon that affects virtually every aspect of people's daily lives. Gender operates in concert with motivational and self-regulatory mechanism, and its conception and roles are the products of broad network of social influences operating independently in varieties of the societal subsystem (Mischel, 1970). There are various theories with regard to gender differentiation and development. The psychological-oriented theories tend to emphasize on inner-psychic processes governing the gender development (Kohlberg, 1968). The sociological theories focus on the social and cultural determinants while the biological-oriented theories focus on the differential biological roles played by males and females in the reproduction under gender role development and differentiation (Trivers, 1972). Finally, the gender schema theory focuses on both social and psychological basis and centres mainly on individual differences.

It is a matter of concern whether there is any difference in the performance in psychological abilities among the male and female subjects residing in rural and urban areas. Generally males are considered superior and females inferior without exploring the root cause and antecedents conditions of the environmental factors. The females have to bear the discrimination of the majority in every sphere starting from their own family to the society who provide them a thorny and impoverished environment, and as a result it affects their performance and overall personality including their adjustment to the situation and health. In India the status of females was venerated where the male's uses to respect their ideas, mind and body by considering them as Avatars of Devi's (goddess) but nowadays such concepts do not exist. The discrimination and differentiation on the basis of gender which are causing inferiority complexes among the females in both rural as well as in urban settings and are resulting disparities in achievement. In a study Dona, Scholz, Schwarzer and Sud (2002) have reported a superiority of males with regard to self-efficacy as compared to females in various cultures. This gender differences can disappear when women judges their efficacy to perform the same activities in everyday situation in a stereotypically feminine tasks than in context of male-dominated occupation (Junge & Dretzke, 1995). Women's beliefs about their capabilities and their career aspirations are shaped by undermining social practices within the family, the educational system, peer relationships, mass media, occupational system and the culture at large (Signorielli, 1990).

In tune with Vancouver's findings, Zinta (2006) also found no relationship between self-efficacy and performance. The study has reported the effect of self-efficacy, test-anxiety and short-term intervention on problem solving. The findings show that the main effects of self-efficacy and counselling were not significant whereas the test-anxiety showed a minor effect on problem solving.

Keeping in view the relevant literature the present study was conducted to examine the impact of rural and urban background on performance among the self-efficacious students. An attempt was made to explore the effect of rural and urban background minutely, operationally and empirically by comparing the within and between group performance of rural and urban background students in problem-solving task (anagram solution).

METHOD

Sample

The data were collected on a sample of n = 416 (208 rural and 208 urban) subjects with high and low in self-efficacy (mean age of 16.5 years), studying in various senior secondary schools of Shimla districts of Himachal Pradesh in India. These rural and urban subjects n = 208 in each group were divided into two sub-groups on the basis of n = 104 males and n = 104 females in each group. These males and females in each group were further sub-divided into two equivalent comparable halves based on their high and low self-efficacy that comprises of n =52 subjects in each high and low n = 52 self-efficacy group. So, in all, there were eight groups, four from rural and four from urban background that include both the males and females with high and low self-efficacy. The criterion for selection in the high and low self-efficacy group was followed M ± 1 SD of the general self-efficacy scales scores.

Tools

The general self-efficacy scale was originally developed in Germany and translated into English by Jerusalem & Schwarzer, 1992 and in Hindi by Sud (1998). The Hindi version of the scale was used in the present study which is a four-point scale for identifying the subjects in categories of high and low self-efficacy. This scale has 10 items where the scores range from minimum 10 to a maximum of 40. The scale is highly reliable and its psychometric precision has been tested in 25 countries (Dona, Scholz, Schwarzer, & Sud, 2002). It yields the internal consistencies between alpha .75 and .91 respectively. Its concurrent validity has also been established on the basis of appropriate correlations.

Problem-solving Task

In this study the dependent variable was a problem-solving task. It consisted of anagrams having several letter words placed in a jumbled-up manner. The subjects had to re-arrange and form appropriate words. They were presented 12 anagrams, selected from English adjectives to solve within 10 minutes. These anagrams were presented to the students belonging to high and low self-efficacy and test-anxiety. The subjects in experimental conditions were presented with short-term intervention while the comparison did not follow any treatment. Each word carried equal marks resulting in the composite score of 12.

Procedure

In all 416 subjects were selected from rural and urban areas of Himachal Pradesh. Their selections were based on the criterion of selection M ± 1SD of the obtained scores on the general self-efficacy scale. Those subjects who scored 1 SD above from the mean of self-efficacy score were considered as high self-efficacious and those subjects who scored below 1 SD from the mean were considered as low self-efficacious. For recording the performance 104 males + 104 females from rural and 104 males + 104 females from urban background were selected. Finally these subjects were sub-divided into eight subgroups keeping in view their self-efficacy, rural and urban background and gender. These rural and urban, 52 in each group, were given anagrams-solution task to perform within a time limit of 10 minutes. The subjects were given adequate information regarding the task. First of all comparison was made within rural and urban setting in order to detect the performance of male and female subjects with high and low self-efficacy. Then the comparison of subjects between rural and urban settings was made. This multifarious comparison was made by following, mean, standard deviation and t-test.

Results and Discussion

RHM/RLM: Rural high/Low self-efficacious male; RHF/RLF: Rural high/low self-efficacious females.

Table 1 indicates that the rural high self-efficacious females showed non-significant difference with rural high self-efficacious males ($t = 1.01$, $p > 0.05$); rural low self-efficacious males ($t = 0.15$, $p > 0.01$) and with rural low self-efficacious females ($t = 0.80$, $p > 0.05$). The rural low self-efficacious females did not show significant difference with rural low self-efficacious males ($t = 0.81$, $p > 0.05$); rural high self-efficacious males ($t = 0.21$). There was non-significant difference between rural high and low self-efficacious males ($t = 1.00$, $p > 0.05$) in problem-solving tasks.

Table 1: Mean, SD, t-ratios and probability of rural self-efficacious students in problem-solving task (anagram solution)

	M (SD)	*M (SD)*	*t*	*p*
G-1	RHM	RHF		p > 0.05
	6.03 (2.35)	6.48 (2.11)	1.01	
G-2	RLM	RLF		
	6.56 (2.99)	6.13 (2.29)	0.81	p > 0.05
G-3	RHM	RLF		
	6.03 (2.35)	6.13 (2.29)	0.21	p > 0.05
G-4	RLM	RHF		
	6.56 (2.99)	6.48 (2.11)	0.15	p > 0.05
G-5	RHM	RLM		
	6.03 (2.35)	6.48 (2.11)	1.00	p > 0.05
G-6	RHF	RLF		
	6.03 (2.35)	6.13 (2.29)	0.80	p > 0.05

UHM/ULM: Urban high/low self-efficacious male; UHF/ULF: Urban high/low self-efficacious females.

Table 2: Mean, SD, t-ratios and probabilities of urban self-efficacious students in problem solving task (anagram solution)

	M (SD)	*M (SD)*	*t*
G-1	UHM	UHF	
	7.96 (2.22)	8.67 (2.01)	1.80**
G-2	ULM	ULF	
	8.44 (2.52)	8.34 (2.27)	0.22**
G-3	UHM	ULF	
	7.96 (2.22)	8.34 (2.27)	0.90*
G-4	ULM	UHF	
	8.44 (2.52)	8.67 (2.01)	0.54**
G-5	UHM	ULM	
	7.96 (2.22)	8.44 (2.52)	1.14*
G-6	UHF	ULF	
	8.67 (2.01)	8.34	0.78*

Table 2, shows that there was non-significant difference in the performance of urban high self-efficacy males except to urban high self-efficacious females ($t = 1.80$, $p < 0.10$), urban low self-efficacious females ($t = 0.90$, $p > 0.05$) and urban low self-efficacious males ($t = 1.14$, $p > 0.01$). The urban low self-efficacious males did not differ significantly with urban low self-efficacious females ($t = 0.22$, $p > 0.05$), and urban high self-efficacious females ($t = 0.54$, $p > 0.05$). The same trends were also found in the performance of high and low self-efficacious urban high and low self-efficacious males ($t = 1.14$, $p > 0.05$) and females ($t = 0.78$, $p > 0.05$), who showed non-significant difference in the problem-solving task.

Table 3 : Mean, SD, t-ratios and probabilities between rural and urban self-efficacious students in problem-solving task (anagram solution).

	M (SD)	*M (SD)*	*t*
G-1	RHM	UHM	
	6.03 (2.35)	7.96 (2.22)	4.49**
G-2	RHM	ULM	
	6.03 (2.35)	8.44 (2.52)	5.33**
G-3	RHM	UHF	
	6.03 (2.35)	8.67 (2.01)	6.16**
G-4	RHM	ULF	
	6.03 (2.35)	8.34(2.27)	5.09**
G-5	RLM	UHF	
	6.56(2.99)	7.96(2.22)	2.80**
G-6	RLM	ULM	
	6.56 (2.99)	8.44 (2.52)	3.61**
G-7	RLM	UHF	
	6.56 (2.99)	8.67 (2.01)	4.22**
G-8	RLM	ULF	
	6.56 (2.99)	8.34 (2.27)	3.41**
G-9	UHM	RHM	
	7.96 (2.22)	6.03 (2.35)	4.47**
G-10	UHM	RHF	
	7.96 (2.22)	6.48 (2.11)	3.65**
G-11	UHM	RLF	
	7.96 (2.22)	6.13 (2.29)	4.32**
G-12	ULM	RHF	
	8.44 (2.52)	6.48 (2.11)	4.57**

(Contd...)

(Contd...)

G-13	RHF	UHF	
	6.48 (2.11)	8.67 (2.01)	5.41**
G-14	RHF	ULF	
	8.44 (2.52)	6.13 (2.29)	5.18
G-15	RLF	UHF	
	6.13 (2.29)	8.67 (2.01)	6.01
G-16	RLF	ULF	
	6.13 (2.29)	8.34 (2.27)	4.88
G-17	ULF	RHM	
	8.34 (2.27)	6.03 (2.35)	5.09
G-18	ULF	RHF	
	8.34 (2.27)	6.48 (2.11)	4.32
G-19	ULF	RLF	
	8.34 (2.24)	6.13 (2.29)	4.93

RHM/RLM = Rural high/low elf-efficacious male; RHF/RLF : Rural high/low self-efficacious fe:nales ; UHM/ULM = Urban high/Low self-efficacious male; UHF/ULF : urban high/low self-efficacious females.

Table 3 shows that the urban high self-efficacious males significantly outperformed rural high self-efficacious males ($t = 4.49, p < 0.01$), rural low self-efficacious females ($t = 4.32, p < 0.01$), rural high self-efficacious females ($t = 3.65, p < 0.01$) and rural high self-efficacious males ($t = 4.47, p < 0.01$) as well. The urban low self-efficacious male outperformed rural high self-efficacious males ($t = 5.33,. p < 0.01$); rural low self-efficacious males ($t = 3.61, p < 0.01$); and rural high self-efficacious females ($t = 4.57, p < 0.01$). The urban high self-efficacious females outperformed rural high self-efficacious males ($t = 6.16, p < 0.01$); rural low self-efficacious males ($t = 4.22, p < 0.01$); rural high self-efficacious females (5.41, $p < 0.01$) and rural low self-efficacious females ($t = 6.01$). The urban low self-efficacious females outperformed rural high self-efficacious males ($t = 5.09, p < 0.01$); rural low self-efficacious males ($t = 3.41, p < 0.01$); rural high self-efficacious females ($t = 5.18, p < 0.01$); rural low self-efficacious females ($t = 4.88, p < 0.01$); rural high self-efficacious males ($t = 5.09, p < 0.01$), rural high self-efficacious females ($t = 4.32, p < 0.01$) and rural low self-efficacious females ($t = 4.93, p < 0.01$).

It is clear from the results that there is no difference between male and females subjects from rural areas. They show equally better performance in problem-solving abilities. There was no gender difference between high and low self-efficacious subjects from rural background. The females competed with male equally. The same is the condition of urban students where the male and females with high and low self-efficacy perform equally well. From this study it can be generalised that the females students compete equally with their counterparts in achievement. The females of the contemporary era are not lagging behind in any areas and performing equally in every sphere. In education now girls are showing extraordinary performance, the reason being they realise their past and are concentrating more on their studies as compared to the boys who get abundant affection and social support from their families. Some parents of the rural and urban background follow discriminatory attitude for their children by reckoning girls as inferior and boys as superior. So the excess affectionate relationship with the boys perhaps has caused their failure and underachievement as compared to the girls, who are actualising, reflecting and rationalising to their self by making them as more resilient to tackle the vulnerability.

The result shows that there is a significant difference in performance between rural and urban students in the problem-solving task. The urban students with high and low self-efficacy outperformed the rural students with high and low in self-efficacy in performance. The results showed superiority of urban students in achievement in the problem-solving task. It doesn't mean that the rural students are inferior as compared to the urban ones but requires a further insight why it happens so. The rural students live in fresh environment free from pollution, yet their performance is hampered. For good health the physical factor alone is not sufficient but the social, psychological and cultural factors are equally responsible for their adverse performance. This may be due to the quality of education available in rural areas, and less exposure to an enriched environment.

The reason behind the excellent performance of urban students may be the better quality of education, availability of the information from various sources including mass media and electronic media, their educated families, and peers groups which help them in better performance

The result further suggests that the females residing in urban areas, or getting social support from their parents and society are performing well as compared to their male counterparts by removing earlier shackles of dependence. Females who are getting support, cooperation, financial assistance and approval from their parents, family and society are performing well in achievement as well as in every spheres as compared to their counterparts. Education is proving to be effective instrument raising their self-belief, forethought, self-esteem and self-efficacy. Not only the females but also the youths of undeveloped villages and urban areas, who have not availed basic amenities in the past are trying harder and performing well while attaining higher education which proves effective and working as a liberator for them in every sphere.

The suggestion for improving the performance among the undeveloped rural and urban students with high and low self-efficacy is that they must attain higher education, should understand their environment properly, maintain their inner resources, like self-efficacy and self-esteem, become resilient, and capable by not losing their courage in handling adverse situations. They must take benefit of the mass media, electronic media and other means of information.

References

Agrawal, R., & Misra, G. (2002), A factor analytic study of achievement goals and means: an Indian view. In A. K. Dalal and G, Misra (Eds.), *New directions in Indian psychology*, volume 1: *Social Psychology*. New Delhi: Sage.

Bandalos, D.L., Yates, K., & Thorndike, C. (1995), Effects of math self-concept, perceived self-efficacy and attribution for failure and success on test anxiety, *Journal of Educational Psychology, 87*, 611-623.

Bandura, A. (1967), Behavioural psychotherapy. Scientific American, March.

Bandura, A. (1977), Analysis of self-efficacy theory of behavioural change, *Psychological Review, 84*, 191-215.

Bandura, A. (1982), Self-efficacy mechanism in human agency, *American Psychologist, 37,* 122-147.

Bandura, A. (1986), *Social foundations of thought and action: a social cognitive theory,* Englewood Cliffs, NJ: Prentice Hall.

Bandura, A. (1999), Social cognitive theory of personality, In L. Pervin ,and O. John (Eds.), *Handbook of personality* (2nd eds.), New York: Guilford Publication.

Bandura, A. (2001), Social cognitive theory: an agentic perspective, *Annual Review of Psychology, 52,* 1- 26.

Bandura, A. (2004), Swimming against the mainstream: the early years from chilly tributary to transformative mainstream, *Behaviour Research and Therapy, 42,* 613-630.

Bandura, A., Adams, N. E., & Beyer, J. (1977), Cognitive processing mediating Behavioural change, *Journal of Personality and Social Psychology, 35,* 124-139.

Bandura, A., Adams, N.E., Hardy, A. B., & Howells, G. N. (1980), Tests of the generalisability of self-efficacy theory, *Cognitive Theory and Research, 4,* 39-66.

Cervone, D., Jiwani, N., & Wood, R. (1991), Goal setting and the different influence of self-regulatory processes on complex decision making performance, *Journal of Personality and Social Psychology. 61,* 257-266.

Dona, B. G., Scholz, U., Schwarzer, R., & Sud, S. ((2002), Is perceived self-efficacy a universal construct: psychometric findings from 25 countries, *European Journal of Psychological Assessment, 1,* 21.

Faroqi, M. A. (1981). *Communication and influence processes: a survey of research in psychology 1971-1976,* part-2. Indian Council of social Science Research, New Delhi.

Feltz, D. L (1982), Path analysis of the causal elements of Bandura's theory of self-efficacy and an anxiety passed model of avoidance behaviour, *Journal of Personality and Social Psychology, 42,* 764-781.

Junge, M. E., & Dretzke, B. J. (1995), Mathematical self-efficacy, gender differences in gifted/talented adolescents, *Gifted Child Quarterly, 39,* 22-28.

Kohlberg, L. (1968), A cognitive developmental analysis of children's sex role concepts and attitudes, In E. E. Maccoby (Ed.), *The development of sex differences* (pp. 82- 173), Stanford, CA: Stanford University Press.

Lapan, R. T., Adams, A., Turner, S., & Hinkelman, J. M. (2000), Seventh graders Vocational interest and efficacy expectation patterns, *Journal of Career Development, 26,* 215-229.

Mischel, W. (1970), A social learning view of sex differences in behaviour, In P. H. Mussen (Ed.), *Carmichael's Manual of Child Psychology*, (pp. 3-72), New York: Wiley.

Sanna, L. J. (1997), Self-efficacy and counterfactual thinking: upto a week with or Without a paddle, *Personality and Social Psychology Bulletin, 23*, 654-667.

Sharma, H.L. (2005), Creativity of engineers and civil services personnel, *Journal of Community Guidance and Research, 22*, 3-10.

Sinha, D. (2002), Psychology in rural area: the case of developing country, In A .K. Dalal and G. Misra (Eds.), *New directions in Indian psychology, volume 1: social psychology*, New Delhi: Sage.

Signorielli, N. (1990), Children, television roles: messages and impact, *Journal of Adolescent Health Care, 11*, 50-58.

Subramanian, S.V., Delgado, I., Jadue, L., Vega, J., & Kawachi, I. (2003), Income, inequality and health: multilevel analysis of Chilean communities, *Journal of Epidemiology and Community Health, 57*, 844 - 848.

Sud, S. (1998), Hindi version of general self-efficacy scale, Varanasi: Rupa, Retrieved 12.1.2005 http://userpage.fu-berlin.de/~health/hindi.htm

Ryff, C. D., Singer, B. H., & Seltzer, M. M. (2002), Pathways through challenge: implications for well-being and health, In L.Pulkkinen, and A. Caspi (Eds.), *Paths to successful development: personality in the life course* (pp. 302-328), New York: Cambridge University Press.

Tiwari, P. S. N. (2003), Perceived environment and aspects of social cognition among villagers, In A. Agarwal, and A. K. Saxena (Eds.), *Psychological perspectives in environmental and developmental issues* (pp. 98-112), New Delhi: Concept Publishing Company

Trivers, R. L. (1972), Parental investment and sexual selection. In B. Campbell (Ed.), *Sexual selection and the descent of man* (pp. 136-172), New Delhi: Amerind.

Vancouver, J.B., Thompson, C.M., Tischner, E.C., & Putka, D.J. (2002), Two studies examining the negative effects of self-efficacy on performance, *Journal of Applied Psychology, 87*, 506-516.

Vroom, V.H. (1964), *Work and motivation*, New York: Wiley.

Zinta, R.L. (2006), Effect of self-efficacy, test-anxiety and short-term intervention on problem solving: a preliminary analysis, *Social Science International*, 22, 3-8.

25

Factors Underlying Marks in Madhyamika Examination of West Bengal

—*Rumki Gupta*

The secondary education serves as a bridge between primary and higher education and also as entry into the higher education. All the students enrolled under the West Bengal Board of Secondary Education (WBBSE) participate in a challenging standard based curriculum. First public school leaving examination i.e., Madhyamik Examination which is conducted by the WBBSE at the end of class X in West Bengal. Factor analysis of Madhyamik curriculum subjects score of the students for a particular year 2000 was done considering marks of all subjects and separately for oral part of respective subjects. Three factors were extracted from there. They may be identified as i) descriptive scientific factor ii) language and logical factor and iii) oral or verbal factor. Factor analysis was also done by considering eight subjects. Oral marks were included with the marks of respective subjects. In this case, only one factor was emerged which may be identified as scholastic factor.

In a student's school life the interim period between primary school level and higher secondary level is called the secondary stage and the education at this stage is called secondary education. Secondary education has a vital role to play in any programme of education for the community. It is the stage which in all countries marks the completion of education for the vast majority.

This paper originally appears in the *Journal of the Indian Academy of Applied Psychology*, 2006, Vol.32, No.1-3, pp. 99-105.

Even the minority which goes for higher education cannot take full advantage of the wider opportunities offered by the universities unless they have received their grounding in a system of a sound secondary education.

The main objective of secondary education is to develop among the pupils qualities of leadership needed in different walks of life. Elementary education seeks to provide the basic information and skills needed for survival. Higher education seeks to extend the boundaries of knowledge and is often an end in itself. Secondary education is the connecting link between these two and also serves – or at least should serve – to select those who are to provide higher leadership to the community. Those who complete their education at this stage must acquire knowledge and competence and also develop qualities of leadership and character. Moreover, this stage may be broadly equated with the period of adolescence.

Adolescents are neither children nor adults, and what is more disturbing pass, from one phase to the other with bewildering speed. They are then passing through psychological changes of profound significance to the individual and the community. This is the period through which children are growing into adults, and the growth passes through many phases.

It is too early to take a decision about the future life on the basis of the emergence of any particular trait. A final decision about future profession at this stage may thus lead to grave mistakes. Hence the full benefit from secondary education cannot be derived if the curriculum at this stage has been incomplete or defective.

As curriculum is planned and guided by the school for learning and a set of documents for implementation, that should be implemented effectively, whether it is carried on in groups or individually, inside or outside the school. A curriculum is an attempt to communicate the essential principles and features of an educational proposal in such a form that it is open to critical scrutiny and capable of effective translation into practice

(Stenhouse, 1975). And it is essential to see the curriculum as much more than a mere collection of subjects and syllabi.

Secondary school leaving examination that is called Madhyamika Examination in West Bengal serves as a basis to achieve several aims. For this reason, the importance of this examination has an enormous effect on students' existence and also for their future programme. This examination is conducted by the West Bengal Board of Secondary Education (WBBSE) and by this examination students' attainment level is evaluated after completing study of consecutive 10 years. Students are followed by a scheduled curriculum ascertained by WBBSE to appear in this examination. They must take the examination in seven compulsory subjects, i.e., (i) Bengali (two papers, Beng I and Beng II), (ii) English (Eng), (iii) Mathematics (Maths), (iv) Physical Science (Ph.Sc), (v) Life Science (L. Sc), (vi) History (Hist) and (vii) Geography (Geo). These seven subjects are again divided into three major groups. These are as follows:

i) Language group (Beng I and Beng II, Eng)

ii) Science group (Maths, Ph Sc and L Sc)

iii) India and her people group (Hist and Geo)

Apart from these seven subjects one can opt for one additional subject. It is necessary to mention here that in Madhyamika Examination, two types of subjects are available as additional, such as (i) Pedagogical subjects like Additional Mathematics, Mechanics, Physics, Biology, Fishery, Logic, etc. and (ii) Work education, Music, etc. According to the criteria of WBBSE, besides English and Mathematics, all the subjects contain an oral part of 10 marks and the students have to appear for oral examination also. The performance of the students is evaluated on the basis of a total marks of 100 for each subject (90 marks in written and 10 marks in oral) except Bengali. In Bengali, students have to score out of 200 marks in two papers (180 marks in written and 20 marks in oral). In English and Mathematics, students have to score out of 100 (only written).

Though the curriculum of the Madhyamika Examination is broad and diverse, the essential areas related to this curriculum of various subjects are interconnected and students can progress through this curriculum. The curriculum is planned and guided learning (Kelly, 1983,1999).

As discussed earlier, the curriculum of Madhyamika Examination should include those programmes which will help the students to develop the qualities necessary in different spheres of life. Hence the vision and mission of the present curriculum of this examination need to be set. For this purpose it is necessary to locate the significant components being pertinent to the certain objectives of the curriculum. The above scenario depicts that it would be a major assignment if the factors inherent to the marks of Madhyamika Examination can be ascertained. Further, this study can be extended to extract the existing aptitude of the students.

Keeping in mind the above discussion the purpose of the present article is to find out the inherent factors of the marks of Madhyamika Examination and to predict the type of ability of the students according to his/ her marks obtained in different subjects.

METHOD

Sample

A multistage stratified clustered sampling design was adopted in this study. In the first stage, all 18 districts of WB were divided into four strata. The first stratum was Kolkata. Beside this, other 17 districts were stratified into three strata. Two districts from each stratum were selected by Rao, Heartly and Cochran (1962) scheme. Thus seven selected districts are as follows:

- Stratum 1 Kolkata
- Stratum 2 Jalpaiguri and Malda
- Stratum 3 Howrah and Hoogly
- Stratum 4 Midnapore and Bankura

The name of the schools and the number of schools were obtained from a list of recognised schools published by WBBSE (1989). The selection of schools from selected districts was done following simple random sampling without replacement (SRSWOR). Fifteen boys' schools and 10 girls' schools were selected randomly from each selected district. In the case of Kolkata and Midnapore 24 boys' schools and 12 girls' schools were selected as the number of schools in these two districts are more than other districts. As a result, 197 schools were selected for the purpose of this study. Totally the number of students was 17,978 in the year 2000. The medium of instruction in all the schools was Bengali.

Measures

The marks obtained by the students in their Madhyamika Examination 2000 was considered as the academic achievement score and detailed marksheets were collected from WBBSE.

Results and Discussion

At this level an attempt was made to obtain a picture of how well the students performed in all the subjects under this curriculum. The mean, SD and full marks of each subjects of the students are presented in Table 1.

Table 1: Mean, standard deviation and full marks of the students for Madhyamika subjects

	Subjects		*Written*		*Oral*	
	Mean	*SD*	*Full marks*	*Mean*	*SD*	*Full marks*
Bengali	84.43	37.33	200	15.33	5.43	20
English	31.03	17.72	100	–	–	–
Mathematics	37.78	22.15	100	–	–	–
Physical science	41.19	20.88	100	8.13	2.15	10
Life science	47.88	22.74	100	8.18	2.24	10
History	39.18	19.07	100	7.87	2.75	10
Geography	38.78	20.68	100	7.87	2.75	10
Additional subjects	49.80	30.06	100	–	–	–

It is clear from the results presented in Table 1 that average scores in Bengali, English, Mathematics, Physical Science, History and Geography vary between 30 and 40 out of 100. The average score and SD is minimum in English. English appears to be the most difficult subject in Madhyamika Examination. Bengali being the mother tongue of maximum students, they consider English as a foreign language. And also Bengali being the medium of instruction they can easily avoid English.

The other discrepancy may lie with the educational system and teaching-learning procedure. In the Science group, it is revealed that in Life science the average score is near about 48. In Madhyamika examination the students have scored high in Life science in comparison to Mathematics and Physical science. Similarly, in the case of India and her people group, the average scores in History and Geography of the students are more or less the same. In the case of additional subject, the average is about 50 and SD is as high as 30. It has already been reported earlier that in Madhyamika Examination, two types of subjects are available as additional, such as (i) Pedagogical subjects like Additional Mathematics, Logic, etc. and (ii) Work education, Music, etc. In the case of the latter, high marks are easily available in comparison to the first one. As a result, the SD becomes relatively large and two different distributions are combined into one.

In the case of oral examination, average marks are around 80 per cent. The discrepancies of averages between oral and written examinations indicate certain shortcomings in teaching-learning and evaluation method. Correlational analyses for the 14 subjects (variables) indicate that there are some significant positive relationships among the variables. The results are presented in Table 2.

Next, factor analysis was done considering the marks of all the fourteen subjects (above-mentioned main subjects including the oral part of the respective subjects and additional subject). A factor analysis was done with a notion to identify the common factors underlying these 14 subjects. The principal component

Table 2 :Correlations among the subjects under study **

Sl No	*Subjects Additional subject*	*Beng I*	*Beng II*	*Oral*	*Eng*	*Maths*	*Ph.Sc*	*Oral*	*L.Sc*	*Oral*	*Hist*	*Oral*	*Geo*	*Oral*
1.	BengI	–												
2.	BengII	.90	–											
3.	Oral	.75	.78	–										
4.	Eng	.96	.99	.83	–									
5.	Maths	.83	.84	.65	.90	–								
6.	Ph.Sc	.93	.94	.66	.93	.95	–							
7.	Oral	.57	.59	.55	.63	.71	.68	–						
8.	L.Sc	.63	.63	.27	.68	.75	.91	.59	–					
9.	Oral	.41	.42	.42	.45	.60	.53	.93	.52	–				
10.	Hist	.71	.72	.39	.77	.79	.94	.56	.89	.46	–			
11.	Oral	.62	.62	.35	.67	.70	.82	.57	.78	.50	.76	–		
12.	Geo	.44	.45	.43	.49	.62	.57	.92	.56	.91	.50	.53	–	
13.	Oral	.65	.66	.40	.76	.76	.86	.66	.82	.61	.80	.71	.63	–
14.	Additional subject	.73	.74	.51	.79	.80	.90	.69	.80	.61	.80	.71	.64	.77 –

All the values are significant at .01 level

method including varimax rotation was applied. Table 3 presents the sorted rotated factor loadings of the above-mentioned subjects.

Table 3: Factor loadings and their squares for 14 subjects

Subjects	*Factor 1*	*Sq. of factor*	*Factor 2*	*Sq. of factor*	*Factor 3*	*Sq. of factor*
Bengali I	.487	.24	.786	.62	.167	.03
Bengali II	.477	.23	.818	.67	.173	.03
Oral	.043	.00	.870	.76	.282	.08
English	.523	.27	.863	.75	.187	.04
Mathematics	.602	.36	.601	.36	.362	.13
Physical Sc.	.800	.64	.638	.41	.237	.06
Oral	.325	.11	.354	.13	.821	.67
Life Sc.	.930	.86	.172	.03	.277	.08
Oral	.249	.06	.157	.03	.972	.95
History	.852	.73	.334	.11	.205	.04
Oral	.717	.51	.279	.08	.286	.08
Geography	.297	.09	.184	.03	.927	.86
Oral	.723	.52	.302	.09	.389	.15
Addl. Sub.	.672	.45	.429	.18	.391	.15

Table 3 indicates that there were three factors underlying the 14 subjects. Mathematics, Physical science and Life science had high loadings on Factor 1. These subjects mainly measure scientific ability of the individual and hence Factor 1 may be termed as a descriptive scientific factor. History, History-oral and Geography-oral have considerable loadings in Factor 1. Bengali-oral has high loading on Factor 2 and Physical science-oral, Life Science-oral and Geography have high factor loadings in Factor 3. This effect may be due to the arbitrariness of oral marking. Table 3 shows that Bengali and English have lower factor loadings, and Mathematics, Physical science and Life Science have high factor loadings in Factor 1. At the same time History, History-oral and Geography-oral have considerable factor loadings in Factor 1. History and Geography may be identified as descriptive science. The lower factor loadings of History and Geography in Factor 2 also support this conclusion.

Bengali 1st and 2nd papers including oral part and English have high loadings on Factor 2. These two subjects require knowledge of language to express. So Factor 2 may be identified as a language factor. There was a third factor. Mainly oral parts had high positive loadings on this factor. This factor is identified as an oral or a verbal factor.

The factor loadings given in Table 3 also represent the correlation of each subject with the factors. These correlations are called the factorial validity of each subject (Anastasi, 1976). From Table 3 it can be mentioned that the factorial validity of Bengali as a measure of mathematical and scientific factor is .487, language factor is .786 and verbal factor is .167. The factorial validity of Bengali I, Bengali II, Bengali oral and English, in terms of language factor, are .786, .818, .870 and .863 respectively. The factorial validities of Mathematics, Physical Science and Life science in terms of mathematical and scientific factor are .602, .800 and .930 respectively. The first four subjects have less validity as the measures of descriptive scientific factor.

Since each factor loading represents the correlation between the subject and the factor, the square of the factor loadings gives the proportion of common variance between the subject and that factor. Thus, it can be found from Table 3 that in Bengali I and II, 24 per cent and 23 per cent variance is attributable to the descriptive scientific factor and 62 per cent and 67 per cent variance is attributable to the language and logical factor . In English, 27 per cent of the variance is attributable to the descriptive scientific factor and 75 per cent to the language and logical factor. It may be stated that Bengali and English have greater language factor structure. It can be revealed in such a way that one student may have greater language ability to score high in Bengali and English. In the case of Mathematics, the percentage of variance attributable to the descriptive scientific factor and language and logical factor is same and it is only 36 per cent. So the proportional contribution of the descriptive scientific factor and language and logical factor is same in the case of Mathematics. It may be represented in such a way that the student who scored high in Mathematics has both language and scientific ability. Again in Physical science and Life science 64 per cent and 93 per cent of the variance is attributable to the descriptive scientific factor and 41 per cent and only 3 per cent to the language and logical factor. This result also reveals that the students who have high score in Physical science and Life science have greater scientific ability. And according to that ability one student may select any one stream like Science, Arts, Commerce, etc. in future. In the case of History, 73 per cent of the variance is attributable to the descriptive scientific factor and 11 per cent to the language and logical factor. Geography has negligible percentage of variance to the descriptive scientific factor and language and logical factor. But the variance attributable to the oral or verbal factor in Geography is 86 per cent. This discrepancy may come from certain shortcomings in evaluation method.

Any individual's performance on these subjects depends on the amount of each of the relevant factors he or she possesses as well as the relative weight of these factors in the particular subject. It states that if a student scores high in Bengali or English, he or she has more language ability. Again high scores of a student in Physical science and Life science reveal that he or she possesses more scientific ability. Thus, if a student's score is expressed in the same units in scientific, language and oral or verbal factor then each score can be weighted by multiplying it by the corresponding factor loading. The sum of these three products would provide an estimate of the student's score on the factor.

Thus, if a student secures very high score in language and logical factor, this would help him much more in Bengali and English than in Physical science or Life science. Similarly, if a student scores very high in descriptive scientific factor, this would help him much in the Physical science and Life science. Of these three factors, language and logical factor would have the greatest effect on Life science and oral or verbal factor have the greatest effect on Life science oral.

There are eight subjects in the Madhyamika Examination. The result shows that all the subjects can be represented by only three factors (mentioned above). In the case of 14 variables, 91.5 per cent of the variance in the data space is explained by three latent factors.

In the next phase, factor analysis has been done by considering eight subjects as indicated in the mark-sheet (seven core subjects and an additional subject). Oral marks have been included with the marks of respective subjects. Factor loadings of eight variables are presented in Table 4. In this case only one factor has emerged. This can be identified as the scholastic factor. The variance explained is 81 per cent. This indicates that a Madhyamika student who performs well in one subject is likely to perform well in other subjects also.

Table 4 : Factor loadings on one factor extracted from 8 variables

Subjects	*Loadings*
Bengali	.885
English	.856
Mathematics	.861
Physical science	.919
Life science	.916
History	.858
Geography	.906
Additional subject	.993

References

Anastasi Anne (1976), *Psychological Testing* (Fourth Edition), Macmillan Publishing Co. Inc. New York.

Kelly, A. V. (1983; 1999), *The Curriculum. Theory and practice 4e*, London: Paul Chapman, List of Recognised X - Class Schools (1989) - West Bengal Board of Secondary Education, Calcutta.

Rao, J. N.K., Hartly, H.O. and Cochran, W.G. (1962), A Simple Procedures of Unequal Probability Sampling Without Replacement, *Journal of the Royal Statistical Society*,Series-B, 24, 482-491.

Stenhouse, Lawrence (1975), *An introduction to Curriculum Research and Development*, London: Heineman.

History of International School Psychology Association

As one looks back over a quarter of a century of development of an organisation we now call the International School Psychology Association (ISPA), it is apparent that the main theme that weaves throughout its existence was and still is the right of all children to a safe environment in which to grow and learn to their maximum potential.

In the early days of 1972, Frances Mullen and Calvin Catterall, two School Psychologists who had travelled and worked in many parts of the world, explored the idea of mobilising support for international communication between professionals in school psychology. Because of their effort the concept took a giant step forward when the International School Psychology Committee (ISPC) was formed by the Division of School Psychology at the annual meeting of the American Psychological Association (APA) in September 1972. Then in the spring of 1973, another organisation in Americas called the National Association of School Psychologists (NASP), became a partner in this new visionary idea. Dr. Catterall and Dr. Mullen took the leadership roles as co-chairpersons of the ISPC while both organisations provided financial support.

The ISPC began with four major objectives that would embrace a world-wide purpose: to foster communication between psychologists in educational settings, to encourage the implementation of promising practices in school psychology, to raise the effectiveness of education, and to promote the maximum contribution of psychology to education. Next, with Dr. Catterall's wide range of already acquired professional friends, a network was set up for receiving news of school psychology and disseminating it to various countries. The first *World-Go-Round* (WGR) was published in June 1973. The response to this publication was heartening. A healthy foundation was laid so that the future would see, to date, 93 issues of *WGR* having been circulated to educational psychologists in over 55 countries.

By August 1975, Dr. Frances Culbertson initiated a program called SHARE, an acronym for Sharing Home and Round the World Experience. For more than 22 years, it has remained a leading hospitality programme for psychologists travelling outside their own countries. SHARE is sponsored by several international groups and was the brainchild of Dr. Catterall. However, without the firm foundation given to it by Dr. Culbertson, Project SHARE would not be as strong and viable as it is today.

Throughout the 70s and into the 80s, ISPC flourished, going from 50 members to over 300. This growth in membership and the world-wide interest in ISPC affirmed the need for a more formal organisational structure. In 1982, at ISPC's fifth colloquium in Stockholm, Sweden, several significant steps were taken. The committee's name was officially changed to the International School Psychology Association (ISPA). Anders Poulsen became its first president, and soon thereafter, ISPA's constitution and bylaws were adopted. Unfortunately Dr. Catterall was not able to take over his functions as the Executive Secretary of ISPA, severely marked, as he was, with the after-effects of the meningitis which struck him in 1980. In spite of this his spirits were high as he witnessed his most cherished dream come true; a dream that began in 1972; a dream that set out to enhance communication between psychologists from educational settings throughout the world; a dream that became the bedrock of a quarter of a century of noteworthy accomplishments in the formation and development of professionalism in international school psychology.

It was ISPA's international perspective that moved the organisation in 1979 into a relationship with the United Nations Education, Scientific and Cultural Organisation (UNESCO).

During that year ISPC was represented at an international conference on education held in Geneva, Switzerland, sponsored by UNESCO. At that conference the United Nations General Assembly declared 1979 the International Year of the Child. This prompted ISPC to develop a Declaration of the Psychological Rights of the Child, initiating a world-wide recruitment process to get school psychologists to become 'rights advocates'. Subsequently, ISPA formed a committee, which now works directly with UNESCO and other UN non-governmental agencies to strengthen children's rights and services internationally. Even as late as 1993 national coalitions grew out of this movement. ISPA, to this day, is taking an active leadership role to strengthen its impact.

ISPA has sponsored an annual colloquium for providing a forum for professional interchange between individuals from around the world who are committed to the improvement of the mental health of children. Twenty successful colloquia have been held. From the beginning, the intention was to have a colloquium every year but that was not realised until 1982 onward. The continuity of having a colloquium every year was regarded as essential in order to maintain professional communication in a rapidly changing world. Therefore, since 1982, all colloquia have occurred yearly.

It may come as a surprise to many that the journal, *School Psychology International,* was an original publication of ISPC. It began as an idea in 1978 and eventually became a reality through the efforts of Ludwig Lowenstein in England. The first publication was the July/August 1979 issue, which had 32 pages for the cost of 1 .25 English pounds or 2. 50 US $. The journal was disseminated in a magazine format and printed by the School Psychology Publishing Company. However, in later years, this quarterly publication became autonomous and was not affiliated with ISPA. In 1993, it then became the official journal of ISPA. It highlights information of interest to educational/ school psychologists, some of which are original empirical research, promising procedures, and systems approaches for initiating positive changes within school communities in countries throughout the world.

National and international organisations can become affiliate members of ISPA. From the two original partners (NASP and APA) which supported the inception of IS-PC, there are now twenty-five national organisations around the globe that have chosen to support ISPA by being affiliate members. A delegate from each group is encouraged to give a report at each colloquia and throughout the year national news pertinent to the profession is submitted to be published in the *World-Go- Round*. Other notable accomplishments of ISPA include:

- Summer travelling seminars offering professional programs of educational value;
- Assisting in the formation of national associations in various countries;
- Active contributor to national and international publications;
- The publication of *Psychology In The Schools In International Perspective*, Volumes I, II, and III, which provides information about school psychology in a variety of settings;
- The formation of a Financial Aid Fund to support colleagues from around the world who, without assistance could not attend our colloquia; and subsequently applying for and receiving tax free status allowing donations to be tax deductible in the USA;
- The acceptance of a Code of Ethics which endeavours to set forth standards governing professional behaviour, capturing commonalities that span geographic and national boundaries;
- Plans for an International Institute of School Psychology offering graduate level programmes and research opportunities with cross-cultural emphasis;
- Acceptance and involvement in activities regarding the Young Child and Family Environment Project 1990-95 (UNESCO);
- The development of a *Colloquium Manual* as well as an ISPA Governance Operations Handbook;

- The implementation of a Leadership Workshop held prior to the colloquium;
- The publishing of a Leadership Bulletin to communicate ISPA's committee work to the membership;
- Involvement in the UN International Year for Tolerance 1995; and
- The declaration of a Definition of School Psychology and International Guidelines for the Preparation of School Psychologists as advisory instruments for those interested in better understanding school psychology.

Basically, it is the governance, loyal members and the role volunteers played that has made the International School Psychology Association what it is today. The fact that ISPA continues as a substantial presence on the international scene is certain testimony to the extraordinary human beings who created the ideas and did the work to move this successful organisation from its genesis into its own autonomous stature. Indeed, we can attribute the strength and noteworthy accomplishments of the ISPA of today to the firm foundation of teamwork and dedication of the past. It is a story of generosity, of faith, and perhaps above all, of a fervent desire to make a dream come true.

Bringing the Past Forward—A Retiree's Nightmare

Part I: Beginnings

Can you imagine looking at 30 years of files, papers packed in loose-leaf binders, filling the shelves of ISPA's Central Office as well as at home, and wondering if I will live long enough to go through it all to determine what should be archived? They were all, when received, evaluated as important for a Central Office and of benefit for the association. Now and again it was my intention to begin going over all those papers, determine what is important for the history of ISPA and send them to Betts Rivét as official archival material to be stored in the library at the University of Memphis. Busy working days postponed these good intentions and only occasionally when a binder grew so big that not even one new (and important) sheet could go into it, this binder had to be examined and a number of older papers plucked out ending up in the wastebasket.

ISPA has filled pretty much of my life over these many years. Also my memory has been dominated with the natural "filing in my head" of ISPA information but, as you might expect, growing in age many of these memories have ended up in the "old-age wastebasket." However, now being freed from daily responsibilities, I found myself ready to take on the challenge of reading, sorting, and examining what is needed for future historical importance for ISPA. It seemed overwhelming and, indeed, a retiree's nightmare. Finally I began by starting with the oldest material first. In many a case, I do not know what to keep because some of it may already be in the possession of Betts or Tom Fagan. For that reason Betts and I have agreed that I would make a rough sorting of the material and what I find worth keeping I will send to her for a final decision and thereafter archiving. It has proven to be very time consuming to read every letter, every document. Having worked a day or two with this, I realised that I had, in hand, fundamentally important information related to the origin of ISPA and, in fact, I was one of the few people involved at ISPA's beginning and still active now. I felt strongly that some of this information should be shared with the readers of WGR. This I will try to do in coming issues with bits and pieces in which I was involved and which, I hope, will contribute to the understanding of the decade of ISPA, the years from 1974 to 1984, the period up to the tragic death of Cal Catterall in the train accident in France.

How it all Began

On March 11, 1974, I received a newsletter called the *World-Go-Round* (Vol. 2, No. 1) edited by a Dr. Calvin Catterall, a man fully unknown to me. It was issued by an International School Psychology Committee (ISPC) which was described as 'a joint committee of Division 16 of the American Psychological Association and the National Association of School Psychologists'. The newsletter told that ISPC had two co-chairpersons, Dr. Catterall and Frances Mullen, and it went on to report about plans for an international colloquium for School

Psychologists to be held some place in Europe during 1975. Dr. Catterall requested people to contact him if they were interested and willing to take leadership responsibilities in this. Several years earlier I had held a UNESCO post in Thailand and had, in several other ways, been travelling with professional purposes but this WGR was my first contact with an international group with the same profession as my own. It raised such an interest in me that I, the same day as I received the newsletter, forwarded a reply to Dr. Catterall. My letter began with "I wonder how you found me", a question that was never really answered. After introducing myself, informing him that I was the elected President of the Danish Association of School Psychologists (or chairman as we say), I continued by saying that "Your idea of an International Colloquium of School Psychology is very fascinating. Is Denmark too small a place for that?" After giving more information about the Danish association the letter ended saying, "Please do write if you think we have something to contribute." Soon I received Dr. Catterall's reply. It was a long letter, rich in words which I soon found was a characteristic of his. He wrote to ask me to serve on the international planning group for this coming colloquium.

I accepted, with pleasure, for this was to be the very first international colloquium for school psychologists. A number of letters crossed the Atlantic in the ensuing months and it was decided that the site of the first colloquium should be Munich, a place easy to reach, and with reduction in hotel rates available. I had received a small Danish grant to be used for a study visit to New York during the fall of 1974. This made it possible for me to accept an invitation to attend the Executive Board meeting of NASP to be held in Chicago in October where I also were to meet with Cal Catterall and Frances Mullen in person. I must admit that as I landed at O'Hare airport in Chicago, I felt something important was just ahead of me.

Cal and Frances were at the O'Hare Inn where the NASP meeting was held. Our first talk was held over an awful chicken curry dinner. The NASP meeting was chaired by President Jean Leppaluoto. I was introduced as a member of the planning committee for the next year's colloquium and I addressed the Board with a greeting from the Danish association. Later in the evening I met with a few members of the planning committee to discuss early stages of the colloquium plans. As the following months went by, plans developed well and Cal, supported by Frances, did an outstanding job working out details from a distance. They both possessed a warm, sincere sense of international cooperation, listening to and respecting other cultures as they designed this first colloquium.

The Munich Colloquium (22-26 July, 1975). The colloquium theme was "School Psychology in Changing Societies." Programme booklets were made and distributed during the winter, all adorned with a logo designed by Cal's daughter, Karen. That logo is still the one representing our association today. Also they were very impressive as to the content of the program to be offered in Munich. The actual program presented at the colloquium was almost up to the promised standard, but cancellations or changes did not pose a problem because Cal possessed a very special ability to establish an atmosphere of acceptance. He could, elegantly, reorganise a session so that the 200 participants felt valued and given ample opportunity for international interaction about various aspects of the colloquium theme. An interesting note: more than 10 of those present in Munich have attended most of our colloquia ever since. Two have served ISPA one way or another until this day and Bayard Bartley is one of them. The program booklet announced an evening session from 8 to 10 titled: *The Future Of International Communication in School Psychology*. Added was that it was 'an invitational meeting for the presidents of National Psychology groups, the Colloquium Planning Committee, and members of the International School Psychology Committee. The aim of the meeting was that the invited persons should try to formulate some thoughts about how this first attempt for international cooperation could continue. These thoughts were to be brought up for discussion and a possible decision in a plenary session on the last morning of the colloquium.

Only very few of the above-mentioned types of leaders were attending the colloquium, for which reason it was suggested to extend the invitation to a broader audience and meet in a nearby Bierstube which evolved into a good social evening with an exchange of opinions and ideas which became the basis of proposals that were presented the last day. I believe that Cal originally had hoped that steps could be taken to establish a real membership organisation. This was understandable since, to continue ISPC, funds were badly needed. Until then, Cal and his family not only did all the work but also paid for printing and mailing. Personally, I felt sure (as did others) that it was not a mature time to establish a formalised organisation. Cal accepted this. I was asked to chair this plenary session on the last day. My files show that I presented the following proposals:

- The planning group found it important to establish ways to continue some type of international cooperation but found it too early to try to establish a real membership organisation with elected board and all that follows this. It was found that some sort of structure was needed if it should be realistic to keep a cooperation running and possibly making steps for further development and a minimum amount of money was also required.
- Goals or aims for this cooperation should be discussed and decided upon for the work to be done within the nearest two-three years, but which?
- Should a continuation of the WGR be one of these goals? To be published four-five times annually? If yes, how to provide funds for this?
- Should a new international colloquium be one of the goals to aim for?
- Would it be of importance to have published one or more books about school psychology in various countries, a project Cal Catterall already worked on?

Generally and without much discussion it was met with warm approval that the WGR should continue, that a new colloquium was considered important, and that books about school psychology would be most relevant for promotion of international cooperation and improvement of school psychology worldwide. The discussion about financing was the most difficult part. The group suggested that national associations should be asked to pay 10/15/20 cents per member to this international cooperation. Would that be realistic? Furthermore, each person receiving the WGR should be asked to pay for it. Three or four dollars annually was suggested. Those who did not pay would be deleted from the mailing list. Would that be realistic?

No minutes exist from that meeting but I do remember a long discussion and much doubt being expressed as to the realistic nature of the plans. It came up that the publishing of the books might bring a profit that would help keep the project running. At least, if we wanted to go on, we had to believe that money would come in some way or another!

The final part that was discussed was a mechanism for steering the committee and keeping it of such simple nature that it would cost nothing yet efficient enough to take care of the initial projects. To this purpose the planning group suggested that:

- An executive group of five should be established and this body should be named "The International School Psychology Committee." Two of the members were obviously to be Frances Mullen and Calvin Catterall, (which I gave ground for saying) without their willingness to continue to put their effort and their heart into this international project, nothing whatsoever will be done and the goals not attained. This was accepted along with the suggestion that the group responsible for the day's agenda be empowered to find three people for this committee who would be fairly representative of larger professional groups in major geographical areas outside the United States. Finally it was proposed that:
- The International School Psychology Committee should establish a larger Associate Committee consisting of members of the group involved in the planning of this first colloquium, and others who still wanted to be involved internationally, as well as one representative from each of the various national associations of school psychologists wanting to be involved in this project. The decisions made during this final session of the first colloquium were basic, but important steps in the later development of the International School Psychology Association (ISPA). They were small hesitant attempts and proved, in various ways,

not to be very realistic. For instance, I am not sure that very much more money was paid than what the Danish association allocated (2 DKK per member = 30 cents per member). Right after the colloquium, I was asked to be a member of this new International School Psychology Committee. It took some time to find the two last members, but after long considerations and much exchange of thoughts Odette L van Kolck from Brazil and Avner Ziv from Israel also joined the committee in November.

PART II: JULY 1975-AUGUST 1977

In Munich I had accepted the invitation from Cal Catterall to become a member of the new International School Psychology Committee (ISPC). That was in July. Already early August I learned from a letter that Cal expected me to carry out the following duties:

- Organise the work of ISPC,
- Suggest who to appoint as other members of ISPC, and
- Take responsibility for the next colloquium to be held in 1977 and to find in which Scandinavian country it could be best arranged.

In fast succession, all during August, four more letters came from Cal. Their content included:

- A news release about the Munich colloquium,
- Guidelines for choosing members of the ISPC,
- Organisational guidelines to keep ISPC momentum going, and
- A tentative timeline for the 2nd international colloquium on school psychology listing 19 items/steps and the months each should be finalised.

Needless to say, my breath was taken away because Cal expected me to carry out all of the tasks. Little did he know that I already had more than enough to do. I was the leader of the School Psychological Counselling in my area and wanted here to do a job deserving professional respect among school children, parents and teachers as well as by my employer, the municipal authorities.

I was also deeply involved in official and semi-official associations related to the function of our society which were time consuming. But most demanding was my six year chairmanship of the Danish School Psychologists Association. This post brought along requests for my participating in and contributing to many types of sessions, meetings, conferences throughout the country, and also I was asked to be a member of several official government boards and commissions. All of this were unpaid work to be done after normal working hours. I replied to Cal's five letters before the end of August. This letter crossed in the mail with one more letter from Cal (now, altogether six since we met in Munich). The main content in this letter from him was, "I have been waiting for your answer for the last week and a half. I do not know what would happen to the Steering Committee if you are not able to accept. We need you desperately."

I perhaps should have felt flattered at being seen as important but, instead, I was a bit fearful. I could foresee some problems if Cal, who seemed to spend most of his time on ISPC, could not accept or understand that I had major obligations elsewhere. In my reply to him, I assured him that he could rely on me to do what I accepted to do keeping in mind my other responsibilities. As the fine, warm-hearted man he was, he immediately gave me a positive reply. Generally, we had an uncomplicated, cooperative relationship and I deeply respected his dynamic and visionary leadership. I also believe that he respected my help shaping and defining the direction of ISPC in those early years of 1975-6 as well as keeping plans close to the world of reality.

In 1975 Cal was preparing the first volume of the series of books about *International Perspectives on School Psychology*. It was published in 1976. Subsequently, Volume 2 was published in 1977.

In planning for the 2nd ISPC Colloquium, I suggested that Helsingør, Denmark, be the site for this colloquium. Early in 1976, the Local Organising Committee (LOC) was well on its way in planning for the 1977 colloquium. Even though Helsingør was two hours travelling time away from the airport in Copenhagen, it had all the facilities and attractions beneficial for our colloquium. It is a town with the Hamlet castle, Kronborg, and a new, modern Conference Centre had enough accommodations for the participants which could be supplemented, if necessary, with nearby camping huts, youth hostels, and even local teachers and colleagues opening their homes for us. All the municipalities around Helsingør had well staffed School Psychological Counselling Offices willing to support the LOC is various ways. But one major problem existed. The conference site was owned and run by the United Danish Trade Unions. It was much in demand and required that we sign a contract one year prior to the colloquium. We had to guarantee to rent the whole Centre which included full payment of all 175 rooms and full board for the same number of participants. Cancellation would be accepted no later than three months before the colloquium. If later, we would be obliged to pay 90 per cent of the total sum (an amount of money higher than the value of my private home). ISPC had no buffer-sum available. However, realising the personal risk in signing the contract, I did so on June 2, 1976, with my wife's approval. More about this later.

A torrent of letters passed between Cal and me, his more frequent and longer than mine. Fax and email did not exist, so communication took time and we needed to meet in person to talk over a number of issues. The XXI International Congress of Psychology gave us this opportunity in July 1976 in Paris. Concurrently in Paris, Frances Mullen coordinated and organised the 34th Annual Convention of the International Council of Psychologists and Cal arranged to be there with a Travelling Seminar. I was invited to participate in a seminar on international psychology so with the financial support from my association and the Danish Ministry of Education, I was able to go to Paris and meet Frances and Cal. Staying at a humble side-street hotel where all sorts of perceptible human activities went on all night, I found my experience filled with joyful contrasts: Speaking in a Sorbonne classroom, meeting with Frances and Cal for a light meal at a little café (a favourite hang-out for both Lenin and Hemingway), and finally an evening banquet in the luxury Hotel Concorde La Fayette, were the high lights of my Paris experience.

During our discussions of colloquium items and general ISPC matters, Frances hinted that because of an overload of duties she may need to leave ISPC. She did so formally during the fall and

Professor Gaston Gauthier of Quebec, Canada, accepted to replace her. Upon returning to Denmark, the flow of letters about the planning of the colloquium between Cal and me continued and our local planning progressed. The First Circular, colloquium information, and the registration form were distributed on time. Cal's travel agent planned three Travelling Seminars.

A plan was devised whereby Americans could register to attend the colloquium with Cal or with the travel agent or with us in Copenhagen. Unfortunately, we did not foresee the confusion and how difficult it was for us to keep a general overview of the registration process. We mailed announcements of the colloquium directly to every school psychologist in all five Nordic countries. We were supported by the Danish Foreign Ministry and the Ministry of Education with both addresses and directly forwarding our material via their own channels especially to the East European Countries. To educational institutions in the Soviet Union, we made special letters of invitation in Russian. All of the publicity did not seem to help much because by May 1, 1977 we, in Denmark, only has 10 registered participants and Cal reported 50 "reservations, but some of them just inquiries." Since the dollar was low, we wondered if that was influencing registration from USA.

At this point our signed contract with the colloquium site was causing us great concern. We had 15 days to make a decision to cancel or be bound to pay 90 per cent of the total sum for 175 people. In fact, I was the one to have the final word on this because it was my home that we were gambling with. In a letter we told Cal that the LOC would call him on May 11th and he, by then, had to know how many, in total, had registered for the colloquium with him. But on that day, there was no reassurance from Cal except "they are coming in pretty fast now." The situation was becoming critical. But I had the feeling that the administration of the conference site was not too happy if we cancelled because it perhaps could be difficult to get another group to contract the facility at this late date. I proposed and they agreed to set a new deadline date of June 15th and, further, they agreed to 153 full paying participants rather than 175. But even this lower figure could be a problem since the dollar continued to drop in value, which in itself undermined our budget. It was increasingly more expensive for Americans to travel abroad.

An appeal was sent out to all Danish school psychologists, explaining the situation and asking as many as possible to participate in our colloquium through the financial assistance of their own office budget. By early June we had a total of 109 people registered, but phone calls from Danish colleagues as a result of our letter- appeal gave us the absolute, unquestionable backing we needed from our colleagues. We decided not to cancel and luckily so because we ended up with 250 participants at the colloquium coming from 30 different countries. We will never forget that May in 1977 when panic was just around the corner. It taught me a lesson to strive for ISPC to establish a large enough buffer-sum to survive a necessary cancellation of a colloquium. This we first really took steps to realise after the Chernobyl disaster threatened our colloquium in the summer of 1986.

The Second School Psychology Colloquium, August 14-19, 1977, Elsinor, Denmark The theme was "Child Rearing and Educational Practices: Interaction on Personality Development." Cal pulled off a remarkable feat by putting together a well organised program from a distance and bringing with him nicely designed program booklets. The colloquium was successful, documented in a very favourable way from our 'Evaluation Questionnaire' that participants were asked to complete. We instigated the 'Small Interaction Groups for all Participants' which has continued to be a valued characteristic at our colloquia ever since. Our very successful social programs included the popular study visits to schools and institutions, an evening in the old Carmelite Abbey where a local Amateur Theatre Group presented 'Shakespeare Vignettes', and a special children's program every day. Worthy of mentioning here is that the secretarial staff, reception and information desk personnel, as well as the shuttle service drivers were all volunteers which did not burden the colloquium budget at all. They were offered to us by their employers, the municipal school systems in the area where they were employed.

Financially, we were supported by a grant from the Danish

Ministry of Education that covered pre-colloquium costs for printing and mailing and, further, a special grant large enough to invited a South African colleague to attend the colloquium as well as a special post colloquium study tour in our country. Settling the financial side of the colloquium was not easy because of three accounts (The Travelling Seminars, Call Catterall and the LOC). This led to the future decision that a very clear budget is needed and that money control must be in one place only. In spite of the fears of potential problems we made enough money to pay Cal for Vol. 1 and 2 of *Psychology in the Schools* which we gave to all participants. Also we were able to advance $2000 as a loan for costs of printing and mailing to the group planning the next colloquium in England (an amount that this group unfortunately lost for reasons never explained or understood). By the very end, we were able to transfer the small amount of $1500 to the work of ISPC, administered by Cal Catterall. Not much after all that work, but other types of results were probably worth more than money, such as: The Danish Association of School Psychologists had proved its ability to handle such a task, which gave some benefits externally.

Of some importance it was also that Professor Robert Vallet, after a post colloquium study tour we arranged for him, was interviewed by a newspaper which appeared under the headline "Danish School Psychology Is The World's Most Advanced." Also the professional cooperation inside the Scandinavian countries flourished as a result of the colloquium AND it made ISPC and its work international known, and increased the aspirations for the future, which are documented in notes from internal committee meetings held during the colloquium under the heading: 'Deliberations of the International School Psychology Steering Committee, August 1977'. Members in attendance at all sessions were: Cal Catterall, Gaston Gauthier, Avner Ziv, and Anders Poulsen along with others who were invited when special items were discussed. Highlighted items are as follows:

— A strong group of British participants (Klaus Wedell, Jack Wright, Maurice Chazan, Seamus Hegarty, and the Honorary Secretary for the Division of Educational Psychologists of the British Psychological Society, Ken

Cornwall) suggested the University of York in England as the site for the 1979 colloquium. Ken Cornwall offered to be the Convener if the two British associations, in joint sponsorship, would agree.

- The concept of Regional Meetings held at places where it was not yet practical to hold a colloquium, was discussed and accepted. Also planning Travelling Seminars and/or Study Travel Groups to such places were to be considered.
- A Task Force had been urging ISPC to start a journal entitled *International School Psychology Journal*. Although ISPC agreed on the desirability of a journal, we were not in a financial position to start now. The Task Force would continue to work on this (Ludwig Lowenstein, UK).
- The desirability of a relationship with the United Nations was discussed. Gaston Gauthier and Avner Ziv should explore possibilities and bring up more concrete plans and suggestions, especially considering the International Year of the Child in 1979.
- To increase the level of ISPC activity by building up broader contacts in various parts of the world, special assignments were accepted by committee members along with Anna-Lisa Melldén, Sweden. All would report their activities to Cal.
- Finances were discussed by representatives of present and up-coming colloquia and the Journal Task Force. ISPC was functioning on very limited funds. It should be the aim of all colloquia to produce some money for general operational expenses. It was revealed for the first time that Cal, when funds were available, received $100 a month as an honorarium. Avner Ziv suggested that this amount be increased to support Cal, who invested so much time in ISPC, as it would be unlucky for ISPC if he had to find other paid work, consequently, limiting his involvement in the development of ISPC. As soon as the financial status of the colloquium was known, Cal agreed to bring this question back to the committee by mail.
- A discussion about receiving any type of payment for

doing work for ISPC revealed major cultural differences. How would this influence attitudes in the years ahead, what repercussions could be foreseen. North and West Europeans in those days expected such activities to be made by socially involved people, who volunteer their free time trying to move the world somewhat in the direction of their dedication, and not receiving any type of pay for this, but having refunded only their direct expenses.

- The formalisation of ISPC was also an important item for discussion. As a first step, it was agreed to accept the offer from Werner Epp, USA, to begin to look into a Constitution and possibly even a Charter under the UN. It was no time to rest on the credit obtained during this colloquium. What developed hereafter will be reported in Part III.

Part III

In the June issue of WGR I focused on what happened in 1975, when I became a member of the International School Psychology Committee and thereafter in the article mentioned the activities up to the 1977 colloquium in Elsinor and finally gave a survey of what the Steering Committee at its sessions during this colloquium considered most important to have implemented in a nearer future. Right after the colloquium we probably all needed a period to restore to new activities. Cal Catterall admitted this as he introduced a letter to me, dated September 6, 1977 as follows: "I do not know about you, but I am having trouble getting back into the saddle again. I have been home for about two weeks and have only done a few of the things that needed to be done when I got home." These words were followed by five pages giving evidence that he was very well 'back into the saddle' mentioning what he in fact already had been doing (which was far more than most of us would ever manage in the same timespan):

- Made an agreement with Peter Burzinsky to serve as a "production manager" of WGR in cooperation with the advanced printing facilities at Vincennes University in Indiana (which proved to be very positive for WGR and ISPC during its period of functioning).

– Already had forwarded to the British a long organisational letter as a support to their initial planning for the next colloquium.
– Pre-planned the coming summer's Travelling Seminar But most of the five pages dealt with finances, a continuation of the discussions by the Steering Committee in Elsinor. Cal did not like to discuss money. At the time, he had no regular job, thus no regular income. Support for ISPC came from various US sources such as the California School Psychology Association (CASP), American Psychological Association (APA) and mainly from the National Association of School Psychology (NASP). Very few people paid for the WGR which Cal generously distributed (about 1,000 copies worldwide). He used his own funds to publish the volumes of *Psychology in the Schools in International Perspective*. But as the optimist he was by nature, and as he believed so much in the importance of ISPC, he always tried to find ways to raise funds. When he did not succeed, he paid out of his own pocket. We urged him to discuss this because the Steering Committee felt strongly that we could not let him go on doing this. We knew that a solution to this would not be found as long as we were a loosely structured Committee with no formal financial accounting system in place. Finding a solution became even more difficult when the continuity of the work in the Committee was broken when Gaston Gauthier vacated his seat and was replaced by Dr. Blanca M. De Alvarez from Mexico.

New Initiatives: The International Year of the Child (1979)

The period between the Elsinor colloquium in 1977 and York in 1979 was, in reality, the Crown of Achievements for Cal. The Liaison network was tremendously expanded by Cal in co-operation with Anna-Lisa Mellden from Sweden but it brought on some operational function problems.

However, the core of this period was the International Year of the Child (IYC). It was roughly touched on in Elsinor but nobody imagined how successful it would be for Cal, personally, and for ISPC. Looking back it is unbelievable how Cal had already started setting up the ISPC's agenda for the IYC in the October 1977 issue of the WGR. By June 1978 he published a draft of "The International School Psychology Committee's Declaration of the Psychological Rights of the Child". He named ten tentative 'Psychological Rights' along with a well-structured four phase plan indicating how these rights could be discussed worldwide.

Cal was an untiring, creative visionary. He succeeded in mobilising a large number of people worldwide and set the agenda for discussions in wide educational and school psychological groups in many countries. He obtained visible and lasting results, not the least of which were the many successful Travelling Seminars. Not only did he bring the 'rights' to the knowledge of colleagues in many countries but also to political and administrative circles as well. After a final polishing of these 'rights', they were approved by the participants of the York colloquium in July 1979. Cal was the drive behind all of this! He was the only one who had the insight and imaginative power to formulate these psychological rights using ideas set forth by the UN in the 1959 document "Declaration of the Rights of the Child." AND, it is worth noting that, as was characteristic of Cal, the 1979 document was published under the name of the ISP Steering Committee, so we all were given the credit that he and he alone really deserved.

I do find it fair to mention one special IYC initiative even though it is from my own country. The Danish Association of School Psychologists made a major contribution to the success of the whole campaign by publishing 20,000 copies of a well designed booklet of the ten psychological rights, each illustrated with a photograph. We added a one-page text for each of the 10 rights explaining and illustrating the content of each. This booklet was distributed free to most schools, libraries, practitioners in Denmark as well as colleagues in neighbouring countries where it was well received and widely quoted. The Swedes and the Germans succeeded in having made reprints in their own languages. Furthermore, the Danish association published a special issue of the journal Skolepsykologi in which Danish cultural and political leaders wrote articles about the ten psychological rights and their importance.

During the York colloquium a Task Force under the direction of Stuart Hart finalised the ISP Psychological Rights of the Child which was presented to a plenary session the last day of the colloquium. In the 1979 October issue of the WGR, Cal reported, "As was anticipated, the Declaration of the Psychological Rights of the Child was adopted by the majority of the participants at the closing session of the York colloquium. What had not been anticipated, however, was the rather strong opposition to the idea of making such a declaration at all. Although, like all rights statements, it is admittedly somewhat idealistic and various countries are at different levels of readiness to work on these rights and for most people who had been working on the wording of the declaration we had experienced a 'who can be against them?' reaction." After mentioning some of the reservations, he continued by saying that the majority signed in support of the Declaration. "And so, although there were different reactions to the process, we have now passed the major milestone of having adopted the first international Declaration of the Psychological Rights of the Child. If this has to be more than an exercise in futility, the task before us is to find a variety of ways and the manpower to help move this process beyond where it is now to where it should be, a guiding force, helping to improve the quality of life for the world's children."

Good documentation and follow-up related to the whole process around the IYC can be found in the WGRs from 1977-1979. In my opinion, this was the most successful, effective and memorable task that Cal did for children and for International School Psychology. But the opposition disappointed him immensely. Cal also was let down when some participants raised the question about the loose structure of ISPC and possible consequences. It was meant as a serious concern. Everything would fall apart if something should happen to Cal 'on the way back over the ocean' (as expressed by some). There was scepticism related to the funding of the work done.

"Where are the needed funds coming from and how are they spent?" It was difficult for some to understand how Cal could afford to use so much time, as his level of activity for ISPC indicated, without getting money from somewhere. From whom and why? However, the ISP Steering Committee was still in agreement that the 'movement' was not yet mature enough for establishing a formal association which, naturally, would require membership and official treasuring which was what the critics were asking for. It was decided that Cal, who had taken care of everything related to money, would make a formal annual accounting of money received and spent. This would then be published in the WGR.

Unforeseen was that in less than a year thereafter, the Steering Committee was, indeed, confronted with the need to reconsider the structure of the ISPC. But first, a few words about:

The 3rd International Colloquium, University of York, July 7-12, 1979 which had the theme: *Psychology for Children - Today and Tomorrow.* Ken Cornwall was the competent convener and worked together with a strong group of British School Psychologists along with the backing of two associations representing the British School Psychologists. A total of 300 participants came to York, the largest group being British, many Americans, and 30 countries being represented. In my experience, the British are good conference hosts so most participants felt that social and cultural offers were fine and well arranged and that the professional program was interesting. Personally, I found the setting at the university campus excellent and the city of York was unique as an outer frame to the experience.

The colloquium was seen as valuable for the British and, certainly, for the development of ideas and thinking connected to school psychology in various parts of the world. A major contribution was Volume 3 of Cal's books about *Psychology in the Schools in International Perspective.* His second part of the "History of the Movement" such as 'factors affecting the development' and the 'four levels of development' were core questions in several sessions during the colloquium. Not everyone agreed with his deliberations but they stimulated discussions and brought forward ideas for the future.

Finally to be mentioned a sad fact. Many months after the colloquium the British Local Organising Committee (LOC) informed me that they were unable to refund the loan of $2,000 given to them by ISPC to cover the initial basic costs for printing and mailing. The reason for this was never properly explained. We can only speculate that poor financial planning or some internal friction which surfaced after the colloquium might have been the cause. From that we tried to learn for the future, but not always have we been successful.

The 4th Colloquium, Jerusalem, Israel, June 29 to July 3, 1980

At the end of 1979, the planning of the colloquium in Israel was well on its way. Sweden seemed ready for 1981 and other countries were explored for years thereafter. Cal planned a Travelling Seminar bringing a large group from USA to Jerusalem. I tried to arrange a Scandinavian group to go but the interest was not there. I also had to inform Cal that I was unable to attend because of my own financial reasons. I was somewhat surprised that I did not receive the usual quantity of mail from Cal and especially startled that he never commented on the fact that I could not attend the colloquium. I sensed something was not as it should be. Phone calls then, for me, were an expensive luxury and only used when urgent. I felt now was the time to call him and I did so several times. No response. Now I felt somehow I ought to attend the colloquium and, luckily, with the help of the Ministry of Education and the Danish Association, I was able to find the basic $700 needed for travel and registration. I forwarded a note to Cal about this.

It was a fortunate circumstance that I was able to book my travel and register for the colloquium because it was on June 23, 1980 that Cal's wife called to inform me that Cal was seriously ill with meningitis. She asked me, on behalf of Cal, to take over his duties and responsibilities at the colloquium. Of course I said yes, not knowing what that implied before I arrived in Jerusalem. *Uriel Last*, the convener, was helpful by giving me a list of my main duties. Among these were:

- Give the Welcome Address to participants at the opening activity,
- Speak at the concluding session,
- Head a number of sessions during the colloquium, and

- Prepare a 'Thank You' at a reception at the home of a psychologist being The First Lady of Israel, Mrs. Ofira Navon, married to Yitzhak Navon, the country's President from 1978-83.

Those were busy days and evenings, trying to prepare myself to represent ISPC reasonably well. The colloquium was held under the auspices of the Hebrew University of Jerusalem with participation of three more universities and, of course, the Division of Educational and School Psychology of the Israel Psychological Association.

The theme of the colloquium was *Psychology and Changing Education* and the high quality professional programme was very well organised. The social and cultural programs did not give many opportunities to meet colleagues partly because of the 500 participants, 450 were Israeli and were present mostly only during the professional sessions. The remaining 80 (60 from USA and 20 from other countries) were spread out in various hotels all over the city. Travelling to and from the colloquium site, Mount Scopus, was somewhat problematic, especially in the evenings.

Calvin Catterall Seriously ill. What now?

In Jerusalem I received a letter from Gretchen, Cal's wife, with more details. The meningitis was diagnosed in May but, even before that, family and friends noticed some signs indicating that Cal was not quite himself. Doctors were not optimistic and a full recovery, if ever, would take time. At the colloquium, one of Cal's duties was to head a meeting of the ISP Liaison Network but now it was my responsibility. The following eight people were present at the meeting on June 30th: Avner Ziv (from Israel and on the ISP Steering Committee), Peter Burzinsky (from USA and Co-Editor of the WGR), Ludwig Lowenstein (from England and Editor of the journal *School Psychology International*, SPI, which will be discussed later in detail), Jean-Claude Guillemard (from France who had already at the York colloquium involved himself in ISP activities and, I might add, has served ISPA on various important and demanding posts to the present day), Bob Germain, (from USA, liaison from Missouri), Michael Schnur (on the colloquium LOC and member of the Israel Psychological

Association), Elizabeth Guillion (from USA who had the latest news from Gretchen Catterall). A person from South Africa was there also whom I had not previously met.

The meeting centred around the sad fact of Cal's illness and our hopes for his recovery all of which led to a discussion of the future of ISP. In fact, we were now in a situation for which we had been criticised - loose structure of ISPC and what if something happened to Cal? Those weaknesses were now clearly manifested, however, the present forum of eight could not make any decisions. It was the duty of the whole Steering Committee. Fortunately, this little dedicated group of ISP people was willing to debate the situation, bring up suggestions for what was necessary to be done and how this could possibly be implemented. The following ideas came up during the meeting:

- Probably necessary to postpone the planned 1981 colloquium in Stockholm to 1982,
- Find ways to continue with (1) the International Network, (2) planning for future colloquia, (3) SPI Journal, and (4) *World-Go-Round.*

  Would Peter Burzinsky keep on with the WGR? If so, practical issues should be investigated. Are any articles ready? Is there money for printing and mailing?
- It would be necessary to find a person willing and capable to function, for some period of time, as the head of the Steering Committee.
- I was asked to take the lead in this process and accepted to approach the whole Steering Committee and inform widely within ISP about the present situation and return to this group with a status report by the end of August.
- I was back home from Jerusalem on July 5th and the next day I immediately began writing letters to inform the extensive ISP constituents of the situation.

PART IV

Part three of the early history of ISPA, published in the September issue of the *WGR*, reported about the period covering the colloquia in York (1979) and Jerusalem (1980) and informed you of the serious illness that befell Calvin Catterall in the spring of 1980. How would his recovery develop and how would it influence his work fo the ISPC? Nobody could know when we met in Jerusalem but the predictions were not too good. Fortunately it seemed at the beginning to turn out better than expected. Already in his letter of July 18th he reported, "... my memory functions seem to be about average... I am currently somewhat weak and temporarily a little confused at times but I feel that I can take of some of the ISPC work that I have had to give up over the past few weeks...hope I will be able to carry the thought content...."

Sadly, he probably had been too optimistic as very few letters followed from him during the fall and they, indirectly, told that he was not back on track. The impression was that he continued to feel tired and short of energy. That was confirmed also in communication from US members who had met him. Yet he outwardly tried to prove that he was well by mentioning a number of initiatives to be implemented. The major one was in a December 1980 letter: "The big news is that I have decided that it is time to formalise the organisation. The idea was suggested to me by someone who was at Israel...."

Years later, considering how this evolved, the following thought came to my mind: Was that decision his signaling that now he felt well and back to his usual standard OR could it be that, subconsciously, he felt that it was high time to realise his dream? Whatever, the reason, Cal began a period of a high level of activity. He presented a draft of a constitution, based on already existing US associations' constitutions. People who were close to him then say. that he probably composed the constitution without help from others. This constitution was published in the May 1981 *WGR* and a vote was asked for from the readers along with a vote to indicate whether or not to establish a more formal association. That *WGR* also indicated that the International Liaison Panel had already approved both issues.

In the August 1981 WGR he announced that the constitution was now "formally accepted by the majority of those who voted.... and that our new association can be established during the Stockholm colloquium in the summer of 1982." Even though he did not communicate very much with me during this constitutional process, I had the impression that he was now back to his former, almost hectic, level of activity and full of initiatives and ideas, as usual. For example, he arranged a travelling seminar to China in June 1981 and worked successfully with the Psychological Rights of the Child and kept in touch with Stuart Hart's newly established Centre for the Study of Children's Rights in Indianapolis, Indiana. During the fall of 1981, Cal made a European Trip. He visited Sweden for discussions about the 1982 colloquium. He stayed in my home for a few days during which first and foremost two items were discussed:

> He, on his side, still trying to convince me to run for the first president of ISPA as in his previous letters. I, on my side, reminding him of his many promises to supply ISPC with an audited survey of its financial status. From Copenhagen he went on to Wurzburg, Germany to meet Bernhard Meissner (BM). He spent several days there and from Bernhard's reporting from then I am here to mention, that Cal at a conference arranged by BM gave an interesting keynote titled "The Development of School Psychology and its Perspectives from an International Aspect." Further Cal during his stay tried to convince BM to run for being elected as the treasurer in the association to be formalised during the Stockholm colloquium. BM argued that he had no idea of how to handle financial affairs of an organisation, but Cal held out a prospect that he himself as the Executive Secretary of the new association would handle all the daily financial matters. BM finally accepted to run, also because he felt a real personal need for professional international contacts being one out of a total of only about 15 school psychologists at the time working in the whole of Bavaria.

He also visited Italy and England and met members for discussions about coming events and initiatives. I was informed that the material for a ballot for the election of officers was ready by December 1981 and would be distributed with an issue of *WGR* in late 1981 or early 1982. But no *WGR* came and no communication from Cal either. I should have been aware that something was not as it should be but I had just taken a new job and was, in fact, responsible for running my old job as well as my new one. My hands were more than full. Since I had tried, in vain, to speak to Cal about the financial accounting of ISPC, I had a foreboding feeling that the account was empty and that he had drained his own personal bank account as well. At last a *WGR* came in late April 1982 and had the ballot material enclosed. Later I learned that its production and mailing was made possible by The Brain-Wave Technologies Corporation Ltd., Montreal as pay for an order form for the "Mangina diagnostic tool of visual perception« printed in this issue of WGR."

Late April was almost too late to carry out the election process but somehow Cal succeeded because by July 25 letters were mailed to the people who had been elected. These were: Anders Poulsen as President; Herbert Bischoff (Anchorage, Alaska) as President-Elect; Bernhard Meissner (Wurzburg, Germany) as Treasurer; and Ludwig Lowenstein (UK) as Secretary. These people were elected to the job of putting together a viable organisation called the International School Psychology Association (ISPA). The circumstances surrounding its beginning were somewhat shaky, to say the least, but more about that in the next instalment.

Part V

In the previous section, I explained the circumstances surrounding the late election of officers as the formation of ISPA began to take shape. When I received the letter from Cal about the election results, he also told that his travelling seminar plans had fallen through but he managed to find money enough for his air ticket to Sweden for the summer colloquium. Furthermore, he made a surprising and unexpected remark saying that he moved out of his home and was now living alone at a new address. This message was alarming and signalled that he was now facing personal problems which, perhaps, could be understood as after-effects of his meningitis in 1980.

A few days after this letter we were to meet in Stockholm. When Cal arrived at the airport, his personal situation was such that the immigration authorities would not let him leave the airport. I was called to come there to possibly help. I met him quite ill at ease and depressed but he claimed that no medical was needed, only rest. The next day he was better and we, once again, had to admire his willpower. As a result of his year-long dedicated work, it was very important for him to be present during the forming of the foundation of the *International School Psychology Association* in spite of his health and money problems.

No minutes or personal notes are in my possession from this founding session that took place on Wednesday, August 4th, 1982, but fortunately Bernhard Meissner (BM) has some handwritten notes from this meeting. The colloquium attendees were invited to participate. According to Bernhard, 37 were present, and let me add that 12 of these are still ISPA members and all of them have for longer periods been actively involved in leading ISPA functions. From the elected Executive Committee (EC) only myself as President and Bernhard Meissner, Treasurer, were present. Cal had beforehand stressed that he would make it easy for the EC by continuing all of his functions as usual but now under the title of Executive Director. But what now? Would he be able to function? And we had a totally broken economy! Also Bernhard's notes (which will go into the ISPA archive) clearly shows that he had very mixed feelings about the future. As President I seriously worried about what I had engaged myself in. What is left in my mind about this founding meeting and about the business meetings during the following days is that I felt scared, helpless, and completely uncertain about ISPA's future. I expressed my feelings in a letter to Anna-Lisa Mellden after the adoption of ISPA by saying, "I will fight for the survival of ISPA but, if I have to accept that it is to die, I will do my best to leave behind that it passed away in a decent manner."

The Fifth International School Psychology Colloquium, August 1-6, 1982, Stockholm

It was held at the University of Stockholm and the theme was "Children - the Mirror of Society." The location was very good and it was well organised by the LOC, chaired by Anna-Lisa Mellden, who later took her good turn on the EC of ISPA. The approximately 200 participants, made up, for once, of very few Americans, met a large, well organised and qualified professional program. It was held in an epoch when nuclear weapons was a worldwide issue. This led to an important decision to form a task force to prepare an anti-nuclear resolution. That gave much reason for discussion of the pros and cons regarding that issue. The resolution was signed by more than half of the participants and published in the November, 1982 *WGR*. The LOC also succeeded in organising an excellent social program, among which was an invitation by the City of Stockholm for a buffet dinner at Stadshuset, the famous City Hall, where the Nobel Prize Celebrations are held. Here in this beautiful hall, I gave my first official speech as President of ISPA. That was something very special for me and THAT I have not forgotten. This colloquium was very successful and also was favoured by exceptionally fine weather for Stockholm.

The First Steps of the New Association

With no money and Cal, as disabled as he was, as our Executive Director, the EC realised that we had a difficult period ahead of us. We had no way of fully knowing about Cal's personal situation except from results of his work. With the deepest respect for Cal's personal integrity we did try to have him do the basic jobs for the association that he himself had outlined as his duties, not the least was keeping a membership list and the dues status updated. However, most urgently, he was to make a report of the financial status of ISPA. We could not move forward until we had these facts. This we did not receive from him.

In December 1982 a WGR came, which seemed to prove his ability to function organised and structured, and happy was I for this signal of progress in his situation, but after Cal passed away we received information saying that my interpretation had been false. Besides reporting about the Stockholm colloquium and the founding of the association, it also informed about an interesting and rather time consuming task in which he had been involved during the fall. That was a report about his successful cooperation with the newly established Centre for the Study of the Psychological Rights of the Child, at Indiana University, Indianapolis, initiated and under the leadership of Stuart Hart. With the support of a large grant, Stuart was planning a convention on the *Psychological Abuse of the Child: In the Home,*

School, and Community, to be held in August 1983. Stuart had already in Stockholm generously invited ISPA to be a co-sponsor and offered to add $10 US to the conference fee as a financial support to ISPA. Additionally, he would organise home stay for ISPA members from abroad. I do see all of this as Stuart's tribute to Cal personally for all he previously has done in relation to the Rights of the Child and, also, as a support to stabilising ISPA.

During the early months of 1983, the EC members received unclear signals from Cal and had the impression that his personal situation was very poor. This was confirmed by some ISPA members who had visited him. We also received requests from members who were troubled by not receiving any response to their membership fee payment. Many times during the winter, I sent letters to Cal in which I requested him to reply to matters related to the basic financial questions he had promised to handle. The whole situation was so sad and I did my best to be firm in a polite and respectful manner. But it seemed that he did not understand how serious the situation was for ISPA and also for himself. I felt that he possibly was unable to act in an organised and structured way, being caught in a world of positive ideas and plans for the further development of ISPA but not realising his own disability in carrying these out. The EC felt obliged to have the total state of affairs of the association cleared up, and in June, I again requested Cal to supply a full survey of finances and provide other basic information to be given to members in an annual report at the Delegates meeting that would be held in Indianapolis in August 1983. This meeting would take place prior to the "International Conference on the Psychological Abuse of Children and Youth."

When that day came, Cal had not prepared any of the material that was expected. The next days were difficult and unpleasant for everyone there. In short, the participating members demanded that Cal no longer should handle ISPA finances which the EC could only support. As a result, that brought up a number of subjects that had to be dealt with in order to implement this. Busy days followed. The members present really proved their dedication to the survival of ISPA by doing the following basic jobs sorely needed:

- Preparing a membership list showing the dues status everyone present spent many hours helping to try to make such a list by copying Cal's handwritten index cards which was an almost impossible task;
- A committee worked on needed amendments to the constitution in order to meet a now changed role of the Executive Secretary. From now on the elected treasurer would handle all daily financial functions including the recording of membership fees and keeping a membership list;
- In relation to the above, a bank account was needed in USA which Stuart Hart was very helpful in establishing;
- A membership form had to be designed.

During those days of intense discussions many things came up that everyone felt were crucial to ISPA's survival. I have thought long and hard about what to, and what not to deal with in reporting about this period of the early history of ISPA. Some may find that I have been too detailed in my attempt to give an overall understanding of the situation this new and vulnerable association faced. However, what I have reported here, I have found needed in order to be just and fair to all involved.

The Child and Youth Abuse Conference in Indianapolis was considered ISPA's 6th International School Psychology Colloquium. Of the 200 participants, most were Americans, of which 25 were ISPA members and of those 25 very few non-Americans. Because of our essential internal ISPA strategy discussions, few ISPA members took part in the conference sessions. However, Stuart found it generally successful and promising for further work.

Source: www.ispaweb.org

Index